"WOMEN FORGET THAT MEN ARE THE MASTERS"

Gender antagonism and socio-economic change in Kisii District, Kenya

Margrethe Silberschmidt

NORDISKA AFRIKAINSTITUTET 1999

Indexing terms
Gender identity
Gender relations
Social values
Social change
Kenya

This book is published with support from The Danish Council for Development Research, Danida, Ministry of Foreign Affairs, Copenhagen.

Cover design: Adriaan Honcoop
The picture shows dancing Kisii women swinging their pangas, singing vulgar songs and mocking men during the celebration of their daughters' circumcision.

Photographs: Margrethe Silberschmidt

Language checking/copy editing: Roger Leys

ISBN 91-7106-439-7

Printed in Sweden by Elanders Gotab, Stockholm 1999

Contents

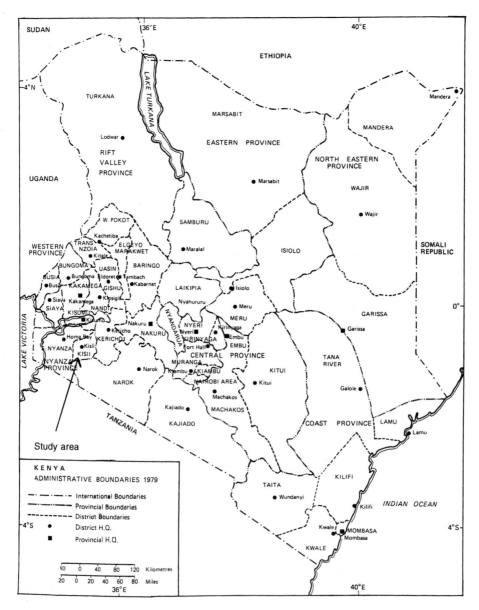

Study area

KENYA
ADMINISTRATIVE BOUNDARIES 1979

—··—··—	International Boundaries
—···—···—	Provincial Boundaries
—————	District Boundaries
●	District H.Q.
■	Provincial H.Q.

Source: *Population and Development, 1984*

Preface

This study investigates the antagonistic relations between men and women in Kisii district, Western Kenya and analyses male-female relationships and the way in which gender identities are formulated.

The study is the result of research that started way back in 1984. It involved frequent periods of fieldwork in Kisii in 1984, 1985 and 1986. Most of this fieldwork focused on women, in particular their use of family planning services and the relations between genders. The intention was to include men—when appropriate. As the research progressed it became clear that men could not just be included and a study of male attitudes to women's use of family planning was undertaken. In 1990 and 1992 supplementary research was undertaken, focusing on men.

Contemporary Kisii is, on the surface, a male dominated society. But any analysis of relations of gender in contemporary Kisii confronts many paradoxes. Socio-economic change in this century has had profound but different implications for women and men. The main contention of this book is that change has affected men more deeply than women. Men's roles and identities have been challenged and undermined, whereas those of women have, in some ways, been strengthened. Traditional institutions are breaking up and cohabitation is replacing marriage since men cannot afford to pay brideprice. Many activities that, in the past, have been crucial to male identity and social value have disappeared. Socioeconomic change has brought with it new social obligations and economic expectations: among others, that men are expected to be bread-winners.

Due to land shortage and unemployment, most men are unable, or unwilling, to fulfill this new role and the expectations linked to it. So men are often reduced to 'figureheads' of households, their authority has come under threat as have their social value, identity and sense of self-esteem. Antagonism between men and women is rife. Women are often the sole providers of the material needs of the household. Moreover, for many women, having children is often a strategy for stabilizing their precarious situation in partnerships where no bridewealth has been paid. But these extra burdens have often strengthened women's identity and sense of self-esteem. This is one of many paradoxes and it raises the question as to whether they are to be found elsewhere, particularly in Sub-Saharan Africa.

Societies in Sub Saharan Africa are often described as dominated by patriarchal norms, practices and values. The term patriarchy has been widely used to analyse conditions of male superiority vis-à-vis women. The general view is that patriarchy *and* socioeconomic change have benefitted men at the expense of women. This view is not "wrong" but requires qualification. To be sure, both customary law and some consequences of socio-economic and political change have put women in disadvantageous and subordinate positions. Women do not have equal access to family property, they seldom have the right to inherit land and other assets and, when marriages break down, they do not even have 'custody' of their own children. Yet, as this study tries to demonstrate, the stereotypes of male domination and female subordination can be misleading. Such stereotypes are static and can be deceptive when used in the analysis of societies undergoing massive change. For not all men are successful patriarchs and not all women passive victims.

But, in Sub Saharan Africa, few studies have tried to investigate these paradoxes. There is an urgent need for gender studies that *also* investigate the situation of men qua men. For example, as shown in this study, the lack of income earning opportunities and men's inability to provide for their families tend to undermine male identity. Massive unemployment and underemployment have also become a general feature in other parts of rural and in particular urban Africa. Yet how this affects male identity, masculinity and self esteem is still unexplored. In Kisii male identity seems increasingly linked to sexuality, to men's control of women's sexuality and reproductive behaviour and to alcohol abuse, violence and rape. Possessing no means to change their economic situation, many men seem to translate their frustrations into other forms of behaviour: sexual activity with many partners being one of them, an activity that seems to boost male identity. Yet a wife must be sexually faithful, she cannot refuse her husband's demand for sex nor can she even ask him to use condoms. One result is that women's reproductive and sexual health is threatened and, in the case of AIDS, often terminally so.

During my fieldwork I have come to know many people in Kisii without whose insights and help this study could not have been carried out. I am particularly grateful to my research assistants; especially Mary Kemunto, Helen Kerubo and Clemencia Kwamboka. Warm thanks also to Mr. and Mrs. John Oigara for all their insights, their help and their hospitality.

I want to thank my always inspiring Ph.D. supervisor, Susan Whyte, Knud Erik Svendsen for his support of the study, and Eva Rosander for her encouragement, particularly towards the end of the writing-up. I am also grateful to professor Leshabari, the Director of the Institute of Public Health, Muhimbili University, Dar es Salaam for his interest in my work and for his support. This study could not have been possible without the support of my children, Eva and Noah, and my husband Ole Therkildsen. The Development Research Council of Denmark funded the research, the Centre for Development Research in Copenhagen provided a work environment and the Institute of Development Studies of the University of Nairobi granted me research clearance. My thanks also to Roger Leys for his final editing.

Chapter 1
Background to the Study

During my research in Kisii District,[1] Western Kenya, men and women's deep frustrations about each other, their conflicts of interests, constant negotiations and, in particular, women's contempt for their husbands were persistent themes. I was often confronted with acts of domestic violence, rape, and poisoning—mainly women poisoning their husbands to 'tame' them—or one spouse kills the other. Or as I was told 'this woman and her children had stayed for more than four days without eating and here was her husband just drinking with another woman and not caring at all about the children who were starving. So she went and killed her children as she could not revenge on the husband'. The reason was that 'children belong to the husband, so when a wife gets angry at him, the only way to really hit him is by killing the children'.

The aim of the present study is to investigate the underlying reasons for the antagonistic relations between the sexes. Escalating gender conflicts and lack of domestic harmony have been documented in many East African contexts, and are seen as reflections of the deepening contradictions provoked by profound socio-economic transformations in this century (LeVine, S., 1979; Oboler, 1985; Hay and Stichter, 1984; Kandiyoti, 1988; Moore, 1988). My own research in Kisii clearly supports these observations. But it also reveals that behind existing interpretations are a number of much more complex, less accessible and less visible reasons for the increasingly tense and antagonistic relations between the genders (Silberschmidt, 1991a and b, 1992, 1993). These are linked to the fact that traditional social and economic structures, male and female economic and social roles, institutional arrangements, beliefs and values have all been deeply affected. Competition to survive economically has become intense due to population pressure, increasingly tiny land plots and rising unemployment. With an increasing number of elopements and no transfer of bridewealth the institution of marriage is changing. And with an increasing number of 'broken' homes and female-headed households the idea of the household is changing. The value of children is questioned and new ideas about fertility and, in

---

[1] In pre-colonial times Kisii was called Gusiiland. The British colonizers changed the name of Gusiiland to Kisii (in 1907), and today the District is called Kisii. The people were the Abagusii or Gusii. Today they are called Kisii in the English language but refer to themselves as Abagusii or Gusii. The term Gusii is derived from Mogusii, the person that the Gusii people claim as their ancestor. In the following I shall refer to the inhabitants of Kisii as the Gusii.

particular, sexuality are appearing. This new situation has serious implications for both genders and for the relations between them.

Gender relations are socially constituted, shaped and sanctioned by existing and changing norms and values. Central to these relations are culturally specific notions of masculinity and femininity as well as notions about appropriate behaviour for each gender. These notions are based on codes of behaviour and expectations. They are underpinned by ideology, reinforced by the different access to socially valued resources and sanctioned by a number of different mechanisms. As such they are relations into which people enter involuntarily. In situations of change and the breaking up of traditional structures, new norms and values are created. While old norms and values seem to die hard in Kisii a new set of ideas—another competing moral universe—has been created, and people are caught between conflicting values.

So far these issues have not been much researched. Consequently, I find myself moving onto new ground, challenging existing conclusions and perhaps—but hopefully not—arriving at speculative conclusions. In order to contribute to the on-going debate on gender relations, the aim of this study is to develop a more profound theoretical understanding and more refined conceptual tools. The wider perspective of the study is to acquire more sophisticated and in-depth insight into changing relations of power and hierarchy, changing male and female identities as well as continuity and discontinuity in gender positions.

In most literature on gender and gender relations there has not been an equal focus on men and women. Women have been at the centre of the investigation. In this study, and in order to place individual gender concerns and motivations at the centre of the historical process that contextualizes their lives, equal emphasis will be put on women and men. Efforts are made to address questions linked to both male and female perceptions of selves and each other and to let the 'actors' speak for themselves.

Iona and Philip Mayer, who were among the first anthropologists to work in Kisii—in the mid-1940s—refer to Kisii as a society 'organized for overt competition' with acknowledged rivalry at every point where "brothers fight for the mother's breast" (1965:53). Forty years later, during my fieldwork—also in Kisii—Gusii had the reputation of being 'extremely violent': 'husbands kill their wives, and wives kill their husbands'; 'Gusii men are terribly jealous and possessive'; 'the worst offence of a married Gusii woman is to show that she can make it on her own'; Gusii men are 'proud and terribly self conscious'; 'they ego-trip a lot'; 'they are highly emotional'; 'they get upset very quickly'; 'they overreact and explode'. Robert and Barbara LeVine identified four general patterns of behaviour: authoritarianism, emotional restraint, interpersonal hostility and last but not least sex antagonism (LeVine, R. and B., 1966/77:184). In the relationship between women and men there was one with a strong association between sex and aggression:

> Coitus is an act in which a man overcomes the resistance of a woman and causes her pain. This is not limited to the wedding night but continues to be important in marital relations (1966/77:54).

According to LeVine and LeVine, such aggression is not a new phenomena. The relations between the sexes were always antagonistic. Men used to marry women from other clans which were potential enemies—in order to create friendly relations: 'we marry those we fight' men would say. LeVine and LeVine take the hostility as almost axiomatic—as a given—as if it was an inherent characteristic of the relationship between men and women. While I find it problematic to treat the relationship between men and women as a given, my data support the above notions and indicate that the relationship between the genders seems to have become even more antagonistic and harsh: it is the site on which masculinity and femininity are fought out. Fights between clans have stopped, and men no longer marry 'those they fight'. Nevertheless, fighting between the sexes continues.

There seems to be a need—particularly by men—to carve out their masculinity and their masculine identity from that of women. With socio-economic change, new gender roles, new norms and values—dual models of gender roles have emerged. While, on the one hand, women and men do realize the emergence of fundamental changes in their lives, the interaction between past and present norms and values is unclear. What everybody is perfectly aware of is that households have become violent battlegrounds; wives have become increasingly rude and abusive, husbands have become increasingly irresponsible towards their families, and the number of 'broken homes' is on the increase. The following comments by Gusii women and men, emerging from my research in Kisii over the past ten years, are typical.

Women's comments about men: 'a husband is like an extra baby in the house'; 'husbands contribute with nothing'; 'they use their money on drinking and other women, not on school fees and clothes'; 'they never buy sugar and tea and not even soap'. 'Men do not know how to plan': 'they forget about bridewealth, so we are ashamed to go and see our parents'; 'when they are finally at home it is only to ask for food'; 'women cannot count on husbands'; 'our sons have nobody to take as a model'. 'Men want all the eggs in a woman's womb to be used'. 'Men are so delicate; they break so easily; women have no time to break'; 'women would be better off without a husband'.

Men's comments about women: 'Women are rude to men. We are the masters, but they order us about and refuse to listen. This is the reason for so many 'broken homes'. 'Women complain all the time; they speak up at Barazas (local community meetings) and complain to the chiefs about their husbands'. 'They want all our money'; 'they don't have the food ready, when husbands get home. Sometimes husbands do not dare to eat it for fear of being poisoned'. 'When we come home (drunk), they do not let us in, and we have to sleep outside'. 'Our daughters elope with boys without asking us, and we never get any bridewealth'. 'If wives use family planning (contraceptives), they will roam about with other men; men can 'misbehave', women cannot'.

How to interpret these comments? Both genders seem deeply frustrated—but their frustrations are different. Economic pressure has become intolerable, and women are aggressive because husbands tend not to contribute economically to the survival of the household. Women feel left on their own—alone with all responsibilities in terms of making ends meet, providing food, even school fees, and raising their children. They want husbands who are responsible heads of households and 'family providers'. But men do not live up to the expectations of women. Consequently, 'men are a burden; they are weak; they are useless'; 'a woman would be much better off without a husband'. A woman's access to land, though, is dependent on a man. This means that women 'need' a husband in order to get access to land which is their means of production.

Men are also aggressive. However, their comments express both more defensiveness and sense of injury. This has struck me as very unusual in a society where patriarchy is the dominant structure, where women are structurally subordinated to men and considered 'minors' all their lives. It is also paradoxical that, in a situation where men are the acknowledged heads of households, women have little respect for them.

In short, judging from what men and women say about each other, the relations between the genders are loaded with tensions. Men do not behave as they should, nor do women. Women and men do not live up to the expectations of each other—nor to the prescribed norms and values which still seem to figure profoundly in the minds of both sexes. Most importantly, values which form the basis for male and female expectations seem to be given different weight and priority by men and women. There is a tremendous need for households to find some or other extra income. Women engage in all types of income generating activities to make ends meet. Many men are not able to find regular employment, and the little income they get is seldom spent on the household but rather on personal consumption (alcohol and girlfriends). This is contradictory, because men as well as women agree that the duty of the head of the household is to contribute to the needs of the household and provide school fees.

Kisii landscape today—Setting the stage

Kisii District is the highest part of the South Nyanza highlands. It consists of rounded, steep sided hills intersected by narrow valleys which are rich in red laterized volcanic soils. There is normally sufficient rainfall, and the area

View of Kisii

is well served by the tributaries of three main rivers which flow into Lake Victoria. The highlands cover an area of 2196 sq. km. The hilly terrain makes communication by road difficult, particularly during the rains when the roads become impassable. The climatic conditions allow for a large variety of crops ranging from tea and coffee, pyrethrum, wheat, and maize to various kinds of vegetables and fruits. The District is among the most productive cash and food crop regions in Kenya, and the land is classified as high potential. Virtually every square inch is used for cultivation. From this point of view, Kisii is one of the most 'developed' districts in Kenya.

Kisii is populated almost exclusively by the Bantu-speaking Gusii people. Before the British began establishing authority over Gusiiland (1907), Gusii institutions were not, as they are now, differentiated into political, economic and religious spheres. Social life was based on kinship and patriarchal authority which called for axiomatic reverence not only from wives and daughters, but also from sons (Mayer, I., 1974). Clusters of patrilineal clans lived in clan villages. Clans and lineages were politically significant in that they provided a framework for territorial organisation (LeVine, R. and B., 1966/77). In the colonial period, important political activities that were male domains were taken over by the British rulers. At the same time, a process of migration was initiated, and men were often more or less forced to migrate to other parts of the country to serve the colonizers' needs and to provide cash for paying tax.

Since the turn of the century, a number of different Christian missions have been operating in the District. Catholic and Seventh Day Adventist denominations constitute the vast majority. Most of the Christian churches

Kisii Town

were started by European missionaries who built up large congregations of a scope unknown to the Gusii and transcending communal and tribal loyalties. Until the 1980s the main Christian denominations served as effective agents of social control. It is questionable whether this will continue. The KANU government's increasing abuse of political and human rights and tolerance of a high level of corruption have provoked a debate on the role of religious groups in politics.

In 1907 the population of Kisii was estimated by the British Administration at 75,000 . The population has increased steadily over the past century— and has multiplied about 20 times to date. Today, Kisii is one of the rural districts with the highest population density. In 1988, for administrative reasons, the District was divided into two: Kisii District and Nyamira District. According to the population census of 1979 the then Kisii District had a total population of 869,512. Projections for 1991 were 850,000 for Kisii District and 540,000 for Nyamira District. These projection figures are outdated since the population of Kisii and Nyamira Districts amounted to 1,559,253 by 1993. Thus, the total population has increased by 56% between 1979 and 1993 (*Kisii District Development Plan 1989–93*, 1992:13). Between 1969 and 1979 Population density increased by approximately 29.9%, from 304 persons per square km to 395 per square km (Were and Nyamwaya, 1986:134). Average population density in the District was 604 in 1988 and projected to be 710 by 1993 (*Kisii District Development Plan 1989–93*, 1992 Appendix, tables 1–4). At present projected population growth rates, the population of the District will have doubled by the beginning of the next century (Were and Nyamwaya, 1986:138). (In the following, no differentiation is made between Kisii and

Nyamira District, as data collection started before the District was divided and data on which this study is based has been collected in both Districts.)

According to the 1979 census data, infant mortality rates were 85.1 deaths per 1000 infants. Projections for 1989 were 69.6 (*Kisii District Development Plan 1989–93*, 1992:38, Appendix, table 5). The census data yield a general life expectancy for Kisii District of 54.4 years compared with 59 on a national scale (Egerö and Hammarskjöld, 1994:35). Since over 70% of the population consists of children and young people, Kisii can boast a high potential in manpower over the present and coming years (1994:43). By the year 2000 the proportion of persons under 15 years of age will be between 45%–50% of the total population (Were and Nyamwaya, 1986:132).

The change in the ratio of people to land has not been followed by any significant change in reproductive attitudes or behaviour in Kisii , though recent KAP (knowledge, attitude, practice) studies indicate a decline in fertility rates (Silberschmidt, 1991a; Egerö, 1994). The total fertility rate in Kisii was 8.7 in 1979. In 1991, the rate for the District was estimated at 7.6 children compared with 6.5 for Kenya.[2] Sexually transmitted diseases flourish, and the AIDS epidemic has not left Kisii untouched. In 1992, according to the local gynaecologist, 30% of the sexually active Gusii were HIV infected.[3]

Considering that land is essential for subsistence, the population concentration is extreme. Pressure on land has become a main issue as well as the cause of many conflicts. The majority of households only dispose of 1/2–2 acres of land—nowhere near enough to feed a family. This means that most families are not able to feed themselves from farming, and there is an increasingly urgent need to supplement this with income from other activities.

The expansion of smallholder production has been the dynamic element in the Kisii growth process since the mid-forties, and today agriculture constitutes the backbone of the Kisii economy. Agricultural tasks are almost entirely carried out by women as was the case in pre-colonial times. Cattle herding, which used to be a traditional major male activity, has become very rare. Men's cattle villages were eliminated by the British, and most grazing areas are now being used for farming. This means that while women's traditional area of work has expanded, that of men has shrunk.

Male dominance still pervades the structural framework; men are the acknowledged heads of household and residence is virilocal. Men own the land, and women only get access to land through marriage. As most men have difficulties in providing bridewealth, which is the means to make a marriage legal, 'official' marriage is increasingly being replaced by cohabitation. Polygamy has declined drastically, and today less than 15% of all

---

[2] Kisii has one of the highest population growth rates in the country (3.8%) exceeding the national growth rate of 3.4% (Egerö and Hammarskjöld, 1994).

[3] Personal communication.

households are polygamous. According to statistics, one third of the households are female-headed (Central Bureau of Statistics, 1986). No clear definition of a female headed household is given, except that it is assumed that the
household is female headed when a woman has no husband. My research
indicates that many more households are female headed. Even if the husband is the official head of household and living permanently on the farm,
an increasing number of women are left with the total responsibility for the
survival of themselves and their children with no or only sporadic support
from their husbands (Silberschmidt, 1991a, 1991b).

During colonialism, male migration figures for Kisii were very high, and
all males had at one point of their life worked outside the District. Nowadays migration figures show only about 5,000 working outside Kisii. (*Kisii
District Development Plan 1989–93*). At the same time Kisii is said to have the
biggest unemployment rate in the whole country (*The Nation*, 6.3.1992).
Some men work seasonally as extra hands on larger farms. However, most
men find it below their dignity to do farm work—which they equate with
women's work. Total wage employment for the District is low.[4] While the
hunger for education, particularly for boys, is as fierce as anywhere in
Kenya, unemployment is seen as a particularly serious problem among
school leavers whether they leave primary or secondary school—especially
because there is not enough land to make a living. As noted by Raikes in his
study of Kisii and in agreement with my findings, these depressing facets
are only one side of the coin. Enormous amounts of energy and ingenuity,
though not all well-directed, are expended by men and women in finding
solutions to their problems. However, the very level of activity on many
different fronts has reduced the potential returns (Raikes, P., 1988).

Alcohol abuse, mainly by men, is very common throughout the District.
In 1978, Kisii had the highest rate of alcohol abuse in the country (Otieno,
Owola and Oduor, 1979). There is no indication that alcohol abuse has decreased. On the contrary: 'Men drink to drown their problems'—men and
women agree.

Poisoning seems to occur more in Kisii than in any other district in the
country. While in 1989, Nairobi had 144 cases of poisoning registered, Central Province (about the size of Kisii and Nyamira Districts) had 636 cases.
But 1,145 cases were registered in Kisii (*Kisii District Development Plan 1989–
93*). As to cases of unregistered poisoning, there are no studies available.

Kisii has never been in the forefront of political developments. Kisii was
not linked to the militant wing of the nationalist movement (Mau Mau) in
the struggle for independence. During the 1992 elections for a multi-party
system, which coincided with my last fieldwork, Kisii suddenly became
very aware of its own ethnic identity. Kisii became a violent place, particularly along the borders to Kericho, where old antagonisms particularly over

---

[4] 33,750 in 1987 according to the *Kisii District Development Plan 1989–93*, 1992.

land, were reinforced by political differences. Kalenjin on the Kericho side (belonging to President Moi's tribe) and Gusii men started fighting along the borders. Killings, burning of farms and shootings were reported daily.

In sum, Kisii is part of a wider society and has been confronted with profound processes of change where boundaries are constantly transgressed and contested, and new norms and values are emerging. At the same time— and very paradoxically—Kisii has managed to stay very enclosed in its own moral system, deeply embedded in rigid norms, values and ancient traditions. So new and old forces co-exist: 'Dallas' and 'Dollars' along with advertisements for fancy washing machines are being eagerly watched in bars, mainly by men. But old traditions, morals, norms and values are being forcefully perpetuated. Even if both sexes agree that 'men have often taken the back seat' the belief in male superiority and female inferiority still dominates male and female ideas of gender relations. Men frequently engage in open assertive displays of masculine behaviour, and they constantly assert the privileges automatically accorded them as males. Regardless of the socio-economic circumstances in which they find themselves, men are consciously and constantly preoccupied with the fact that they are men, and that this condition differentiates them radically from women. Men almost invariably claim to be more knowledgeable and intelligent than women. 'We are the masters, so says the bible'. 'From creation men were given more power than women, this should remain the same'. Christian church services are attended more or less regularly, and most Gusii refer to themselves as Christians (mainly Catholics or Seven Day Adventists). But old ancestor cults and beliefs are still observed; spirits and witches are fully recognized; and while boys are circumcised girls are clitoritectomized. In a survey carried out in 1983, more than 80% of the Gusii claimed to be Christians. However, despite the campaigns of the Christian Missions to colonize Gusii spiritually, the majority still believe in traditional religion (Were and Nyamwaya, 1986:31).

Themes and assumptions of the study

From the above description of Kisii and the antagonistic relations between the genders, a number of overlapping and contradictory themes have emerged. These constitute the framework of this study.

First, in spite of ample evidence and documentation of the deteriorating effect of socio-economic transformation on the situation of women, and in spite of pervading patriarchal structures subordinating women and benefiting men, the effects of socio-economic transformations in Kisii have perhaps been even harsher for men than for women.

Second, men seem to have been submitted—to a larger extent than women—to new obligations and expectations breadwinners and following this—new systems of social values.

Third, while women's traditional roles have expanded and their burdens increased, traditional male roles have almost disappeared. Coupled with unemployment the result has been an emasculation of traditional male roles and lack of access to new social roles.

Fourth, female self-esteem has increased whereas male self-esteem has decreased. While the traditional obligations and responsibilities of women have intensified, their expanded role has often acted as a 'booster' to female identity and competence. The contrary has been the case with men.

Following this, a main assumption of this study is that women in Kisii have a strength that men seem to lack, a tendency which is not necessarily contradicted by evidence of the prevalence of men's increasing violence against women. This seems to be connected to the fact that women have been able to retain their traditional role within the household and also in the wider context of society to a much greater extent than men. Women seem to be able to draw on traditional cultural norms and values much more than men. Consequently, women seem to have been able to maintain their sense of identity to a much larger degree than men. As a result of the conflicting demands and expectations embedded in the Gusii 'male code' men seem to be faced with many more obstacles and contradictions than women.

Inspired by the work by Ortner and Whitehead, I shall assume a) that there is a close link between gender identity and social value; b) that social value is pertinent and fundamental to women's and men's identity, self-esteem as well as gender relations, and c) social value 'is the domain of social structure that most directly affects cultural notions of gender and sexuality (Ortner and Whitehead, 1981/89:16). Thus, the concept of social value constitutes an important key to understanding the construction of gender, the dynamics of gender relations and also the antagonistic relations between the sexes. The study is based on three main hypotheses:

–   Women can more easily than men relate to traditional and current social values connected to being a woman. Despite fundamental changes in the lives of women, there has been a greater continuity in the lives of women than in that of men. This continuity has made it possible for women to pursue and expand traditional (occupational and social) roles. In contrast, the continuity in men's lives has been disrupted. Traditional male (occupational) roles have been emasculated and the possibility of access to new roles which give social value is often very limited. This has serious consequences for men's self-esteem.

–   For men, social value and identity are closely linked to fertility and, in particular, sexuality. A high level of sexual activity seems to give social value and self-esteem when other activities that provide social value are non-existent. Sexual control of women is fundamental to male identity and masculinity. Lack of social value seems to be compensated for by increased control over women (including their fertility) manifested in macho-sexual behaviour and violence against women. For women, social value and identity are closely linked to their fertility patterns. A high level of sexual activity is negatively linked to the social value of women.

– Ideas about social values are often shared by women and men. However, in practice, men and women seem to have conflicting priorities .

Analytical frame

With no direct way or any readily available analytical tools to explain gender antagonism I shall take a roundabout route in my attempt to do so. Useful analytical tools have been provided by feminist anthropological research where attempts have been made to combine symbolic and sociological approaches to the study of gender and enquiries have been made into the cultural construction of self or person through an analysis of gender identity. Other useful analytical tools are provided, in particular by Igor Kopytoff (1990).

Gender as symbolic construct

As mentioned above, I have been particularly inspired by the work by Ortner and Whitehead which takes its point of departure in the systematic asymmetry of gender relations, an asymmetry which favours men and constrains women. Their work is not concerned with explaining gender antagonism and cannot be used directly to explain such antagonism. However, it provides this study with useful tools because it analyzes 'man' and 'woman' as symbolic categories or constructs. As such 'masculinity' and 'femininity' are not given by nature or rooted in individual characteristics, but are socially constructed:

> What gender is, what men and women are, what sorts of relations do or should obtain between them—all of these notions do not simply reflect or elaborate upon biological "givens" but are largely products of social and cultural processes (Ortner and Whitehead, 1981/89:1).

Gender, sexuality, and reproduction are treated as *symbols*—as cultural and symbolic constructs—invested with meaning by the particular society in question. These *symbols* can only be understood when their place in a larger system of symbols and meanings is appreciated. Thus an inquiry has to be made into the processes and consequences of their construction and organization. Behind current gender notions and notions of norms and values is a long history of complex codes 'designing' the cultural categories of male and female. It is the opposition between these categories which constitutes the origin of the qualities, the norms and values attributed to these categories (1981/89).

Prestige/social value, marriage and sexuality

According to Ortner and Whitehead, the structures of greatest importance for the cultural construction of gender and identity are the structures of prestige/social honour/social value: it is the prestige/social value dimension that has the clearest and most intelligible implications for gender ideas. Consequently:

- a gender system is first and foremost a prestige structure;

- prestige structures in any society tend toward symbolic consistency with one another;

- gender constructs are partly functions of the ways in which male prestige-oriented action articulates with structures of cross-sex relations.

- the cultural construction of sex and gender tends everywhere to be affected by the prestige considerations of socially dominant male actors (1981/89:12).

Marriage is one of the most important institutions within which gender ideology is produced and reproduced and is fundamental for the construction of gender identity and sexuality. Special emphasis should, therefore, be put on analyzing marriage and, in particular, sexuality. Sexuality is a cultural construct constituting the cornerstone of marriage, and marriage and sexuality affect, in particular, male prestige and social value. Consequently, prestige is the domain of social structure that most directly affects cultural notions of gender and sexuality (1981/89:16).

Critique of Ortner and Whitehead

I have three criticisms of Ortner and Whitehead. First, they do not deal with change. Gender as well as gender relations—being largely products of social and cultural processes—are neither universal nor static but dynamic and changeable. Referring to Weber's reflections that prestige systems are both structurally significant and historically dynamic Ortner and Whitehead do argue that a particular prestige system and its deeper social supports must be viewed as historically specific and complex (1981/89:15–16). However, when focusing on sources, processes and consequences for the construction of gender, they do not deal with transformations of societies—not to mention the changing lives, norms and values of the actors. Consequently, their approach becomes purely theoretical (Collier and Yanagisako, 1987) and remains static.

My second argument is that Ortner and Whitehead do not differentiate between male and female perceptions of prestige and social value. They stress the importance 'of not only focusing on the formal characteristics of the structure, but on the ways in which, in operation within such structures, actors' perceptions of the world, of nature, of the self and of social relations—are shaped in certain ways' (Ortner and Whitehead, 1981/89:5). But their prestige system, as they present it, reflects the male perspective. They seem to assume that social value has the same meaning for both genders. While Ortner and Whitehead emphasize that 'having a wife is a prerequisite to adult autonomy and status' (1981/89:21), they do not mention what having a husband means for a woman. As a result women disappear from the analysis; they become mute and it is not possible to capture conflicting gender interest and values.

Third, Ortner and Whitehead argue that 'For men ... although the issue of sexual control does not actually generate categories of masculinity, there is nonetheless a correspondence between status and sexual activity that is the inverse of the female system—higher-ranking men are supposed to be more sexually active and expressive, lower-status men less so' (1981/89:9). Their emphasis on the correspondence between male status and male sexual activity which is the inverse of the female system, is inspiring. However, my data show that their argument about sexual control not actually generating categories of masculinity needs to be qualified. As shall also appear below, my findings seem to indicate quite the contrary.

The present study will deal with the following questions and issues: 1) What type of new social value systems have emerged in Kisii? 2) What gives social value to men and women respectively? 3) Are male and female perceptions of social value the same? Do women and men have identical perceptions of social value, or is it rather a question of different priorities? Do women and men agree on social value in theory, but differ in practice? 4) How does sexual control of women relate to masculinity and male identity?

This approach makes it possible to investigate to what extent social values remain constant, are changing or are contradictory. Surprisingly, such an approach and such issues have not been central in the gender debate so far. As a cultural, social and psychological construct, gender is embedded in and interacts with the cultural framework, norms and values. As such, gender is formed by complex unfinished processes, is never static and cannot be studied in isolation. Given the close interaction between the construction of gender (identity) and social value, the aim of this study is precisely to develop a dynamic approach which encompasses change. Therefore, it becomes crucial to make an inquiry into the *changing* cultural contexts and spheres which shape *changing* gender notions, *changing* male and female identities and also *changing* social values. Such an approach requires an historical analysis in order to capture—step by step—what is actually taking place in Kisii.

The concepts of prestige, social honour or social value assume slightly different qualities and fall in different degrees on different persons and groups within any society) (1981/89:13). In the following I shall use the term social value. It is a much broader concept: a person can have social value and no prestige; and while prestige indicates hierarchy and one type of social value social value does not necessarily indicate hierarchy. Moreover, social value is negotiable.

Perception of self and existential and role-based identities

The founder of identity theory, Erik H. Erikson, defines identity in terms of continuity, 'persistent sameness with oneself' and stresses the fact that there are different identities in different phases of a person's life. (Erikson, 1959/80). Erikson's concern with the consistency of cultural values (or 'moral universe') and the actual structure of a person's social universe is particularly illuminating for this study. According to Erikson, when a person's moral universe is suddenly invalidated because of lack of 'fit' with social reality, the identity—i.e. the conceptions of an individual self in relation to others—will be invalidated too. Such an invalidation may be the outcome of its confrontation with a changed social structure, in which the person's own role is changed too. If—as a result—the self image does not correspond to the actual social reality, the centre of gravity of personal identity may disappear. This is what Erikson calls 'acute identity diffusion' (1959/80:132) or what Jacobson-Widding refers to as 'identity-crisis' (Jacobson-Widding, 1983:14). While Erikson's approach makes it possible to encompass concepts such as perception of self and 'identity crisis' and hence to encompass change, it does not take into consideration that conceptions of self/person or identity are cross-culturally as variable as the concepts of male and female.

Moreover, no particular effort is made to distinguish between male and female identity. From this point of view, I find the analytical approach and tools developed by Kopytoff in his study of the Suku in Zaire particularly useful for this study. This is precisely because he permits a distinction between male and female identity. Moreover, Kopytoff's distinction between existential and role-based identities opens up for the link between social value and different types of identities as well as an understanding of how changing social values affect male and female existential and role-based identities differently.

The point of departure for Kopytoff is that some identities are based on what a person *is* (= existential identity), others are based on what a person *does* (= role-based identity): some identities are negotiable while others are not (Kopytoff, 1990:80). Kopytoff stresses the importance of distinguishing, in the representations of gender, those aspects of female and male identity that are culturally defined as 'existential' or 'immanent' (in the very nature of being female or male) and those that pertain to the roles people play.

While the existentially based identity is composed of features that are intrinsic, or 'immanent' in a cultural definition of what it is to be male or female—and not negotiable (mother/father)—the role-based identity is based on what a person does (farmer/craftsman) and is negotiable. Thus, existential identity indicates a state of being (mother/father) rather than of doing: it is difficult to renegotiate, relatively immutable, and surrounded by strong social and ritual sanctions that punish deviant behaviour. In contrast, features of role-based identity may be negotiated and the identities themselves relinquished with no sanctions.

The breaking up of identity into two 'ideal types' or models also makes it possible to explore and understand apparent paradoxes and contradictions in the construction of male and female identities, ideas about social value and the wider implications for the relations between genders.

However, Kopytoff, does not deal with the fact that, for example, a head of household or a father has social functions: that certain social functions pertain to certain roles. As will be shown in this study it is not enough just to *be* a father or to *do* a certain type of work. It is also important *how* these roles are performed. This dimension does not figure in Kopytoff's model. This has implications for the dynamics of his approach. This is precisely because—as shall be demonstrated below—the social functions linked to men's and women's roles have changed dramatically during this century, and these social functions, for men in particular, have become central issues of negotiation and disagreement between men and women.

Methodological approach

Data for this study was obtained during several periods of fieldwork, from a number of different sources and by using many different (and perhaps unorthodox) methodological approaches: collection of quantitative data, participant observation, interviews, case studies and life histories. As a historical perspective was crucial to the study, I have also relied on a number of secondary sources.

According to Keesing and Keesing,

> The anthropologist has no elaborate bag of methodological devices to depersonalize and objectify his encounter with other human beings. In a sense, he has only his common humanity. To see what he does, and can do with it we must turn to a mode of exploration that is peculiarly anthropological. (Keesing and Keesing, 1971:11).

> Whatever analytical abstractions the social scientist uses to carve out formal patterns that he can manipulate with the tools of science—whether models of 'culture' or 'social structure' or whatever—the richness of everyday human experience and the uniqueness of real people remain essential sources of insight. That he himself is human may be the social scientist's best means of understanding man and his social life. (1971:27)

Of course, common humanity is important, in fact, a prerequisite—but far from enough. At times I have felt extremely frustrated as an anthropologist. To obtain my data I have to get very close to my 'objects', get involved in their very personal life: the more personal—the more interesting. It has been particularly frustrating to watch impossible situations. As a compensation, I have at times acted very much as a social worker and a chauffeur—the only things I had to offer. As I have been involved with the Gusii over a period of 10 years, I have developed a number of close relations, precisely because I have taken part in people's daily struggles. I have taken beaten up women to the District hospital, accompanied women to the Health Centre to give birth, been at the prison in Kisii town to inquire about arrested family members. I have accompanied desperate women who were infertile, to an old 'witch' at the other end of the District, who had remedies to make them fertile. I have been discussing for hours with desperate men, who wanted to give up drinking, but were unable to do so. I have argued with many school headmasters, who did not allow pupils to attend school if their uniform was torn etc. etc.

As a methodological frame, I have used a practice/grounded approach. At the outset I did not consciously plan to use such an approach. In retrospect, and in terms of the type of data that I needed, this turned out to be the approach that I automatically ended up using. This means that I have been particularly interested in the agency of both women and men; their self perceptions, cultural and social forms and practices, and the ways in which individuals are caught up in dialogues and relations between themselves and the structures in which they are placed; how actors formulate conflicting views and disclose problems and interests; their fears and dreams. Linked to this, direct quotes are used extensively in order to let men as well as women speak for themselves and with each other.

Data collection

My first research project in Kisii was entitled 'Women's position in the household and their use of family planning and antenatal services: A case study from Kisii District Kenya'. Part of the study was carried out together with a medical sociologist, Alanagh Raikes (Raikes, A., 1990). In 1984, 1985 and 1986 (altogether over 11 months) data was collected from all over Kisii District, partly through interviews by means of questionnaires, and partly through informal (qualitative) repetitive interviews. Interviews by means of a questionnaire were carried out with 723 women (aged 17–45) from all seven divisions in the then one District. Twenty women from Matunwa and 20 from Mosocho, were interviewed regularly in depth. Eight family health field workers from Kisii Hospital were put at our disposal to carry out the survey. Health field workers from Matunwa and Mosocho assisted me in the qualitative interviewing.[5]

The informal interviewing which was concentrated in two different areas—Matunwa and Mosocho—(I have always come back to them during the following years and they constitute my 'core areas') consists of interviews carried out, mainly with women but also with men individually, in groups of each sex and in groups with both sexes. This means that I have collected two types of data: quantitative data, that is data collected by means of a questionnaire and qualitative data i.e. data collected in informal and repeated in-depth interviews. The quantitative data collection was carried out for comparative reasons and in order to get a wider perspective on my qualitative data (and vice versa). The quantitative data was computerized.

Hence my first study was mainly directed towards women, and the intention was to include the views of men to the extent that this would contribute to an understanding of women's use of contraceptive measures. As the study progressed, it became increasingly clear to me that men could not just be included. How to understand why most men were, in theory, in favour of birth control (bombarded as they are by daily broadcasts supporting birth control) but in practice were against (according to their wives). How to understand why women made their own decisions without consulting their 'owners'? Why did women often try to limit the number of births without their husband's knowledge? How to grasp women's complaints that they could neither depend on the economic support or the labour of their menfolk, and that 'a husband in the house was like having an extra baby'. To understand these attitudes it was necessary to incorporate men much more directly in the study. A number of questions needed to be dealt with. What did the men feel about their life situation? How did it affect their attitude to their wives' use of contraceptives? Did men feel that their contribution to the household was unsatisfactory? Or did they feel that women were trespassing on their traditional areas of authority? I could not be content just with women's views of their husbands. Such a view would be too

---

[5] A random cluster sampling methodology was developed to select a random number of sites in Kisii District where both users and non-users of the services were interviewed in their homes. The methodology was based on a modified version of the World Health Organization's sampling procedure for the selection of 30 sites in a given geographical area, a random selection of a starting point (the household) within each site and a selection of seven individuals of the appropriate age from within each of the 30 sites. In Kisii we increased the cluster numbers from 30 to 35. Standard I primary school children were used for the selection of households.

Partly because of the unknown number of family planning users in the District, and partly because of the resources provided to us by the Ministry of Health, it was possible to obtain a larger sample, and 10 interviews per cluster were opted for instead of the sampling index of seven. This meant that in each cluster interviews were carried out with 10 women who were either pregnant or had given birth during the last year and were, therefore, potential family planning users. In the same cluster, a comparative group of women was interviewed. This group was selected precisely because they were not pregnant and not breast feeding and might therefore be family planning users. 10 women were interviewed in this category in each cluster. For more details see A. Raikes (1990) and M. Silberschmidt (1991a).

partial. Thus it became imperative to have a parallel study of men. To start with, my female interviewers refused to carry out interviews with men. It would affect their reputation. 'How can we approach men. It would be indecent'. Somehow I managed to talk them into giving it just one try. They came back to me, very surprised, saying that it had been very interesting to talk with men; that men were very communicative; that men told them that nobody had ever asked them questions like that. In the end, most of my female interviewers said that they preferred to interview men: unlike women, men always had plenty of time.

Informal interviews were then conducted, and a questionnaire with very much the same questions as those asked of women was worked out. Sixty men were interviewed. Priority was given to interviewing the husbands of women interviewed. Apart from questions linked to men's attitudes to their wives' use of health facilities, including modern contraceptives, how soon after delivery and how often they 'met' (had sex) with their wives, questions were asked on husband's labour and economic input into the household, if they stayed permanently on the farm or not. In addition, questions were asked on decision-making patterns in relation to various household tasks. These questionnaires were also computerized. Another 60 men were interviewed with a mini-questionnaire, focusing on what had turned out to be major issues in relations to the entire study: attitudes to family planning, value of children and men's expectations about their future situation as well as that of their children.

In order to get a representative sample the interviews were carried out in all seven divisions of Kisii with men of different age and with different socio-economic and educational backgrounds. As the incorporation of men in the study was not included originally in the project preparation, the 120 interviews were the limit of our capacity in terms of labour as well as time.

During fieldwork in 1990, (in connection with my second study: 'Rethinking men and gender relations'), men were in the centre of the research. Forty men were interviewed in-depth and a number of interviews were also carried out with women. However, it was not possible to select the men as intended i.e. men from Matunwa village and according to whether or not they had migrated, whether or not they were living permanently on farm, whether or not they were contributing regularly to the support of their family. This was first and foremost because my very best interviewer (from my earlier study) who was living in Matunwa was seriously ill except for the last 10 days, when I worked with her. My short field work period (3 months) did not allow me to find another person with her qualities and with the same in-depth knowledge of this particular village, where I had made in depth interviews during my previous fieldwork. Instead, I decided to reorganize my approach and to rely on a few of my excellent assistants (from my previous study) whom I had contacted before my arrival in Kisii. With their assistance I succeeded in making the 40 in depth interviews with men. Some of these men were interviewed on several occasions.

In addition, a questionnaire survey on men—with many qualitative and open-ended questions—was also carried out by my assistants. In order to compare male and female ideas, values, attitudes and reactions, an adjusted questionnaire was worked out for women with the same questions. As my assistants had to combine their daily work as family health field workers with the interviewing, I had no set goal in terms of the number of interviews. These interviews were carried out in different parts of the District. The main criteria for selection of men and women were that they were 'married', had children and different educational and economic background. I ended up with 80 questionnaire interviews with men of different ages (19–65) and 20 with women also of different ages (25–45). A few men refused to be interviewed unless they were paid, given alcohol or food.

Both in the formal and informal interviewing with questionnaires men were confronted with questions linked to the domestic sphere: access to resources, division of labour within the household, male responsibilities and contributions to the household, economic input and labour. In addition, questions were asked on men as husbands and relations between genders ('what do husband and wife quarrel about nowadays', 'how can a man be overpowered by his wife', 'why are many men afraid of being poisoned by their wives'). Men were also questioned on their role and obligations as fathers; how they saw the future of their children; what were their major problems right now; if/why they were depressed; what type of dreams they had at night etc.

Other types of questions were also addressed. Where and when did men socialize? How often did men meet with other men? Where did they meet? What did they discuss among themselves? Drinking habits were also taken up: why do so many men drink to-day'? Are men irresponsible, compared with women? Questions linked to male perceptions of selves were asked: what is a good man? Are you such a man? What should a man do to be respected by others? Are you respected by others? What would you like other people to say about you when you die? If you had the choice what would you like to change about your life? etc. Information was also collected on men's sexual life; when did they start their sexual career, the number of partners they had etc. To provide a detailed picture of men's daily activities, all men were asked to explain how they had spent the day (and were going to spend the rest of the day) from 6 a.m. to 12 p.m.

In order to be as representative as possible, these interviews were carried out in various parts of Kisii. To start with I also used some male interviewers, assuming that men would perhaps speak more freely to other men. I was wrong. Men were not at all as free with other men as they were with my female health workers. Moreover, it was also more legitimate to speak about fertility and sexual concerns with women than with other men.

At a conference on alcohol problems in developing countries in Oslo in 1988, I was introduced to the chief psychiatrist from Nairobi University Hospital, Dr. Acuda (who had participated in a study on alcohol problems in Kisii in 1978). I was told that a psychiatrist was to be employed in the near future at the Kisii District Hospital. Thus, on arrival in Kisii in 1990 I immediately contacted the hospital, and it turned out that a psychiatrist had worked there for one year. I attended Dr. Badia's consultations once a week from 8 a.m.—1 p.m. over a period of two months with about 50 patients (mainly men) during each session. I was also allowed to carry out interviews separately with patients as well as with patients in the psychiatric ward.

In 1992, I was back in Kisii to collect additional data for this study. The political situation, however, was extremely critical. Nevertheless, I succeeded in contacting most of my old friends and assistants both in Matunwa and in Mosocho. I carried out qualitative interviews, exclusively in households that I already knew, focusing on (changing) social values, men's and women's perceptions of social value and changing perceptions of social values. Unfortunately, Kisii became an increasingly turbulent and unsafe place because of the coming elections, and after having been involved in a number of violent episodes I was forced to leave prematurely.

Background data on women and men

The data on women interviewed—as well as men—is extensive, and it is difficult to be very systematic. With this reservation I shall give a brief and— I hope—illustrative picture of the general background of the type of men and women interviewed. Neither men nor women were homogeneous groups and social differences were very apparent in the interview sample. Yet having said this, women had much in common, and so did men. Most strikingly, in spite of the fact that both women and men came from different social strata there was often a surprising unanimity in their responses to the questions asked.

All women surveyed in the first study (723) said that they were married (except for a few widows and a few very young girls who stayed at their parents house with a baby—or two). To ask whether bridewealth had been paid turned out to be a very sensitive question. Most said that bridewealth had been paid, but as became apparent later, this was far from the case. 33% of them had no schooling (compared with 11% for the men). 12% lived in polygamous unions. 67% had attended primary school, but most of them had dropped out before reaching the 8th grade. 15% had some secondary schooling.

The women referred to themselves as housewives. Only 6% said that they had off-farm employment (mainly as teachers). This, however, did not mean that they were not involved in income generating activities in the informal sector. Nor did it mean that they had no control over family income.

76% said that they were responsible for the decisions related to the growing and trading of vegetables. Another 31% said that they were the ones who made the decisions in relation to cash crops. They all had children (1–10). Their use of modern contraceptives was low. At the time of interviewing, barely 10% made use of a contraceptive method. To start with, we asked if they had been circumcised—not realizing the magnitude of this practice. This question was an insult to them and had to be dropped almost immediately.

The men interviewed in my second research study were between 19 and 85 years of age. The vast majority were between 25/30 and 45 years. Efforts were made to reach this age group. The reason for this was men in this phase of their lives were confronted with demands as heads of households, husbands and fathers. A few younger men were included in the sample in order to get their opinions. It was also considered very important to draw on the experiences of old men. All men interviewed said they were married, at least in the sense that they were living with a woman (see below). They also said that they had paid bridewealth—or were in the process of doing so (which it turned out was not the case). A few lived in polygamous unions, mainly the older generation (though a few prosperous businessmen maintained that they were planning to acquire a second wife). They all had children (1–14). Their educational background ranged from no schooling at all to a few with Form IV and VI completed (form VI is equivalent to 14 years of schooling). The majority had between 4 and 8 years schooling. In terms of 'occupation' the vast majority defined themselves as farmers. A few said they were businessmen (which included small scale business men, duka owners, matatu drivers, transporters, small-traders, banana sellers etc). There wer a few were government employees, including school teachers (both white-collar categories). A few others worked occasionally as casual labourers.

Outline of the study

The following gives a short outline of each chapter, and how it develops and unfolds my overall themes. Chapter 2 is a historical sketch of the construction of gender and social values. Its point of departure is male and female roles, norms and values in precolonial Kisii and it explores the impact of social change in this century on gender roles and the relations between the sexes. The division of labour, marriage and sexuality—that are critical in shaping and are shaped by cultural conceptions of maleness and femaleness—is explored along with the transformations that these 'spheres' have undergone. The chapter discusses: the consequences of the disappearance of traditional male activities; male migration and men's increasing alienation from the household; women's expanded roles and responsibilities along with a certain independence; the emergence of the 'bread-winner'/provider ideology—and in the wake of this a new moral universe with new social values, new expectations and increasing gender antagonisms.

Chapter 3 explores male and female initiation rituals and how they are linked to the cultural construction of males and females in contemporary Kisii. With initiation still emphasizing 'the moral code of the tribe' it examines the extent to which both female and male initiation rites are integrated and inevitable parts of the Gusii culture, and how these rituals are related to men's and women's present role-based and existential identities and fundamental for their social value.

Chapter 4 explores the relationship between marriage, gender identity and social value. With all the features surrounding the institution of marriage under redefinition and renegotiation the implications for men's and women's gender identity and the relations between genders are investigated. With their gender identity and social value at stake, and with women and men involved in strategizing, the relations between them are becoming increasingly tense. Particular focus is given to the implications of increasing elopements and no transfer of bridewealth for female existential identity.

Chapter 5 closely examines what is taking place at the household level where men and women are engaged in daily struggles and competition over scarce resources. It discusses men's and women's roles, responsibilities and frustrations, and, in particular, the fact that many men find themselves in the contradictory situation of being head of household and at the same time being very marginalized from the household. Based on this, the chapter examines 1) what type of new social roles and new social value systems have emerged for women and men, respectively; 2) how present images of a respected man and woman mesh with old ones; 3) how new social values interact with male and female role-based and existential identities and self-esteem, and 4) how the relations between genders are affected.

Chapter 6 explores the relationship between fertility, gender identity and social value. It discusses why fertility rates have not decreased when both genders recognize that children are becoming economic burdens—and when modern contraceptives are increasingly available. While fertility and children are fundamental to male and female identity, in particular their existential identities, and social value it examines the extent to which men and women are struggling with conflicting and paradoxical rationalities, ideals and reasons.

Chapter 7 explores the relationship between sexuality, gender identity and social value. It discusses the conflicting norms and values which are connected to male and female sexual behaviour and social value, the threat that female sexuality seems to constitute to male existential identity, self-esteem and social value, and the (seemingly increasing) need for men to be in control of female sexuality.

Chapter 8 is the concluding chapter which briefly recapitulates the main points of each chapter. It discusses my findings in relation to the guiding themes of the study, the hypotheses and the theoretical tools that have been used. Particular emphasis is given to trying to come to grips with the underlying reasons constituting the antagonistic relations between the sexes.

Chapter 2
Historical Background—Gender Constructions and Social Value in Pre-Colonial and Colonial Kisii

One of the major problems facing a reconstruction of pre-colonial times is, of course, the lack of source material. Studies by foreign and African scholars based on oral history and interviews with old people who can recall various traditions from the beginning of the century have their limitations, as 'traditions' are sometimes reinterpreted. The outline below should therefore be taken with some reservation.

This being said, I shall rely on studies from Kisii which have been carried out by foreign researchers[6] as well as local scholars from the mid 1940s and more recently. The material produced by the Historical Society at the Cardinal Otunga Secondary School, Mosocho in Kisii, based on a large number of interviews with very old Gusii men and women, is very useful and provides a detailed picture, in particular of men's lives and their activities before colonial times (Cardinal Otunga Historical Society, 1979). The *Kisii District Socio-Cultural Profile* (1986) based on studies carried out by the Institute of African Studies of the University of Nairobi has also provided useful baseline information.

Kisii in the 'formative period'

The Gusii and other peoples like the Kikuyu, Akamba and Bukusu originated from 'Misiri' just to the north of Mount Elgon. Tradition has it that the Gusii settled in Kisii about two centuries ago. The three settlements in Gusiiland, Nyagoe, Manga and Isecha seem to have formed the first localities the Gusii occupied in the highlands. It was from these settlements that Gusii clans sorted themselves out and then expanded into the rest of the highlands. Gusii can be divided into four main groups: namely Abasweta, Abagirango, Abasi and Abanchari (Were and Nyamwaya, 1986:12–17). From the time of settlement in their present territory to the time of the arrival of the British, the Masaii, Kipsigis and the Joluo were the major threats to the survival of the Gusii. Not only did these external enemies attack the Gusii in their heartland, but cattle raiding from Gusii was a lucrative business for these groups. One of the most famous battles was that between the Kipsigis and virtually all Gusii in 1892. If the battle taught the Kipsigis the lesson of

---

[6] In particular, Robert and Barbara LeVine, Philip Mayer, Iona Mayer, Sarah LeVine, and Thomas Håkansson.

not returning to Gusiiland, it also taught the Gusii that unity is strength (1986:22–24).

According to Ochieng, a Kenyan historian, the themes of conquest, assimilation and ecological hazards featured prominently prior to 1900 i.e. the "formative period" (before British administration). These "creative tensions" were necessitated by the natural struggle for survival. In the true spirit of shared destiny, the various ethnic groups were highly dynamic, adaptive, innovative and accommodating (Ochieng, 1974:7–13). Contrary to the parochial view of traditional societies as closed subsistence systems governed by inertia and inward-looking conservatism, pervasive evidence exists of local initiative, dynamism, surplus production, exchange mechanisms and spontaneous innovation. In short, the picture that Ochieng presents of Gusiiland is one of a well-ordered, self-regulatory, self-sufficient society with an inbuilt mechanism for self-perpetuation, production and reproduction and local initiatives, which the colonial intrusion served to dampen and stifle, rather than promote.

According to Bogonko (1976), Gusii pre-colonial education was moral, progressive, comprehensive, gradual and practical. It was not something apart from actual life and its experiences. Education comprised the value, knowledge and skills of society continually transmitted and renewed by word and deed. It was deeply rooted in the history of man's struggle with nature from time immemorial. It was characterised by its collective and social nature with a clear separation of male and female spheres, roles and duties, and every member of the family or community was responsible for imparting knowledge. It had close ties with social life besides being of a polyvalent character and providing moral qualities, developing physical aptitudes and combining manual activity with intellectual exercises.

Gusiiland came under full British rule in 1914. Gusii response to the British was quite negative. When the Gusii realised that British firepower was superior to theirs, Mumboism, a quasi-religious movement developed which glorified Gusii culture and emphasized Gusiiness. The movement eventually died out because of severe repression by the British. Compared with other Bantu-speaking groups in Kenya as well as their Nilotic neighbours, the Luo, the Gusii lagged far behind in Christian conversion and sending children to schools. This 'backwardness' was (according to the British) a result of their negative response to Christian missions which controlled education in the District (Were and Nyamwaya, 1986:25). Prior to the Second World War, the Gusii did not form any political associations, and it took a long time for an educated elite to develop in the District (1986:26).

Men and women and social organization

The extent to which the rather rosy picture of precolonial societies is true or not is difficult to substantiate. However, it is a fact that land in Kisii was abundant. Clusters of patrilineal clans lived in clan villages, and men were the heads of household (LeVine, R, and B., 1966/77). Each household supplied its own food and met many of its other needs as well. The head of the household, the husband, had access to as much land as his family could cultivate and use for grazing. Agriculture was combined with animal husbandry. Cattle herding, however, overshadowed agriculture by far—in social significance if not actually for subsistence. Men acquired large herds of cattle, and numbers were augmented through breeding and raids on neighbouring clans. Thus, cattle herding together with the protection of it—i.e. warfare—went hand in hand and constituted an extremely important basis of both male activities and the male image, not to mention social value (Cardinal Otunga Historical Society, 1979).

Gusii institutions were not differentiated into political, economic and religious spheres but were run on patriarchal lines based on patriarchal mystique which called for axiomatic reverence not only from wives and daughters, but also from sons. There were no temples or shrines; most rituals were performed at home in the same setting in which all other activities took place, often with the patriarch as chief officiant (Mayer, I., 1974).

The intermarrying clans occupied distinct territories. A cardinal feature of the domestic group was its virilocal residence i.e. men were permanent residents from birth to death, while women came from other clans (LeVine R. and B., 1966/77). The household functioned as a unit of economic expansion and social control. The more wives a man married, the more land could be cultivated, the more daughters he would get whose marriages would give him cattle as bridewealth, and the more sons he would get to herd the cattle and to defend the homestead from outside attack. The ideal was proliferation of wives, children, herds and crops, and economic conditions permitted these modes of growth to be mutually reinforcing. Polygamy, then, was a cardinal feature of the household. The head of the household had at least two, ideally four and occasionally more wives. (Some, I was told had up to twenty, a number which may have been possible, partly because large numbers of men were killed in warfare and, partly, because land was abundant). Each wife had her own house with its own yard. The husband allocated fields to her which she was responsible for cultivating. Her produce was stored in her own granary. The wife and her children were supposed to be agriculturally an independent self-supporting unit (Were and Nyamwaya, 1986:39).

Men owned land, property and cattle. Inheritance was always on the male line. As a result, boys were looked upon as the future 'fathers' or heads of the extended family, whereas girls were expected to leave the family and join another. Women then were essential to the lineage process as the instruments of procreation. If a woman's husband died, she had no basic rights to the house, land or household properties, other than certain material possessions clearly defined as her own. A widow however, was not simply tossed out. In most cases she was taken over by a brother of the former husband (see below).

Women were clearly defined in terms of their relations with men (daughter, sister, wife, mother). Men were also defined in terms of their relations with women (son, brother, husband, father). On top of this—and contrary to women—men were also defined in terms of their roles or statuses: head of household, cattle-keeper, chief, elder etc.

The division of labour

Men were administratively responsible for the family's interests i.e. land and cattle. This included apportioning land for the various women of the homestead to cultivate, cattle for the males to marry with and the settling of disputes and lawsuits:

> ... the homestead head was formally the absolute ruler of this group and owner of all its property, with sole power to resolve all its internal difficulties, including intra-familial homicide. The internal allocation of livestock and land was entirely in his hands, and he was also the principal performer of sacrifice to the ancestors ... . There were generally accepted customs concerning allocation of property within the domestic group but if the homestead head chose to disregard them, no one within or outside the homestead could challenge his authority and the matter would wait until after his death for the adjudication of other elders. He had the power of putting a curse on his adult sons, which would kill them or drive them mad unless rescinded after a public apology by the son. Everyone in the homestead was obliged to show deference to its head in their everyday behaviour ... . Each homestead head wanted to have the most populous domestic group possible, with numerous sons as a potential fighting force ... . This drive for numerical expansion of the homestead was a fundamental tendency in Gusii domestic life (LeVine, R. and B., 1966/77:67–68).

Thus men had (at least ideally) a very important role as owner and ruler of the household and its members, and men had both power and authority.

The male head, together with his sons, was also responsible for safeguarding the well-being of all family members. Clan loyalty passed from father to son, and all disputes were directly mediated through male family heads. Informally, and regardless of genealogy, the mature men of the neighbourhood were collectively the neighbourhood bosses. They would meet regularly as a clique to relax, drink beer and talk about local business affairs. Local cases would be brought to them to be judged in accordance with Gusii law which all adult men were supposed to know.

The women were responsible for the food producing cycle, for general domestic services (the procuring of firewood and water, preparation of food), for tending and training young children and nursing the sick, for helping to keep good relations with neighbours and kin. Most activities were carried out on a cooperative basis, in the sense that men would go out hunting, cattle keeping and to war in groups, and women would work together in groups when carrying out their agricultural activities.

In the 18th century it had been discovered that by heating a certain kind of soil, iron could be obtained. Many men were busily involved in the handling of iron and many worked as blacksmiths manufacturing agricultural tools such as jembes, pangas, spears and arrow heads, ankle rings for married women and bracelets for old men. Iron production required digging by men as well as cutting down trees and splitting them into firewood which was turned into charcoal. The digging was hard work. Holes to a depth of 10 feet had to be dug in order to find the right kind of soil. Women participated in the sense that they filled their baskets with the 'iron soil' brought it back home where it was their job to dry the soil and remove unwanted particles (Cardinal Otunga Historical Society: 1979).

The division of labour 'etiquette' set adult males apart from women and children along lines which contributed to their position in the social hierarchy. There was a very clear sexual division of labour which was manifested in two separate hierarchies, where the male hierarchy (sons, husbands, elders) was superior to the female hierarchy (daughters, wives and elder women). The division of labour, then, was characterized by separateness and separate spheres; special tasks and roles were reserved for one sex only. Only men could herd the cattle. In hut-building, men put up the wooden framework while women plastered it. Only men could make ropes, or work with iron. Only women could cook, tend the household fire and brew beer.

Male and female spheres were also divided in the literal sense of physical space. Men did not climb into the rafter storage place where women kept their pots and threshed grain. Women did not go into the men's day hut. Similar separation was practised between old and young, children and circumcised youth, the married and the unmarried. And while men could eat fowl, women could not.

The fact that the ideology of the society was based on separation of the male and female spheres gave certain limits to male domination. In addition, the fact that men depended on women for food provided women with a 'counter-control' and possibilities of sanctions against men. However, there seems to be little doubt that male superiority and dominance were accepted and respected—at least in theory.

Values of maleness and femaleness

In the traditional Gusii code, manliness was based on a father's and a husband's dignity, reflected in respect from juniors in his family, his wives and most importantly, his own self-restraint (Mayer, I., 1965). The male head of the household was its decision-maker and controller of wealth i.e. land, cattle, money and labour, including that of women. As long as he lived, he was the only person who could officiate at sacrifices to the ancestors, whose goodwill controlled the health and fertility of the whole family. Moreover, men had the unchallenged control of political and legal relations and institutions (LeVine, R. and B., 1966/77).

Manliness was also strongly related to men's 'role' as a warrior i.e. men in Kisii (as men elsewhere) were defined by violent deeds (Ortner and Whitehead, 1981/89). The warriors in charge of the *ebisarate* (cattle camps) were subjected to rigorous training and to a number of very strict rules—an education towards manhood—which was to ensure that each warrior was capable, strong, quick-acting, courageous and disciplined (Cardinal Otunga Historical Society, 1979).

> After the boys had successfully gone through the circumcision trials, they were now men who could marry and be admitted to Gusii governing councils. But their education in the ways of men and tactics of war was not complete until they lived in *ebisarate*, (*egesarate* sing.) ... . The young people were instructed that to succeed in life they had to co-operate ... . In short, *ebisarate* helped to unite all the inmates in a strong brotherhood ... . Those who did not co-operate were cautioned about their obstinacy, selfishness and unco-operativeness. In fact a disobedient *egesarate* dweller could be denied his share of milk, meat and *amaguta* even if these items were produced by his own cow. If he remained obstinate after such a ruling, he would be asked to quit and start his own *egesarate*. If he pulled out and went back home to his parents he was laughed at and ridiculed by the elders who heard that he had failed to comply with *egesarate* rules. Pulling out actually meant that the young man was a coward who was not ready to defend his nation; he had run back home to hide under the aprons of his mother. *It was believed that no-one would learn much if he stayed in the company of women* (Were and Nyamwaya, 1986:125–26 [my emphasis]).

> After a boy had passed through all the educational stages up to and including *egesarate*, he was regarded as almost fully educated as to the potentialities and weaknesses of the economy of his society and on the social, moral and political fibres that bound his society together and made it work smoothly. The young men who had lived together in *ebisarate* became mystically and ritually in effect one body, one community, one people (1986:128).

Education acquired from infancy to the *egesarate* stage was put into practice in adult life during which it was tested and refined. An adult was regarded as 'medicine'. He was expected to discuss problems objectively and suggest solutions. Adult men should store knowledge and wisdom (1986).

The *ebisarate* were officially abolished by the British administration in 1912. Until the 1920s, fathers still sent their unmarried sons out together to camp in the bush and jointly look after their fathers' cattle. The boys would practice fighting with spears, and sometimes they would attack other cattle camps. This could escalate into feuding and warring with other villages until the older men met to negotiate peace (LeVine, R. and B., 1966). Gusii men were highly respected as fighters/raiders (Nyasani, 1984).

The traditional ideal of a woman was of one who knew her place as a female, to 'be her age' and to be less 'strong-minded' than the average man.

A woman was also respected when, apart from her childbearing capacities, she was strong, capable, energetic, entrepreneurial and a good manager of her household (LeVine, R. and B., 1966/77). Despite so called subordination to men, women traditionally had essential, semi-autonomous roles as producers and distributors of goods (1966/77). While men were in control of women, they were also dependent on women for their personal wealth (wives, children, cattle and land); for respect, honour and esteem from others; and (by marriage) for peaceful relations with potential enemies from other clans.

In sum, there seems to have been a foundation of respect towards men. Manliness was a quality that all men sought and was closely linked to self control and dignity. Dignity was in turn linked to wealth, to having many wives, many children and particularly to obeying the prescribed norms. Rich men were respected and honoured, poor men despised. (To this day, the term for a 'poor man' continues to be an insult). Conditions permitted the majority of men to ensure that their wives had access to land and that they could pay bridewealth. In terms of labour, there was a certain complementarity whereby each sex took care of their domains of activity and responsibility. Consequently, women seem to have had the expected sense of reverence—'for the offices of father and husband, if not for the individual concerned' (Mayer, I., 1974). Husbands who did not fulfil their obligations towards the household (and there must have been some) certainly did not receive the same respect as those who did.

Just as gender roles were clearcut—what gave social value was also clearcut. Thus, the use of sanctions vis-à-vis transgressors was seldom necessary, given the established value system. The very clear norms and values preserved the established social order, and made the actors accept their place in society and carry out their given roles without asking too many questions (1974). Interestingly enough, in the existing literature on Kisii, traditional ideals of Gusii women are often linked to what women should not be i.e. 'uncontrollable, faithless, disloyal to family interests, jealous, quarrelsome and they should not roam about and 'choose men for themselves'. This supports the suggestion that not all women did in fact play their required role. Women represented a threat to men, and male control over women was therefore essential.

Marriage and fertility

Marriage was bound by three rules:

- marriage between clan members was not allowed, because all clan members were considered relatives. Intermarrying clans were enemies, and marriage was meant to create bonds between fighting clans. Thus the proverb 'those whom we marry are those whom we fight'(a proverb even referred to in Kisii today).

– when a woman married she had to leave her natal homestead and settle in that of her husband and his parents. Here she was given access to a piece of land, and eventually she would become incorporated in her husband's kin group (after she had given birth to at least one son);

– a respectable marriage required the payment of bridewealth to the bride's father. The payment of bridewealth would give the husband exclusive sexual rights over the wife and the custody of all children to whom she gave birth. Thus, the marriage system was characterized by clan exogamy, patrilocal residence and transfer of brideweath (1973).

As such, marriage was a strategy of alliance with other clans and intra-clan marriage was not permitted. The transfer of women at marriage was highly formalized and—from the bride's point of view—highly coercive. She had no influence on the choice of her husband, she had to leave her home and settle in that of her husband, and often she was very reluctant to do so. Marriage negotiations, including settlement of bridewealth, were undertaken by clan elders. Bridewealth was paid in cattle, and a wife could easily cost 20–30 cows. The transfer of women could only take place when bridewealth was paid.

While, on the one hand, women constituted the principal channels through which men could arrange for their access to resources, including children, (the more wives a man had the more land could be cultivated, and the more children he could get), and through which men could create alliances with neighbouring clans, the position of women was clearly inferior to that of men. Moreover, women were never considered 'real' members of their clan and family. 'Women are enemies' (Mayer, P., 1949:7). Only men could be real clan members.

Gusii beliefs, practices and values clearly reflected the notion that human procreation was to be regarded as a blessing, while infertility was one of the greatest tragedies of life. Thus, in terms of social value, the more wives and children a man had, the more he could hope to be respected in the local masculine world—as well as the feminine one. He would have a larger homestead, control more land and dispense more hospitality. He would have a larger faction to side with him in neighbourhood conflicts and judicial cases; sons were expected to side with their father automatically. He would have a wider, more influential network of connections by marriage. And he would be much commemorated in the ancestral cult (male ancestors of the living members of one's lineage):

> The central institution of the ancestor religion was the sacrifice of a goat or bull offered to the shade (soul or spirit) of a dead man by his sons and his grandsons. All the sons were to offer sacrifice, once they were married, not just the eldest son. It was a religious and moral duty to offer these sacrifices regularly so that the father or grandfather 'will not be forgotten' and 'his name lives'. Since nobody but the sons and grandsons could offer these sacrifices, a man who died

without leaving such relatives had his name forgotten, whereas a large number of such relatives meant that his shade would be commemorated often. The desire to be commemorated was seen as axiomatic. One could say it represented the desire to leave a certain influence after death—to be regarded as 'somebody' in the world of living men. A man wanted to be assured of this posthumous commemoration in the same natural and elementary way as he wanted to be 'somebody' in his lifetime (Mayer, I., 1972:125).

Sexual behaviour

Gusii ideas about sex seem to have been rather strict and repressive concerning public manifestations of sexuality, but relatively permissive concerning sexual feelings and clandestine sexual acts (LeVine, R. and B., 1966/77; Mayer, I., 1974). After circumcision (see below) and before marriage young people were allowed to engage in sexual games with each other—as long as this did not result in pregnancies. The newly married couple would, separately, be thoroughly instructed on sex. The male would be enlightened by his male counterparts and his paternal grandmother, who was allowed to discuss any topic with her grandsons. His male advisers would only be interested in his performance and competence as a lover. The grandmother, however, would give her grandson a real lecture on the issue. In bed, the man always was to lie on the left side of the woman, and the wife was never to turn her back to the husband. If she did so it meant that he was a very incompetent lover.

In spite of the relative permissiveness, adultery—when discovered— was a serious offence. The offence, though, was much more serious when committed by a woman than a man, as she was supposed to be faithful to her husband, whereas men had much greater latitude in their sexual activities. Though women were supposed to be sexually faithful to their husband during his life, they were not to stop bearing children after his death. It was a basic principle of marriage that a widow of childbearing age should go on producing children. Brothers or cousins of the dead husband either had to accept the widow(s) as 'wives' themselves, or allow each to choose 'a warmer of the house' from among the men of the neighbourhood. The 'warmer' would then beget children with her and be of general help.

Through polygamy men had access to the sexual services of several wives. Only poor men had one wife, and men with only one wife were ostracized. Even today the proverb has it that when a man with only one wife goes to the bar he should always sit next to the door. In polygamous households wives sometimes succeeded in organizing themselves for mutual benefit. In most households, however, there was a fierce competition between wives for the husband's favour, particularly for his sexual attention. The husband was supposed to treat all his wives in the same way and give them the same sexual attention. While it was common practice for the husband to place his little stool in front of the hut of the wife with whom he intended to spend the night, 'underserved' wives used to snatch the stool and place it in front of their hut—forcing their husband to give them sexual attention.[7]

Kisii—an inflexible system?

In sum, pre-colonial Kisii was a society in which everybody was subject to a large number of prescriptions, social taboos and norms. According to Iona Mayer, daily life was like a theatre in which the actors performed their parts and established their identities. Each had his place and role and all were expected to live up to the prescribed rules. In the terms of a structural functionalist mode of analysis, punishments were far less important than the established system of norms i.e. the rules of behaviour were largely kept, and deviations were rare. Linked to this, and most crucial to this study, Mayer observes that the clear and well established system of norms helped preserve the social order and promote unquestioned obedience; the more the system of prescribed rules and norms was adhered to, the less the problem of identity.

The beginning of a new era—Colonial rule

> There came a time when the *ebisarate* (cattle village) had to disappear for good. This period was a very bad one for the people, because with the disappearance of the cattle villages they feared there would be no life for the Gusii people any more in the future. They felt like that, because they used almost exclusively things that were produced by their cattle. For marriage they needed cows, they used their skins as clothes, their horns as containers, their milk and meat as food.—The decline of the *ebisarate* came with the coming of the white men, who did not like the existence of groups of warriors, who might form the nuclei for rebellious armies (Cardinal Otunga Historical Society, 1979).

Gusiiland formally came under British control as a Native Reserve as early as 1894. The invasion by the colonial power had an undermining effect on the pre-colonial structure of Kisii and its economy. The early stage of colonial administration over the Gusii focused on the maintenance of order. Thereafter, while strengthening administrative authority and initiating a new judicial system, attention turned to the collection of taxes. This should stimulate a supply of labour from inside and outside the District, and encourage trade—based on a money economy—in animals, animal hides and agricultural produce. The development of a cash oriented economy was not enforced directly, but maintenance of colonial law and order and the extraction of goods and services were enforced. The rural population had no strong interest in building the infrastructure of colonialism and had to be induced to work through taxation, a method that had already proved successful in southern Africa (White, 1990:35).

---

[7] Personal communication with old people.

As early as 1907, the colonial administration recorded that the Gusii were very industrious and excellent cultivators (Burnes, 1976). But there is no mention of *who* performed the agricultural work. In the early 1930s, heavy rains and other disasters devastated agricultural production to the point that famine relief programmes had to be set up. Even though production gradually came back to normal, prices received for agricultural produce were low (1976). In spite of this, government taxation remained high, and tax collection became increasingly difficult.

The introduction of chiefs and headmen who had to collect taxes, maintain law and order and control over resources and economic stratification was the start of a process of political and economic differentiation (de Wolf, 1977). This in turn initiated a process of role differentiation. In short, colonial policy consisted of keeping Africans under proper control so that the economic interests of the settler community could be safeguarded. This was to be done in the least expensive way. The cost of the administration of Africans was financed by taxation. This in turn forced men to leave their traditional work and responsibilities and to migrate out of Kisii, in order to earn cash for taxes. With no white settlement in Kisii, European owned plantations in neighbouring districts, the construction of a railroad, the construction of Nairobi etc. all attracted large numbers of Gusii labourers, mainly on a seasonal basis (Mayer, P., 1949). A pattern of male labour migration developed, and Kisii became a major labour reservoir. Records from the 1920s show that the greatest number of migrant workers in the whole country came from Kisii. The early twenties was the heyday of labour recruitment from Nyanza Province (Hay and Stichter, 1984:81). This can be associated with men's marginal role in agriculture and the fact that cattle camps were gradually abolished by the colonial administration. In the early twenties, government persuasion and compulsion were prominent features of the labour market. In the later years of the decade the poor income from crop production also encouraged men to migrate. Increasing economic competition made wage labour a necessity for the very poor, and for most others an essential element in the struggle for upward mobility (1984:98).

Changing male and female roles

1919 and 1920 were years of intense exploitation. The African reserves were recovering from World War I, famine and epidemic, while the areas settled by Europeans required increasing amounts of cheap labour to take full advantage of the postwar boom. To increase the supply of labour to settler farms and state enterprises, 'legislation to prevent idleness' was called for by settlers and Governor Northey (White, 1990:52). After 1919 increases in the Hut and Poll Taxes obliged men to seek wage labour. District Officers, private labour recruiters, and chiefs were to 'advise and encourage' this by every lawful means. Nairobi, along with other cities in colonial Africa, was in part designed to contain and maintain pools of competitively cheap male labourers, who in theory would return to their rural families as soon as their contract ended. They all supposedly had families whose farms would provide them with the foodstuffs their wages did not allow them to purchase.

Despite somewhat conflicting accounts of the extent and length of male migration, there is a general consensus that migration reached its peak in the period between 1930 and 1960. It is interesting to note that Gusii men were highly appreciated by the colonial administration as hard working labourers (Hay and Stichter, 1984). As men came to work in the new colonial cities, ports, railheads and plantations, they became part of the tradition of male labour migration. Policies governing wages, housing and migration tried to guarantee that these men would have neither the interest nor the funds to stay in town any longer than their labour contracts allowed, only to return when the next tax payment was due. Normally, workers had no long term contracts but could be hired and fired at will. They often lived on 'survival' wages in humiliating circumstances—often with 8 men sharing one little room and one prostitute in another room (White, 1990)—with limited possibilities to tend to their own 'consumption needs' and certainly with very little surplus for their dependents in the rural areas (Tostensen, 1986). By 1915 an identifiable role of the prostitute, complete with dependent males, had emerged. Thus, men who left Kisii to work for cash in Nairobi or in other parts of the country became familiar with prostitution.' Men were hungry for sex, and women were hungry for money' (White, 1990:44).

Gradually, migration became more and more long term. Some men migrated for periods of 15–20 years (Hay and Stichter, 1984). In fact the rate of long-stay migration was underestimated, due to the very poor labour statistics of these years (Kitching, 1980). Long term migrants changed work and residence with bewildering rapidity in the 1930s and 1940s and were not in a position to establish a stable life pattern.

Although women continued to provide most of the labour power in agriculture, the extra demands on them were not great and they were aided by the new implements and crops. The extra labour demands in cultivation were still rather small and could be met from an amount of under-utilised women's labour time. Further, quite a number of the migrants were young males, who would normally have been warriors or herdsmen. Thus, high rates of migration out of Kisii in the years up to 1930 seem to have had only little impact on the sexual division of labour (Hay and Stichter, 1984). After 1930, the plough and the hand grinding mill were adopted, and there is the first indication of a rather different pattern of labour use, which was to become far more marked in the 1930s and 1940s (Kitching, 1980).

During this latter period, migration out of Kisii increased markedly along with the development of capitalism. New ways of replacing male labour and of utilising female labour more intensively were needed. In spite of improved technology, enormous burdens were placed on the women left behind. Women's labour-time became increasingly over-utilised—it was actually exploited. Women had to increase or at least maintain agricultural production, feed themselves and their children, and perhaps other dependents, not to mention their absent spouses and sons, while at the same time providing cash crops for export or market sale. Between food and cash crop production, the amount of time women spent cultivating increased dramatically (1980). The sex-segregated division of labour became even more pronounced. At the same time women's labour domain expanded and, I shall argue, so did their decision-making roles—in spite of the fact that they were 'supervised' by the older men who had remained in Kisii.

Kisii—and in fact the whole of western Kenya—was by 1940 a society of women, children and old men. These women were faced with tremendous burdens in the transition toward an increasingly commercialized agriculture (Hay and Stichter, 1984). Female headed households emerged i.e. households where women were often the sole supporters of the needs of the household (since remittances from husbands were non-existent or irregular).

Consequently, the pre-colonial type of households which functioned as units of economic expansion and social control became increasingly rare. Gender roles and relations were subjected to fundamental changes. Money, sex and children were increasingly becoming the sole areas of common interest between husband and wife (LeVine, S., 1979). Anthropological 'network' literature and 'situational analyses' of the 1950s and 60s underline the constraints that male migrants in Central and East African contexts were submitted to, trying to cope with their split lives between rural and urban settings; their attempts to assimilate; their alienation from their local contexts and their difficulties in switching from one context to the other (Mitchell, 1959, 1987; Mayer, P., 1961).

Changing marriage and sexuality patterns

The disappearance of cattle camps had a very negative effect on the payment of bridewealth which used to be paid in cattle. This, in turn, affected marriage patterns severely. While in the pre-colonial period the bride would only take up residence with her husband when bridewealth had been transferred, it became increasingly common for the bride to move in with her husband when a first down payment had been made. Instalments were then supposed to be paid each time the bride had proven her fertility.

While there was no conceivable alternative to marriage, women resented the traditional procedure of obtaining a husband and wanted increasingly to make their own choice. Girls preferred young husbands and did not want to become second or third wives with junior status. Thus they resented the tendency for parents to choose wealthy old polygamists who could afford to pay a lot of bridewealth. Hence they rebelled against their parents by eloping with young men who promised to pay bridewealth, but—as was often the case—never did.

Bridewealth negotiations, when they took place, continued to be carried out by older men. An ever increasing number of men, though, were not able to pay the instalments. As a result, the meaning of bridewealth as well as bridewealth negotiations were attenuated, and contradicting tendencies emerged. Male control over women started to weaken, while at the same time women's (legal) access to their husbands' land became insecure. Women's position in the household became insecure in the sense that when transfer of bridewealth had not taken place, a husband had no 'legal' obligations towards his wife (Håkansson, 1988). It is in this period that 'runaway' and 'roaming' wives became an increasingly common phenomenon (Mayer, I., 1974; LeVine, S., 1979). Through polygamy men were accustomed to have access to the sexual services of several women. However, while sexuality had primarily been an activity within the homestead, sexuality was now taken out of the homestead.

Women's access to resources had always been associated with their access to land. Transfer of bridewealth constituted the key for women to get access to land. Through bridewealth, the wife gained managerial and use rights to her husband's land, the right of maintenance for herself and her children as well as the right for her sons to become legal heirs to the land allocated to her. The husband gained rights in his wife as a domestic worker and to her reproductive capacities. As he became the 'owner' of his wife, he also became the 'owner' of the children he fathered. The absence of bridewealth made women's access to land insecure. It should not be forgotten, though, that at the same time husbands' rights to their children became questionable. Very importantly, daughters' elopements deprived their fathers of bridewealth for their sons to marry with, and run-away wives threatened the household labour force—not to mention the husbands' social value and self-esteem.

For a man, marriage was still a prerequisite to adult autonomy and status—just as it was for women. But men no longer *needed* marriages in order to make peace among themselves. It can be argued that marriage lost some of its original function and meaning, from the point of view of men. But men became fearful that their wives might leave them. Moreover, men needed to marry to have rights to their children. Their meagre wages, however, did not allow them to scrape together a decent bridewealth—or money was used on girlfriends in town. Thus elopements became more common; so did monogamous unions and last but not least so did men's but certainly also women's feelings of insecurity.

Absent men, present wives

When Gusii migrants returned to their homes, most of their former way of life had died out. Grazing areas were giving way to cash crop production; partly because this gave greater cash income, and partly because there was not sufficient male labour for cattle herding. In 1927 cattle camps were abolished by the colonial power despite the fundamental social and symbolic value of cattle. Local political influence was now in the hands of the British. Feuds with other tribes were banned, and warfare and men's role as warrior disappeared. Men were left with participation in minor political decisions of no importance to the colonial administration. As pointed out by Cohen and Odhiambo in their study in Siaya District—also a classic example of a labour reserve—the activities from which Luo men could gain respect from both themselves and their surroundings disappeared (Cohen and Odhiambo, 1989). The same was the case in Kisii.

In the 1950s, when Robert and Barbara LeVine carried out their study in Kisii, women did almost all the cultivation—from breaking ground with hoes to harvesting. They milked the cows—formerly a masculine prerogative—and tried to keep an eye on the herding carried out by pre-adolescent boys who had replaced young men in this job. Women, on top of their traditional responsibilities in the production of food crops, also became involved in the production of cash crops. Thus, with increasing involvement in productive as well as reproductive activities and left with their children and other dependents for long periods of time, women's traditional life pattern was deeply affected.

Given that men had always been more mobile than women and that men had always had less routine tasks, LeVine argues that no drastic restructuring in the division of labour occurred. Rather, what happened was an accentuation of trends already existing in the traditional division of labour (LeVine, R., 1966). However, women became more bound to the homestead than before and had to assume responsibility for tasks that were once their husbands', in addition to their own. Men, though, still retained rights to land, to cattle, and even to the sale of the cash crops their wives had planted, weeded, and harvested. In spite of the emergence of households where women were alone in supporting the family, men were still 'legitimate' heads of household. Thus, while women's burdens had increased, dependence still remained.

The separateness of men's and women's spheres of activity was undoubtedly being reinforced. Men, in particular, became increasingly separated from the domestic domain. In terms of male involvement in public matters, the colonial administration had taken over many of these male functions. By introducing new systems of law, disputes which used to be settled locally were now taken to public courts. To what extent did men continue to dominate their wives' lives and domains? I agree with LeVine that women's dependence still remained, despite absent husbands. Male control was still exercised over women by older men. In principle, cash derived from the sale of tea and coffee could not be collected by women, but only by their husbands on their rare visits. But it should not be overlooked that women exercised independence as daily managers and decision makers of the household. As such, women developed a wide range of strategies in order to get access to the product of their labour. For example they would often sell their produce directly to middlemen—though at a lower price—instead of delivering it to the official authorities. This practice is still widely used today. Hence, one clear result was certainly that more and more demands were made on the women left behind, and men were forced to leave more and more decisions to women. Male superiority and dominance were still accepted and respected. But the fact that male and female activities and spheres had become even more separate limited the extent of male domination. The analysis by Boserup of what happened to women in regions with high male out-migration underlines some of my above arguments, namely that the women became heads of households and sole providers for non-working members of the family. Women became independent, because men went away for years or even forever (Boserup, 1980). Moreover, I shall argue that husbands also became increasingly dependent on women as shamba (farm) managers, for food (women sent big sacks of maize to their husbands in town), for giving birth to children, not to mention respect from others. For instance, a husband who had an 'uncontrollable' wife was not respected by the rest of society, and with the increasing number of women who started 'roaming', men's social value and 'honour' was at stake.

Even if women often acquired a double role and became unpaid family workers in men's cash crop production, they continued to be independent producers of food crops for family use, and sellers of food surpluses which were not needed for family consumption. Nevertheless the change in women's work was less radical than that in men's work. The main role of the women continued to be food producers for the family and performers of domestic services (1980). Boserup's observation that the change in women's work was less radical than that in men's work is crucial and very much in line with my own findings (Silberschmidt, 1991a, 1991b). This argument has been mostly overlooked both in (feminist) anthropological writings and in the existing literature on Kisii.

In addition, I have not come across any reference to the fact that a totally new role was actually imposed on men: the role as family provider and, along with it, new expectations and values. To be sure, men had always contributed to some extent, but not to the extent that was now needed and expected. Robert LeVine (1966), in an article on sex roles and economic change, discusses the changed occupational roles of women and men. However, his interest lies in examining the effect on women's status.[8]

---

[8] The same applies to the analysis by Håkansson who discusses the impact of social change in Kisii (1985, 1988). The observations mentioned above by Cohen and Odhiambo in their study from Siaya District are most interesting in terms of this study: this is precisely because they point out that because the men—husbands, fathers, brothers and sons—were away from home for so long, women became daily 'heads' of rural households. And most importantly, they note that new activities from which men could gain respect from both themselves and their surroundings were lacking (1989).

The development of the 'provider' ideology and new values

Trying to summarize what actually happened during the colonial period is not an easy task, because the situation was rather confusing and contradictory. The division of labour was upset; the meaning of marriage changed; sexuality was taken out of the homestead; new social values emerged—meshing (obscurely) with old ones. A process was started which—using the distinctions of Kopytoff—affected both the existential as well as the role-based identities of Gusii men and women.

In the pre-colonial period, men commanded the surplus product of women's labour and were dependent on their labour for the agricultural production of their family. The rise of wage labour external to the household economy began to change this situation for the men involved. No longer was their survival completely dependent on the family in the short term. The possibility arose that these men could live on their off-farm earnings—quite separate from their families—without re-investing those earnings in the household economy. However, as long as wage labour remained completely external to the household and only short-term, such men would eventually have to return to the household economy for their very survival. This was why the labour migration system served incipient colonial capitalism so well. The costs of reproducing labour, other than the costs of immediate survival of the labourer while outside the home area, were met by the household economy rather than by the employer.

Traditionally, land was abundant, food was generally sufficient (if no droughts occurred), and so was household labour (LeVine, R., 1966). Gradually, however, a new situation emerged whereby women were no longer able to feed their families and satisfy their increasing needs. These could only be met by the husbands' and the wives' joint efforts. It can be argued that the household had always depended on men's and women's joint activities and efforts. However, during colonialism 'joint efforts' came to include men's financial assistance. This was new since employment and trade were regarded as supplements rather than substitutes for the produce of the fields and pastures. Linked to this, Barbara and Robert LeVine observe that the financial aid for the household had become very important—along with store bought items for family members. Moreover, great symbolic value became attached both to the financial aid and the giving of commodities. The LeVines also emphasize the great economic anxiety arising partly from the overcrowding of the land and partly from economic values emphasizing invidious distinctions based on wealth.

Traditionally, male labour time was not used in material production for a large part of the working year. Younger men were mainly engaged in fighting, raiding, hunting and cattle herding. But these activities were not directly productive. Older men (30–50 years) were engaged in ritual and judicial functions to a large extent. These functions were not productive either. As mentioned above, men as heads of households were administratively responsible for the family's interests, land and cattle. Cattle herding, together with the protection of cattle (warfare), went hand in hand and constituted an extremely important basis of both male activities and the male image. With the disappearance of cattle there were no skins to wear, and it became necessary to buy clothes. With the expansion of education, cash for school fees was needed. Men were expected to provide this.

As heads of household, men were closely connected to the domestic domain. But it was through their activities in the public domain that men were responsible for safeguarding and protecting the domestic sphere: wife, children, relatives. Thus, men's traditional role had never been one of a family provider in the new sense of the word which developed during colonialism.

The substantial change in the need for both men's and women's contributions to family support challenged the ideology of separate spheres. On the one hand, it initiated a shift from men's dominance and responsibility as head of household to a pattern of absent migrant—tax-paying men with responsibility towards the state—rather than toward the household. On the other hand, the role of head of household became closely associated with economic responsibility. A new type of social value system, the 'provider' ideology, emerged with new obligations and new responsibilities for men.

Thus, a new discourse began. New values were created and along with them new logics—meshing with old ones. Male existential and role-based identities were particularly affected. The elimination of cattle camps, men's difficulties in providing bridewealth, land shortage, and the decline in polygamy and control and authority over women seriously undermined men's social roles as heads of household. These changes also undermined men's social value, not to mention their role-based as well as existential identities—and their self-esteem. Moreover, just as new expectations emerged, so did new sources of status. However, male employment did not necessarily replace traditional male functions generating identity, status and respect from others—on the contrary.[9]

Along with the intensification of women's roles and responsibilities within the household, women's existential and role-based identities seem to have been reinforced. While women started complaining about lack of male responsibility and their lack of contributions to the household, they became increasingly aware of their own importance. This seems to have nourished their sense of identity. Even though structurally subordinate to men and dependent on men for access to their means of production, women actively responded to the new situation. In order for them to survive with their children, they created a new social role for themselves—a role which was not in contradiction to the image of the 'entrepreneurial and strong woman'. This,

---

[9] As observed by Cohen and Odhiambo in their study from Siaya (1989–98). Similar observations are made by Robert LeVine (1966).

however, had fundamental consequences for the relations between the genders in the sense that the antagonistic relations which already existed intensified. It can be argued that when women complain they take a position of
power. If women were victims they would never have developed a discourse (though, of course, some discourses are subordinate). Linked to this, I
shall argue that a process was started whereby women began challenging
men and their position as heads of household. While a remoulding of
authority in the Siaya rural household took place (Cohen and Odhiambo,
1989:11), the same seems to have occurred in Kisii. Though in a structurally
submissive position, more and more women took 'command of the home'.

Crisis and change in migrant labour

By the eve of the Mau Mau rebellion (1952), profound contradictions were
emerging in Kenyan society (Hay and Stichter, 1984:128). The symbiosis between the peasant and migrant labour modes of production which had held
through the growth period of the 1930s began to break down in the late
1940s and early 1950s. The contradiction over labour supply re-emerged in
reverse form: the peasant economy began to supply more labour than the
wage economy could absorb. Moreover, after World War II, a shift towards
increased production of industrial goods began. These changes were beginning to make the long term outlook for unskilled labour even bleaker. The
growth of industry was beginning to create a demand for skilled and factory
semi-skilled workers rather than for large numbers of unskilled workers.
Only few could qualify for such work, and the stage was being set for a
profound change in the migrant labour system. Some Gusii migrants were
skilled artisans and mechanics, but the majority were unskilled and casually
employed workers. Their wages did not keep pace with living costs and the
situation of these workers was increasingly precarious. The urban minimum
wage only providing the barest essentials of a single man (1984:130–31).

The effects of these changes on the labour force became more apparent
between 1955 and 1963—the year of Kenya's independence—but they
reached fruition in the decade after independence. Between 1955 and 1964,
while output expanded and gross domestic Product rose by 6 per cent a
year, employment in the 'modern' sector of the economy decreased. Obviously, employment did not keep pace with population growth (1984:140).
Gusii migrants started to return to Kisii.

Contemporary Kisii

Today, men are back in Kisii, and they have been back for at least the past
two decades. As noted above, current migration figures (out of Kisii) are
very low with only about 5,000 (mainly men) registered as working outside
Kisii (*Kisii District Development Plan 1989–93*). The most important labour
migration stream consists of rural school leavers who flock to Kisii town in

search of jobs. The less successful ones (which constitute the majority) have turned into a growing army of thugs called *kebago* who terrorize Kisii town and other urban centres in the District (Were and Nyamwaya, 1986:93).

Returning male migrants were not absorbed in the local work force. Today Kisii is recorded as having the highest unemployment rate in the whole country (*The Nation*, 6.3.1992). According to the recent Kisii Development Plan, with agriculture being the leading productive sector in the District, the high potential agricultural land is the most important economic resource (*Kisii District Development Plan 1989–93*, 1992:29, 40). More jobs are planned in agriculture and in small-scale manufacturing and trade. In order to expand the informal sector it is necessary to develop the urban and market centres. The informal sector will play a significant role in employment creation. However, with poor infrastructural facilities in these centres, the informal sector will not absorb the surplus labour to the maximum. There are a few government-supported tea and coffee factories as well as a number of small scale industries. Among these are textile and garment industries. Clothing output, though, has declined markedly since 1990 because of competition from the sale of imported 'second hand' clothing (Billetoft, 1995). Wage employment in Kisii was 33,750.[10] These numbers only account for 'official' wage employment and not for the 'unofficial' types of other income generating activities that many men are involved in.[11]

But in spite of the fact that enormous amounts of energy and ingenuity are expended by many men in finding ways to get access to cash this income is not automatically vested in the household: on the contrary. This is a major source of frustration, particularly for women. As also mentioned above, alcohol abuse, mainly by men, has become very common throughout the District. Men and women agree that 'men drink to drown their problems— and they are many'. Though men are now back in Kisii, the pattern that developed during colonialism whereby men became increasingly alienated from the household, where women's responsibilities increased and gender antagonisms intensified, this pattern is very alive.

Male 'sociability' has become a subject of dispute, as have men's increasing visits to drinking places. Local bars have often become daily meeting places where considerable amounts of alcohol are consumed. As a local Seventh Day Adventist (non-drinking) Gusii politician put it during my first fieldwork in Kisii: Colonialism had been so tough on men that when independence was finally won, men had to celebrate, and they have continued

---

[10] In 1987, according to the *Kisii District Development Plan 1989–93* (1992:30), but only 6,621 according to the Ministry of Work in Kisii.

[11] *Jua Kalis* ('hot/fierce sun' in Kiswahili)—a Kenyan African version of entrepreneurship— refers to the many micro activities which are carried out in the open air. Since the 1980s the term has become the official designation for all kinds of micro enterprises engaged in manufacturing and repairing. There are 250 *Jua Kalis* in Kisii town employing from 2–8 persons. About 30,000 persons in the District (no differentiation by gender) were involved in more or less regular small scale business in 1987 (Billetoft, 1995).

doing so ever since. Besides, he added, what else should they do? In spite of the fact that restrictions on the sale of alcohol were introduced in the beginning of the 1980s, this does not seem to have had any effect.

Kisii is one of the areas in Kenya with the most serious alcohol abuse (Otieno, Owola and Oduor, 1979). A growing number of people drink to escape from problems, and to relieve worries and boredom. It is mainly bottled beer, the locally produced *busaa* (made from fermented flour from maize, sorghum or finger millet) and the locally distilled alcohol (*changaa*) which are consumed. The distillation of *changaa* has been increasingly refined, and some *changaa* is said to contain up to 60–70% pure alcohol. The majority of people with alcohol problems drank mainly *changaa* either alone or in combination with *busaa*. Both types of alcohol are easy to make and cheap. The increasing consumption of *changaa* has completely changed the drinking pattern and may be a major cause of the reported increase in alcoholism (1979). In 1992 the picture was still the same—if not worse. In all villages, a number of households, mainly female-headed, live from their production of *changaa*. They sell it from their houses which they have turned into local 'bars'. Many of these women have succeeded in giving all their children a secondary education on the basis of income from their alcohol production. Thus, instead of investing their income in their own household, paradoxically, men often 'invest' whatever income they may have in another household—often female-headed.

According to Dr. Badia, psychiatrist and attached to Kisii District Hospital since 1988, mental disorders seem to be increasing rapidly, though no base-line statistics exist. These disorders are often reinforced by alcohol intake (personal communication). Also in the rest of the country, psychological and mental disorders are an increasingly important issue. The appearance of the Kenyan 'Psychological Digest' suggests an 'outbreak' of psychological problems or the establishment of a new discourse in the country, and so does the daily column in the daily newspaper *The Nation* with information and advice on how to deal with such problems.

'Real' men and women—Contemporary key values

> The way we were brought up, we were made to have an image of what a good wife or husband is. This is put to us by our parents, teachers, religion, the community in general, friends and peers. These factors combined are called the imago and they are a kind of a jig-saw puzzle which, when brought together, gives us the image of the perfect man or woman. ... when one is marrying, he or she expects to have a perfect partner based on the imago. It is after sometime, however, that one realises he or she has married a REAL man or woman who does not rise to this image of perfection. It is when this reality hits one that unwarranted or justified frustration arise (Ndetei, 1990).

Current stereotyped notions, shared by Gusii women and men, are that 'a man should be the head of his family'—'not just a figure head'. A husband should provide his wife with land, a house, clothes and other necessities which must be purchased in shops or market. He must also clothe the children and pay school fees. The head of the family is not only expected to be its protector, councillor, decision-maker—as in the past—but also the provider of the cash needs of the household. A good husband is somebody to rely upon, to trust: 'a woman needs somebody to plan with'; 'somebody who should at least pay for hired work'; 'somebody who should see to it that the children are getting education'. A man who fulfils these functions is a respected man—a man who has social value.

When 80 men were asked how to identify in more detail a respected man (implying one with social value) they came up with the following answers in this order of priority—and with no hesitation. A respected and good man

– takes care of his family;
– educates his children and pays school fees;
– his wife does not roam about;
– he marries many wives and gets many children;
– he is friendly and shows respect towards his people;
– he assists his people when they have problems and gives good advice;
– he is generous and does not quarrel;
– and, very interestingly, 'he respects himself'.

Further down on the list: 'he plans for his progress', 'he is honest', 'he has land and cattle', 'he does not drink', 'his daughters do not get pregnant before marriage'. He respects his family, relatives and friends. He socializes with other men. He goes to funerals. He contributes to 'development'.' It was also said that a good man should love his enemy, be honest and self-disciplined. He should treat all wives equally and avoid jealousy and quarrels between them. Yet 'if a man has two wives, there is one he loves and another he doesn't love. He will always help the wife he loves most and her children and buy nice clothes, while the other wife will be neglected'. A good man should not stay out late. In short, 'he should be married, have a happy family, a good house, know about God and never have killed anybody'.

Male conceptions of 'a respected and good man' are more or less identical, whether it is the well-off businessman or the poor alcoholic peasant farmer. All are perfectly aware of their responsibility for providing for their wives and children, even if this is more often honoured in the breach than the observance. Confronted with the question : Are you a good man and respected by other people? The first response was generally: 'Yes, I am such a man'. On reflection the majority continued: 'I try to be such a man'. The next question would be: 'How hard do you try?'. And the answer would be: 'you know, even if one tries hard, life is very difficult'.

Elaborating on the concept of who is a 'respected' man, it is by no means a clear-cut concept. It consists of a conglomeration of different, contradictory and also changing elements rooted in both traditional norms and values as well as modern (Christian and Western) ideals. But the majority of men are in no position to pursue these conflicting ideals. Luise White's observations of colonial attempts to create masculinity are food for thought: colonialists had been obsessed with the needs of working men for years. They had put men to work in long and short trousers depending on the job, and legislated what they would earn and where they might reside. And she concludes that beneath the rhetoric of social control, these were attempts to create an African masculinity that mirrored a flattering vision of the officials' own maleness. These constructions of masculinity, though, depended on the climate of the times. Local and external concepts of masculinity were not the same. This created a highly contradictory and conflicting situation, in particular for men, but also for women (White, 1990:3).

When I asked women what is a respected woman—the majority first said:

- one who cares for her family;
- one who teaches her children to be good people;
- one who thinks of the future;
- one who gives food to visitors;
- one who builds her home (keeps it neat and clean);
- one who respects herself;
- one who does not move with other men;
- one who goes to the shamba;
- one who does not gossip;
- one who does not quarrel with her husband;
- one who tries to counsel her husband;
- one who does not drink.

The answers from men and women do not differ significantly. Apparently, both sexes have similar values, and both sexes know perfectly well what is expected of them. As noted by Ndetei, however, 'real' men or women, do not rise to this image of perfection. It is when this reality hits one that unwarranted or justified frustration arise (1990). As shall be shown below there are profound contradictions and discrepancies between men's and women's visions about how to be respected and a 'good' person and how they act out their lives in reality. And this, I shall argue, is a contributing factor to the tense and antagonistic relations between them.

Versions of the past

'People are enchained into acting out versions of the past' (Strathern, 1990:342)

In spite of fundamental ruptures and disorder at all levels of society, Kisii still seems to be anchored in an extremely 'traditional' and inflexible system; in a set of norms and values which put severe limits to the kinds of behaviour which are acceptable—at least in principle. As mentioned above, behind current gender notions, as well as notions of norms and values, is a long history of complex codes 'designing' the cultural categories of contemporary Gusii male and female. While new roles and values have now entered the arena, my experience from Kisii clearly shows that 'versions of the past' are still surprisingly forcefully alive, and that they shape men and women's ideas and images of themselves and others. They also shape ideas of femaleness and maleness, what is proper behaviour and conduct for men and women, respectively, and certainly what is not proper conduct. Among these versions of the past, initiation—in spite of the changes this practice has undergone—plays a crucial role in maintaining traditional values. This will be discussed in the following chapter.

According to Mayer, traditional hierarchies (such as Kisii) seem to maintain themselves by reifying differences of image and identification, which they have actually produced themselves in the first place, through their own definition of "hard-edged" categories and the routine of social separation. As I understand Mayer, and in line with my own observations, Gusii images and identifications seem to be so deeply 'internalised' that they are totally 'natural'. , Mayer, however, argues that it would be naive to think that basic social categories are given their hard edges by 'nature'. They are not:

> True, biological 'nature' does ordain distinctively different roles for each sex in procreation and suckling. Beyond this, however, sex role differences are of a social nature and are socially constructed by ceremonial idiom—such as the ceremonial rule whereby male infants can never outgrow their nourishment from feminine hands. These characteristic patriarchal arrangement will seem 'natural' and inevitable only so long as ... no information strikes home from a different social reality, such as a world where men actually get their own food and yet the heavens don't fall.[12]

Though social reality in Kisii is different from Mayer's example, much 'information' apparently does not strike home. Even today married Gusii men—heads of households—are for example not supposed to get their own food. If a wife does not cook for her husband, it is not only a great insult to his 'maleness' and demonstrates a lack of respect, it is also a lack of 'femaleness', not recognizing one's ascribed duties. Men as well as women still tend to believe that men should get their nourishment from feminine

---

[12] Mayer, I., 1974 and in line with Ortner and Whitehead, 1981/89.

hands—except for the period when young boys at the age of 10 start living in their own hut. Then they cook for themselves until they find a wife. As soon as a wife moves in, the husbands falls back into their 'infant stage'.

'If the wife commands the house it is a weak home', Mary would convincingly argue, knowing perfectly well that she was the one who was in command in her home. Mary, my beautiful, strong-minded and self-confident assistant in her early 40s would always interrupt our work at lunch time to go home and cook for her drunken husband. She had no respect left for Evans. She had lived with him for more than 20 years, and she had been beaten up many times. Nowadays her sons were in their teens, and Evans did not dare to touch her when they were around. When I asked her 'why don't you tell him to cook for himself?', she would send me a wondering look and say 'it is my duty'. 'Why is it your duty? You told me that Evans has sometimes beaten you up so badly that you could hardly walk ... do you have any duties at all towards him? Besides, he may have gone to the bar' I would argue. 'I am a woman, and that is how I have been told'. After some time, she would add 'otherwise people will not follow my advice'. I could never make her change her mind. Mary was very hard working both at the local dispensary and as a farmer. She had great respect in the community; this she did not want to lose. She also had a very good relationship with her in-laws. They admitted that their son was 'a useless drunkard', and they always supported Mary when Evans complained that Mary would not give him any money. He had lost his job as a 'messenger boy' in a bank in Kisii town long ago. So Mary knew very well that she had the upper hand in their household and had taken on all responsibilities. Just as she knew what her duties were.

When I tried to trace where Mary got the notion of 'duty' from, she would refer to the time when her grandmother before circumcision told her how to behave when she became a woman and got married. Her grandmother's teaching was followed up by the instruction given during the circumcision ceremony, where respect and obedience towards husbands as well as the ideal of hard work were emphasized.

In fact, already much earlier, Mary had been socialized into her marital role. As in any other society, Gusii boys and girls are socialized into different patterns of roles and behaviour starting in their early childhood and underpinning their different 'place' and status in the society as well as norms and values. This 'carving' into their minds, I shall argue, is again reinforced by the initiation rituals which are performed on both boys and girls in Kisii. But—of course—not all women were like Mary.

Chapter 3
The Making of Males and Females in Contemporary Kisii

Becoming a male or female is known as sexual differentiation. It is a lengthy, complicated process that mixes biology, learning and social interaction. It begins with genetic sex, gonadal sex, hormonal secretions, internal sex organs, external genitals, the sex label given at birth, and finally the gender identity formed during childhood and adolescence. As you can see it is complicated and a wonder that most people turn out the way they do. (Answer to bewildered male from AMANI, *Daily Nation*, 23, 1990.)

Introduction

This chapter explores the construction of males and females in contemporary Kisii. Gendering, the acquisition of social characteristics of masculinity or femininity, is a highly complex set of processes involving both psychological events and socialization. It starts almost at birth and continues well into adulthood. It involves both acquiring an identity (social and sexual) and learning a set of differentiated behaviours and capacities appropriate to the masculine or the feminine. The acquisition of gender identity is constantly being reinforced and refined by a wide range of other social practices. Identity is created early in life:

> ... in puberty and adolescence all samenesses and continuities relied on earlier are more or less questioned again ... because of the new addition of genital maturity. The growing and developing youths, faced with this physiological revolution within them, and with tangible adult tasks ahead of them are now primarily concerned with what they appear to be in the eyes of others as compared with what they feel they are, and with the question of how to connect the roles and skills cultivated earlier with the occupational prototypes of the day. *In their search for a new sense of continuity and sameness, adolescents ... are ever ready to install lasting idols and ideals as guardians of a final identity.*

Erikson's observations indicate that identity and ideas about social value are created in adolescence if not before, during childhood socialization. In Kisii, initiation rituals are not only fundamental to becoming an adult but—I shall argue—they contribute forcibly to the 'carving' of male and female gender identity. In spite of the fact that the rituals have been watered down over the years, the essence is unaffected and closely interacts with codes of masculinity, femininity and proper gender conduct. An uncircumcised person—

whether male or female—is not considered a full member of the Gusii. Consequently, initiation rituals are essential for both sexes in order to get socially accepted. However, as ideas and values emphasized in the initiation ritual have not kept pace with the reality that both genders are faced with today, the rituals play a contradictory role in the shaping of gender, gender identity and the relations between genders. In the following, I shall investigate female and male initiation rituals; the key values that are emphasized in the rituals and how they interact with the construction of contemporary male and female identity.

Initiation rituals as 'rites de passage'

Practices and ceremonies accompanying an individual's 'life crises'—understood as stages of life—are termed 'rites de passage' (van Gennep, 1908/ 1960). Initiation is a rite de passage and as such a transition from one stage to another. Such rites are therefore closely linked to 1) changes in status, that is, incorporation of the individual into a new status in a group and returning him/her to the customary routines of life, and 2) the critical problems of becoming male and female. The rites have a sexual nature in that they are said to make the individual a man or a woman, or fit to be one (1908/1960:67). In addition to initiation being a rite in which social seniors use an anxious private transition to school people in the public values of responsible adulthood, initiation is also a means to resolve psycho-sexual conflict; and most importantly, initiation is a drama by which men gain control over women's reproductive powers (Paige and Paige, 1981).

Initiation rites in Kisii had caught the attention of earlier anthropologists, who have described the rituals in detail. None of them, though, has developed an analysis of initiation and its impact on the construction of male and female gender identity and the relations between genders. There is an extensive but also descriptive account of Gusii initiation ceremonies for boys and girls as they were carried out in the late 1940s (Mayer, P., 1953). As Mayer was not allowed to attend the initiation of girls, the circumcision of boys is described in much more detail. Initiation rites are also described as are the differences in male and female initiation rites and on parent/child relations (LeVine, R. and B., 1966/77). Comparing my own observations with those of Mayer and LeVine and LeVine, the basic 'meaning' of the rituals is still the same—though some watering down of the ritual performances has taken place.

Initiation in Kisii

Initiation, which is universal for both girls and boys in Kisii, involves genital operations for both sexes. The ceremonies take place every year after harvest (in the beginning of December) and are still an almost 'national' affair. Traditionally, initiation rites for both sexes were performed in late adolescence as preparation for marriage—to make them marriageable. By means of a sacred ceremony, the parental generation transferred to youth the responsibility of regulating premarital sex and initiating the process of mate selection, with peers as a major source of mutual support and regulation in this process. While a certain degree of permissiveness was allowed, girls were not supposed to get pregnant as long as they were not married.

Nowadays, the age of circumcision has dropped drastically. My female assistants, now in their forties, were circumcised at the age of 14–16. Today the rituals are performed with girls at the age of 8–10, and boys at a slightly later stage, as girls are said to mature earlier than boys. While 'younger children heal more easily' was often given as a reason it is more realistic to relate it to a number of complex reasons. One reason for circumcising boys at a younger age would be that there was a need for them to go to Kericho as tea pluckers. Uncircumcised boys could not go (Mayer, P., 1953:11). The lowering of the age of circumcision is associated with the abolition of cattle-villages, the presence of older boys at home and the custom whereby mother and adult sons must avoid each other. As boys gain sexual sophistication at a younger age they have to be moved away from the mothers earlier: mother/son dependency was seen as fraught with sexual overtones (LeVine, R. and B., 1966/77:177). Consequently, boys needed to be initiated into adult status.

In the ceremony that I attended in December, 1985 (51 girls between the age of 8 and 10) initiation took place before the onset of puberty. If children in the lower age range express reluctance, parents say that they will wait until the children voluntarily request inclusion in that year's rites. But most children eagerly volunteer before they reach the upper age limit. Stella, the daughter of Catherine, a poor handicapped widow, ran away during the night of circumcision when her mother was asleep and was circumcised without the mother's knowledge. Stella was 11 years old and thus approaching the upper limit. Catherine, however, could not afford the 'festivities' linked to having her daughter circumcised i.e. to prepare beer and food for the village. Therefore, Stella had been told—as in the year before—that she could still not be circumcised. When I asked Stella why she had run away like that, she was very shy. Little by little it turned out that the most important reason for her to have insisted on her initiation was that if she was not circumcised now, she would be 'left behind' by her age mates. It was certainly not because she could now engage in more prestigious feminine occupations.[13] Catherine was very dependent on her daughter, and Stella had to continue all her normal chores, including digging and weeding the shamba, fetching water and looking after her younger sisters. What mat-

---

[13] Noted as one of the most important reasons for wanting to be initiated (LeVine R. and B., 1966/77:166).

tered most to Stella was that she risked being ostracized by her female age-mates had she not been initiated now.[14]

While circumcision of boys is an accepted practice performed all over the world, circumcision of women—practised in 27 countries mainly on the African continent—has become a subject of international concern. This is reflected in the new term, female genital mutilation (FGM). Attention has been drawn, particularly by feminists and health professionals, to the fact that initiation of men and women cannot be compared. Clitoridectomy is much more invasive than male circumcision: it is a mutilation of girls' genital organs often with serious consequences for their reproductive and sexual health. The practice is seen as a result of patriarchy, reinforced by culture, traditions and superstitions—and closely linked to men's fear of women's sexuality. Linked to this, female circumcision is increasingly becoming an international health issue as well as a political issue (Silberschmidt, 1994).

In Kisii, while Christian denominations condemn female circumcision and governmental decrees forbid this practice, it continues unaffected. As early as 1929, the Church of Scotland united with the Presbyterian Churches of East Africa and initiated a move to abolish female circumcision in Kikuyuland. All church members and those wishing to enrol children in church schools were required to pledge to give up initiation rites in general, and clitoridectomy in particular (Kenyatta, 1938/61:130). The debate over female circumcision even reached the British House of Commons in 1930. Due to an eloquent presentation of the African point of view by Jomo Kenyatta, no edict against it was enacted:

The real argument lies not in the defense of the surgical operation or its details, but in the understanding of a very important fact in the tribal psychology of the Gikuyu—namely that this operation is still regarded as the very essence of an institution which has enormous educational, social, moral and religious implications, quite apart from the operation itself (1938/ 61:133).

In the late 1970s, clitoridectomy was again debated at governmental level. At the beginning of the 1980s a law was enacted which made clitoridectomy illegal in Kenya. While the majority of Kikuyu are said to have abandoned the practice of clitoridectomy, female circumcision continues full fledged in Kisii. However, while the practice was increasingly 'medicalized' before the 1980s (a medical person was called upon to perform the circumcision in the village—or groups of girls were taken to the hospital to have the operation done there) the majority of the operations are again back in the hands of a traditional circumciser who uses the same razor blade for all ini-

---

[14] This is in contradiction to the observations by Robert and Barbara LeVine who argue that the social ties based on the initiation experience are relatively shortlived for girls because—contrary to the boys—they are too dispersed after marriage to continue them (1966/77:175, 183). The social ties may be shortlived for Stella as well. However, they were crucial for her now.

tiates.[15] In a recent survey carried out in Kisii, 308 female circumcisions were recorded of which 224 (72.7%) took place at the riverside, 51 (16.6%) in the bush, 30 (9.7%) in hospital, and only 3 (1%) at home (Gwako, 1995:335).

An uncircumcised woman is almost unheard of in Kisii. Virtually all women are circumcised—even daughters of educated and Christian parents (Silberschmidt, 1991a). This is supported by the latest statistics published in the Daily Nation according to which Kisii is the District in Kenya which is the most 'backward', and where 98% of women are circumcised (*Daily Nation*, February, 1994). This is in line with the conclusions in Gwako's study: clitoridectomy continues to be mandatory. It does not only persist among, but still holds great significance for the Abagusii of Kenya (Gwako 1995:337). I actually met a couple (agronomist/nurse) who had returned to Kisii recently after having spent 4 and 6 years in the UK and the US, respectively. They had 5 daughters and one son. There was no doubt in their minds that all daughters had to be circumcised. Otherwise neither they nor their daughters would ever be accepted in Kisii, and nobody would ever marry them. Thus, female circumcision is closely linked to parents' concern about protecting their daughters from social stigma, as well as to the fact that parents themselves enter a senior age grade i.e. they enter another status group. But the economic factor should not be overlooked. An uncircumcised girl would never find a husband, and fathers would never get a brideprice. Traditionally—but much less today—initiation made male bargains possible within a competitive society. Disciplined daughters allowed fathers to negotiate terms for granting their virginal reproductive powers to approved sons-in-law.

To ask a Gusii woman if she has been circumcised is very disrespectful. As mentioned above, the question had to be taken out of our pilot survey on women after a few interviews: to assume that a woman has not been initiated demonstrates a total disrespect: it is a serious insult. An uncircumcised woman is not a decent woman; she is associated with being sexually uncontrollable: 'women who have not been circumcised cannot control their sexual appetite';'if a woman is not circumcised she will become a prostitute'—a fear which was pronounced over and over by men—as well as women. Gusii men and women are very well aware that removal of the clitoris diminishes sexual excitability—women remain 'controllable'. Women themselves firmly believe that they will become uncontrollable: 'If a woman has not been circumcised, she will become loose'. 'This will cause break-down of homes' both women and men argue.

---

[15] Circumcising women in a health facility with anaesthesia and antibiotics is a compromise which has gained currency in some countries, Egypt for example. At the WHO meeting on FGM which I attended (May 9th, 1994 in Geneva) medicalization of FGM was strongly rejected. Medicalization of FGM, it was argued, will result in a poor understanding of its socio-economic and cultural foundation. It is a justification of the practice and serves to institutionalize it (Silberschmidt, 1994).

A few men, though, said that it was much nicer to 'play sex' with Luo women who were not circumcised. 'Luo women are not like dead logs'. The Luo women that they were talking about were operating as prostitutes in Kisii town. They were in big demand. Some Gusii women had also heard about the 'attractive features' of Luo women. Their outright disdainful attitude was mixed with a jealousy which they tried very hard to conceal: 'Such women should not be allowed to come to Kisii. They are no good for men. They give them wrong ideas'. One Luo woman in her early twenties told that a few days after she moved in with her husband, she was grabbed by her sisters in-law and some women from the village and taken by force to an old female circumciser who performed the operation. Two Kalenjin women who had Gusii husbands said that when giving birth, they had been circumcised by the traditional birth assistant—without being told beforehand. Those women were a great (sexual) threat both to their husbands and to their relatives.

Lonsdale's reflections on initiation in Kikuyuland are also illuminating in a Kisii context: the Kikuyu approach to initiation, he argues, is Freudian (Berman and Lonsdale, 1992:389). To differentiate sexualities by circumcising boys and excising a girl's 'male' member—the clitoris—removed male fear and female aggression as obstacles to fruitful coition. Otherwise men might as well be women and women men; they would not be able to give birth. The clitoris was thought of as an aggressive organ, threatening the male organ. The clitoris represented the masculine element in a girl, and only by removing it did the girl became feminine. Just as a root in the shamba has to be removed, so the clitoris has to be removed:

'Men's preoccupation with fertility made them want to control sexuality—not dominate women. Circumcision and clitoridectomy were like forest clearance; they cut childish nature into adult nature (1992:393).

The ritual of clitoridectomy

The ritual that I attended started at dawn. The 'novices' in the neighbourhood had already been separated according to sex the night before. All novices had been with their 'sponsors' (older girls or younger women who taught them their future duties) and the circumciser all night. Before dawn I joined the mothers of the female novices in the village and went down together with them to the open field where the ritual was to be performed.

On arrival in the open field all the novices were already there, slowly and solemnly lining up. They were covered only by a kanga. The mothers immediately went to their daughters, unwrapped them, held their naked daughters tightly and covered their heads with the kanga. The mothers looked attentive and protective. The circumciser, an old skinny woman, arrived with her helpers—two stout women. They went up to the flat round stone in the middle of the field, and placed a couple of small cans with maize flour next to the stone (for the circumciser to dip her fingers in and to put on the wound) . This stone was the scene of the act. It was here the cli-toridectomy was to be performed. Nobody said a word. There was total silence. Everybody was ready. Helen's daughter was the first to be 'done'. Helen who had worked with nuns at the Catholic dispensary knew that they did not approve of the circumcision of her daughters. Nevertheless, this was her third—and last—daughter to be circumcised. In order to meet both the 'cultural' requirements as well as those of her employers, she had bribed the circumciser. She had gone to her place a few days before, paid her a few shillings, and had agreed with her that her daughter should be the first one to be operated, and that the circumciser should not cut off the whole clitoris, but just make a small incision.

When the circumciser arrived she was not walking steadily. She had been drinking all night—as is the habit. Helen was worried. She was afraid that the circumciser had forgotten their agreement. Helen managed to ex-change a few words with the circumciser, and her daughter was actually the first one to be circumcised. She was pushed forward and placed naked on the stone. The helpers of the circumciser pulled her backwards, held her arms firmly and spread her legs. Helen had pulled me up right to the front, insisting that I took photos. The 'operation' only took a few seconds. Both of us saw that the circumciser did not suffice with just a small incision. Then the next girl was pushed forward and placed on the stone. And the next— and so forth. Not one sound was uttered from the girls. After the operation they lined up on the side and watched the circumcision of the remaining girls. The blood ran down their legs. Nobody complained. And nobody complained during the 30 minutes walk back to the village one hour later.

Mayer, in his study, refers to a letter from a Medical Officer in Kisii in 1944 which states that the Gusii 'remove head of clitoris only, leaving no scar, and not interfering with vaginal orifice' (Mayer, P., 1953:27). In fact, the Gusii are said to perform Sunna, the mildest form of circumcision (compared with excision and infibulation). Based on my own experience of the circumcision of the 51 girls, the operation did not correspond to the ob-servations of the Medical Officer. First of all, for the circumciser to be able to grasp the clitoris (which is smeared with maize flower), she needs a fairly good grasp. The size of the first clitorises that she threw on the ground was not negligible. Second, the circumciser was not sober when she undertook the first 'operation'. Between the operations she sipped *changaa* and needed a better and better grasp in order to remove the clitoris. By the end of the operations, 51 clitorises of different sizes, including vaginal tissue, were ly-ing in the grass.

In a recent study of harmful traditional practices in Kenya, 320 Gusii women (aged between 14–50) were interviewed (Maendeleo Ya Wanawake/ Population Crisis Committee, 1992). The majority were quoted as saying that Sunna had been performed on them i.e. the removal of the prepuce of the clitoris or the clitoris hood only (in accordance with the observations of the Medical Officer). Gusii women in the study also mentioned quite a number of side-effects such as haemorrhage (59%), infection (45%), scarring (85%), painful intercourse (23%), urine retention (57%). This indicates that the operation may be closer to excision (removal of the clitoris and the adjacent parts of the labia minora) than to sunna—which is in agreement with my observations.

As soon as a girl was operated on, her mother would start screaming, shouting, ululating, singing and dancing excitedly, lifting up her skirt, rolling her hips and thrusting forward her pelvis. All songs were concerned with some aspect of coitus. Sexual intercourse with husbands had to be abandoned during the daughter's three weeks seclusion. Mothers had to tend the fire in the hut where the initiate was to dwell until the wound had healed. Keeping the fire constantly alight was most important: should the fire go out their daughters risked becoming infertile. Consequently, mothers had no time to 'service' their husbands. In a very mocking voice women would sing about their husbands being left to their own devices.

During and after the operation, the women shouted obscenities, expressed the desire for prohibited sexual relationships and referred to the sex act publicly. There was indecent exposure and hip movements; all of these ordinarily shocking acts are performed and expected by women. At one point I was grabbed by some women and pulled into the middle of a group of women who were swinging their pangas or wooden sticks wildly high in the air. I was amazed that nobody got hurt. Their movements were indecent and vulgar. I had never seen Gusii women—or any women for that matter— behave like that. I am convinced that none of the initiates had ever seen their mothers behave like that. Nor had their husbands. While the initiate herself recedes into the background the women use the ceremonial occasion as an outlet for their usually concealed sexual lust and their antagonism toward men (LeVine, R. and B., 1966/77:173).

> Many obscene songs are sung, some of them mentioning the name of the novice's father, as the women jerk their hips suggestively and move the phallic sticks, which most of them now hold up and down or punch the fist into the palm of the other hand in a coital rhythm (1966/77:172).

> Women were playing the male sex role: holding sticks which represent phalluses, singing songs of sex from the man's point of view, engaging in mock military combat (1966/77:171).

> ... The novice, preoccupied with her pain ... may be only dimly aware of what the women are singing and doing. In subsequent years, however, she will participate more consciously in the festivities which follow clitoridectomy and attain an awareness of its meaning for women which was not possible for her as a novice (1966/77:173).

Girls waiting in a line for their turn to be circumcised.

The old woman circumciser in action with a razor blade. Maize flower is put on the wound to top the bleeding.

Women celebrating their daughters' circumcision, swinging their pangas, lifting their skirts and singing vulgar songs.

Girl resting in the hut after the circumcision.

A mother is being celebrated by her relatives and the community because her daughter has just been circumcised.

On returning to the village, for the first few hours the girls were left—all alone—behind a shed. In the afternoon each girl was brought to her hut of seclusion. Only women and small children were allowed to see her. Their mothers were feted and lifted up and carried by neighbours who came to drink the home brewed beer and eat ugali and chicken.[16] Thus, by initiation, not only does the girl pass from one stage and status to another but so does her mother—as well as her father. Parents are proud and express relief that they have succeeded in taking their daughter safely into this stage.

---

[16] According to the study by Gwako, the kind of drinks and food served to mark the circumcision have obviously been changing since 89% of the women interviewed (604) said that the mode of feasting was shifting to tea, bread and soft drinks rather than abundant supplies of meat, porridge etc. Almost inevitably the ceremonial slaughtering of a cow (or even a bull) to mark the circumcision of the first born has become less frequent, because the money and other resources needed for such major celebrations are not readily available.

There are also evidence that some of the embarrassing terminologies during the singing and dancing are gradually being dropped, while many Christians carry hymn books and bibles for appropriate citations in the course of the festivities.

The shortening of seclusion periods was noted by 87%, partly due to inadequate supplies of the wood required to keep a fire constantly burning in each seclusion house. The declining role of grandparents was raised by 80%, since they are still expected to educate the novices on matters pertaining to their subsequent contributions to the betterment of the community. Apart from the fact that the latter's educational role is gradually being taken over by the formal school system, many modern parents look down upon the elderly as old-fashioned people whose ideas are not in harmony with the demands of contemporary. Finally more parents (albeit not yet many) are again taking their children to hospitals and having them circumcised by trained medical personnel (1995:337).

During the seclusion period the girls are told to rest quietly, in order for the wound to heal. When I went to see Helen's daughter in the afternoon, the girl was in pain and bleeding heavily. She was on the safe side, though. Her mother had already put her on antibiotics.

Key values connected to female initiation

In the pre-initiation period the initiate is progressively introduced by her instructors to the kind of life and tasks which she will have as an adult woman. Traditionally, grandmothers would also act as instructors. Today, with the dissolution of families and often no grandmothers around, the circumciser also instructs the girls on the night before circumcision.

Through initiation a girl becomes an adult woman. In other African societies initiation is often related to virginity and chastity, in particular infibulation, which 'closes' male access to a woman until she marries (Talle, 1991). In Kisii, initiation makes a woman marriageable and accessible for men. Linked to this, the ritual instruction emphasizes the initiate's relations with men: her first obligation is to find a husband, to be fertile and get children, and behave properly i.e. work hard, be attentive to the husband's needs, helpful to the in-laws and last but not least control her (sexual) behaviour. Traditionally, girls, were taught to protect themselves from getting pregnant with the boys by exercising 'magic' so that boys were incapable of getting an erection. Today, initiated girls are not taught 'magic'. Proper sexual behaviour, however, is most crucial: 'men cannot be expected to be in control of their sexual behaviour', both men and women agree. Consequently, already at this 'premature' stage, young girls are told that 'women should be in control'.

Circumcision of boys

As I was not permitted to witness boys' circumcision myself, I shall draw on the account of others (Mayer, P., 1953; LeVine, R. and B., 1966/77; Were and Nyamwaya, 1986).

> They rise in the middle of the night, for it is customary to reach the circumciser before dawn. The older boys may treat the novice roughly and, as a final test, try to frighten him with stories of the pain and how bad it is to be a coward ... . Fathers and classificatory fathers may not attend a boy's initiation, but brothers, classificatory brothers .. may witness it. The boy is led to a special tree and he stands back to the tree and arms above his head against the tree in readiness for the operation. In contrast to the girls, who are held tightly for their clitoridectomy, boys have to face circumcision on their feet and unsupported by another person. The circumciser kneels before the boy to perform the operation, and the older boys and men, standing behind the circumciser, aim spears and clubs at the boy's head, shouting continuously throughout the operation that he will be killed if he moves or shows signs of pain ... (LeVine, R. and B., 1966/77:179–180).

> Hazing by other boys is an essential feature of the seclusion period. ... . The novices are forced to eat a number of caustic and nauseating substances ... . Refusal to eat brings a beating. They are threatened with being eaten by an animal ... . Toward the end of the night, the novices are beaten with nettles, made to pull up pegs near a fire with their teeth and have their fingers twisted in long bows. Although formalized hazing occurs on this one night only, older boys can come and torment the novices throughout the initiation period. All boys are aware of the respect and avoidance rules of adult status long before their initiation, and hazing helps to make them realize that the rules now apply to them (1966/77:181–182).

Traditionally, during convalescence the novices were taught not only obedience to and respect for the elders and parents but also the importance of courage, endurance and manhood. Courage and endurance were tested when the novice, unquestioningly, had to chew bitter roots and fruits and was beaten with stinging leaves of the *risa* plant. The teaching of courage and endurance was important in that the men had to acquire these qualities now so that when they later joined *ebisarate* the same qualities could be sharpened and finally anchored in their thoughts (Were and Nyamwaya, 1986:122).

One of my informants, who was circumcised 10 years ago, emphasized the very tough disciplining that he underwent before and during the initiation period. He remembered it as a very terrifying but also exciting experience. This experience binds boys together all their life. So it was in earlier times, and so it is today.

The fire in the novices' hut should be tended carefully by the boys themselves and kept burning all the time. The novices were left without matches. If the fire went out it meant serious problems in life: 'your wife will die'; 'your children will fall sick and die'; 'you may even become sterile and never be able to father any children', the boys would be told. 'If you become infertile you cannot 'control' your wife; 'she will be looking for other men to give her children'.

Today, as with girls, the introduction to adult life by elders has more or less been abandoned and taken over by older boys; the traditional seclusion period of one month where a group of boys would have to stay together in a hut has been reduced to 2–3 weeks. Traditionally, girls were allowed to tease the newly circumcised boys, so that they got painful erections. At night the boys were visited by naked girls who would dance and take pleasure in arousing them at a time when they were incapable of coitus. The girls would have their triumph if a resulting erection caused the partly-healed wound to burst open (Mayer, P., 1953; LeVine, R. and B., 1966/77). The girls were not out for sexual intercourse. The idea was to torture the boys who were in pain by adding insult to injury (Were and Nyamwaya, 1986:123).

According to Were and Nyamwaya

> During the ritual nights, those boys who were brave had sexual intercourse with girls. On such nights a party of initiated but unmarried girls gathered to spend the night at one girl novice's place. Young men hung around until everything was quiet for the night; then they stealthily opened the door and crept in. Although the girls were expected to resist genuinely or to pretend to resist, full sexual intercourse was occasionally possible. In fact *ogochobera* was licensed in the sense that the head of the homestead could not prevent the boys from entering his wife's house even if he actually found them prowling around at night nor could the mother of the novice meddle with the boys unless her help was expressly sought by the girls. It is also important to note that during these nights, the girls, through songs and dances, invitingly called in the boys. In full moonlight the girls stripped naked and danced to seductive songs. Though no older men were allowed around, young men were nearby hidden but looking. Naturally their sexual desires were aroused on seeing the naked bodies. The boys waited until the girls went back into the house to sleep and they crept in to *gochobera*. The picture painted so far might indicate that boys found it easy to have sex with girls during *ogochobera*. This is not true. Only a small number of the most daring and swift ones did. *Ogochobera* was not an easy exercise, because getting into the house was a difficult task. Moreover, when the girls danced as they did it did not mean that the boys were going to get them cheaply. During the novitiate and girlhood, girls were warned that it was a curse to lose one's virginity, their greatest honour and pride, before marrying. So if one girl heard boys creep in she alerted the others, and the boys might then receive kicks on their sides, faces or on any other part of the body. They might be greeted with stumps of burning firewood hurled at them to get them out of the house. In short *ogochobera* was an expensive business as most boys never got a girl in the years they tried to *gochobera*. What it taught the boys was that in this world one has to sweat if one is to achieve anything at all. It also taught them sex language and the behaviour of women in sexual matters in general (1986:124–125).

All that the novice boys could do was to reply that they would be seen in their true colours by the girls once they were out of seclusion and could take the girls by stealth, *ogosonia*. *Ogosonia* gave the novices new social status (1986:124). Even if these traditions have come to an end, they are still common knowledge. While women giggle when speaking about this tradition, men still think such behaviour licentious and intended to cause pain.

After the seclusion period it is very important, even today, that the initiates greet parents and elders respectfully. The parents would then tell their son to go and 'cut the rope' i.e. to have intercourse with an older circumcised girl. Boys are now prepared to start their sexual 'career'. Most of my informants started 'playing sex' with older girls shortly after seclusion at the age of 11–12 years. Older girls, I was told, often preferred to play sex with younger boy because they could 'harm' them less.

After initiation the boy assumes adult responsibilities—at least ideally:

> His father expects great deference and obedience from him when he is home and financial contributions when he is working away from home ... . Sex is a forbid-

den topic for discussion with the father but is foremost with the pal (boys circumcised the same year). Pals cooperate in seducing girls together in their
youth. Regardless of whether the specific relationship is continued, the pattern
of contrast between intergenerational relations and peer relations becomes solid-
ified in the post initiation period and perpetuated throughout life ... (LeVine, R.
and B., 1966/77:183–185)

Key values linked to circumcision of boys

Today circumcision of boys in Kisii has not lost its traditional aims and
objectives—namely to introduce the boys to a responsible adult life, increased adult responsibilities and to start their sexual experiences. Responsibility, discipline, respect and self reliance are particular important. So are
kinship duties. A grown man should support not only his own children but
also the children of his brothers. Respect (towards parents and elders) is
essential. Sexual abstinence and respect especially for their mother and
father are stressed.

Moreover, a man should not be a coward; nobody respects a coward.
Boys must stand up not only to the painful experience of circumcision but
also to the threats of their instructors and peers. This is part of the disciplining. Showing courage and endurance to pain is part of becoming a man. If
boys are cowards—if they recoil or cry out when they are cut—everybody
will know. Such behaviour is a disgrace to the parents, and will follow them
for the rest of their lives. They will never be considered 'real' men.

Young boys and men, though, do not show much respect—either to
parents or to elders. Parents complain about their sons. I heard many say
that 'we are afraid of being killed by our sons'; 'sons cannot wait for us to
die to get our shambas'. Once I overheard a very heated discussion between
an old distinguished politician and a young man. The young man inter-
rupted the old man in the middle of his argument. The old man was furious
with the young fellow: 'You must respect me, I could be your grandfather'.
'How can I respect you, when you talk nonsense', the young man answered
back.

Respect, discipline and self restraint do not include male behaviour towards (marriageable) women: only small uninitiated boys are supposed to
treat initiated girls with respect. Consequently, women from now on become
the 'sexual objects' that the initiated boys pursue. Linked to this, male
strength in sexual performance, male potency, virility and fertility are
underlined in the ritual: 'an infertile man is no man' and 'a man without
children has no say'. Masculinity includes command over women in all matters, and, in particular, sexual control. Young men courting girls often
threaten them with rape . There seems to be a need, in particularly among
boys/men, to carve out their masculinity, and rape is one such means. Rape
was already a serious problem in the 1960s when LeVine and LeVine carried

out their fieldwork. Rape, however, has increased dramatically today, according to peoples' accounts. No statistics were available.

Differences and contradictions in girls' and boys' initiation

As shown above, boys' and girls' initiations have different connotations for the sexes. This raises the question of how initiation makes different imprints on adult male and female gender identity and how it affects the relations between the sexes. The following observations are useful as a starting point:

> The difference between boys' and girls' initiation sheds some light on the meaning and function of the male rite. The girl is accompanied to the genital operation by her mother and secluded in her mother's house; the boy is kept apart from his parents from the time of his leaving the house to be circumcised to his emergence several weeks later. The girl is held down during the genital operation, while the boys must stand to face the knife alone ... the boy's seclusion in a special house involves going out to meet others for adventures in hunting and theft. In short, initiation encourages boys to be self-reliant, to do without parental support, to endure hardship unflinchingly, to cooperate with related agemates, and to venture forth with weapons. There is no such encouragement for girls ... . *The emphasis in female initiation is on sexual stimulation while in male initiation, sexual avoidance and respect for parents are stressed.* In augmenting and manipulating her sexual attractiveness in post initiation years, the girl becomes increasingly inconsiderate of her parents' wishes and commands. (Therefore, parents often say) 'If she is bad, let her husband beat her' ... . The parental concept of initiation as *a moral finishing school for boys* and the lack of such a concept for girls thus appears to be related to the patrilocality of ... marriage (LeVine, R. and B., 1966/77 [my emphasis]).

Summing up, boys are faced with different obligations, expectations and a much greater variety of responsibilities than are girls. These differences, which are still greatly emphasized in the rituals, have not been 'adjusted' to adult men's and women's present lives and realities. In spite of the fact that it is common knowledge that men should behave in a respectful and responsible way there are particularly profound contradictions between the respect and responsibility aspects emphasized during boys' initiation and how men later on in life 'perform'.

The ritual is contradictory for women as well—but from a different point of view. It advocates, at one and the same time, women's submission to men as well as disrespect, protest and control. On the one hand, women are taught to submit to 'husbands' and to accept their sexual control. On the other, as shown above, the ritual contains important 'counter acting' elements—in the sense that women (i.e. mothers of the novices) during their daughters' initiation are allowed to indulge in a behaviour which would normally be taboo. Women are allowed to protest against their structurally subordinate position. The fact that the ritual makes it legitimate for women to mock men suggests a certain legitimacy of the disrespect that many women express towards their husbands in daily life. While daughters may be too young to understand the vulgar songs, they do understand their mothers' disrespectful behaviour. Linked to this, I am convinced that they realize, more or less consciously, that in their structurally subordinated situation there are certain 'security valves'. Most crucially, the ritual emphasizes women's control not only of their own sexuality (and fertility) but also of that of men. As I interpret it, circumcision of women is a means for them to control both their own sexuality (and fertility) as well as that of men—because as both Gusii men and women agree 'men cannot control themselves'.

Initiation is not only a drama by which men gain control over women's reproductive powers. Initiation is also a means to resolve psychosexual conflict—and as such the initiation ritual has a therapeutic function (Paige and Paige, 1981). Accepting such an interpretation raises the question whether this is another contributory reason as to why women are still so keen on safeguarding female initiation. Understandably enough, men want to be in control of women—one could argue. But why would women still wholeheartedly support the practice? Of course, initiation is fundamental for the construction of femininity, social acceptance etc. However, I want to go one step further and suggest that there is much more for women in the ritual than immediately observable. That the ritual allows women some 'powers' that they would not have had without the ritual—in spite of their structurally subordinate position. That the ritual may even serve as a something of a 'balancing' and 'compensating' mechanism. To this it is important to add that while mothers'/women's behaviour during female initiation can be strongly associated with an emotional outlet for their usually concealed sexual interest, their frustrations and their antagonism towards men, male initiation does not permit any emotional outlet for fathers/men.

Gender identity, social value and antagonism

With initiation 'messages' in Kisii being confusing, contradictory and in stark contrast to the way which men and women are able to live their contemporary lives, there seems—nevertheless—to be a strong need to demarcate categories as they become more ambiguous. Initiation rituals seem to assert inevitability precisely at the point when reality contradicts it.

In contemporary Kisii, initiation is the public confirmation of the rights of the individual to become an adult social person. Thus, initiation moves each gender into a new social world, and childhood comes to an end. Following the argument that initiation is primarily about rites of separation from an asexual world, followed by rites of incorporation into a sexual world, initiation in Kisii then serves to underpin not only the making of male and female identities—but in particular the difference between these identities. Through the ritual the moral code for each gender is taught and new restraints are imposed upon the individual—to replace an immediate source of authority embodied in the parent with the simultaneously remote and internal one of social obligation.

As such initiation is an 'arrangement' which is considered natural and inevitable—an integral part of Gusii culture—the 'moral code of the tribe' intrinsic to both women's and men's existential identity. In particular, initiation seems to 'shape' existential identities i.e. identities which are very fundamental and also very difficult to negotiate. When told that in other parts of Africa, not only men but women too are circumcised, the Suku fell on the ground with laughter, asking whether women in those places also impregnated women. Among the Suku, to be circumcised was as natural a feature of being a man as the begetting of children and thus an invariant 'natural' attribute of masculinity. Circumcision was above all not a 'natural' attribute of femininity (Kopytoff, 1990:83).

In Kisii, circumcision and clitoridectomy are invariant 'natural' attributes of masculinity and femininity, respectively. However, as the ritual emphasizes a greater variety of responsibilities for men than for women and also different social values, it entails more complicated identities for men than for women. Using Kopytoff's distinctions, Gusii women's intrinsic gender identities can be said to be more narrowly defined than those of men. At the same time there are mixed messages of authorizing independence to females and males. While initiation for men means increased kinship responsibilities as well as self-reliance, initiation has very opposite connotations for women. For women, initiation means first of all a removal from a close proximity of birth relations and immediate family to new social networks revolving around the women married into the husband's clan. While circumcision confirms men's legal rights as well as their sexual rights, women are taught the critical importance of controlling their sexual behaviour i.e. maintaining their virginity and guarding their fertility. There is, however, a contradictory and underlying acceptance of women's disrespect towards men—if not in general then during initiation rituals. There is an acceptance that women have sexual relationships and at the same time prevent conception and that 'controlled' sexual and fertility behaviour is not a male responsibility. Further, that men are not expected to be able to control their fertility and sexuality; that it is legitimate for men not to be responsible; that this is a female responsibility.

My point here is that the social world in Kisii is gendered; the morality is gendered—and the social value system is gendered. What is appropriate and expected of girls is not appropriate for boys. The gendering of the social world is emphasized in the initiation rituals—and this, I shall argue, is strongly reflected in the shaping of male and female identity. What is appropriate behaviour and gives social value to a man is certainly not appropriate for a woman—and vice versa. It is a morality in which—when speaking in sexual terms—virtue is at stake. Not men's virtue but that of young girls and in particular a wife's virtue.

Consequently, the argument that men's preoccupation with fertility made them want to control sexuality—not dominate women—is only part of the truth in a Gusii context (Berman and Lonsdale, 1992:393). Gusii men are preoccupied with fertility—both their own as well as that of their wives. They want to control the fertility of their wife, and they also want to command and dominate her (including her fertility and sexuality). However, with initiation messages underlining the need for women to be in control not only of their own fertility and sexuality but also of that of men, confusions and contradictions arise.

The above arguments could be taken much further. However, I will here just emphasize that there are profound discrepancies between the social roles and values contained in the rituals and women's and in particular men's ability to perform their social roles and live up to these values in contemporary Kisii. There are also contradictions and obscurities within the key values advocated for each sex. Combined with the 'inevitability' of initiation, its importance for adult male and female identity, social roles, and social values in the present Kisii social context, the seeds are sown for tension and antagonisms between the sexes.

Chapter 4
Marriage, Identity and Social Value

Introduction

Marriage is one of the most important institutions in which gender ideology is produced and reproduced. Marriage is fundamental for the construction of gender identity and sexuality, and there is a close relation between marriage and social value (Ortner and Whitehead, 1981/89:20). Just as marriage is a political relationship, it is also a mechanism through which productive relationships, rights and obligations are established—not to mention prestige:

> ... in perhaps the majority of cases, male prestige is deeply involved in cross-sex relations ... having a wife may be a prerequisite to full adult status (1981/89:21).

This links up with the argument that a man needs a wife for the domestic and sexual services that makes him independent and "equal" to other men. Marriage for a man is a prerequisite to adult autonomy and status (Collier and Rosaldo in Ortner and Whitehead, 1981/89:316,). What does marriage mean to women? In the context of such a relationship between marriage and prestige, womanhood is defined largely by wifehood, and the 'essence' of womanhood is that which is of greatest value in a wife—sexuality and economic usefulness (1981/89:326).

In Kisii the institution of marriage has changed dramatically—and so have the relations between the genders. Traditional marriage involving transfer of brideprice to legalize the union is becoming increasingly rare. 'Cohabitations' as a result of elopement have become the norm where no bridewealth has been transferred from the husband or even agreed upon between the in-laws. This, I shall argue, has fundamental and very different implications for male and female identity, social value and the relations between genders. While Ortner and Whitehead provide a useful starting point, their approach—as will be illustrated below—is limited because they do not take the implications of changing marriage patterns into account.

The institution of marriage

In precolonial Kisii, marriage was a political relationship as well as a mechanism by which productive relationships, rights and obligations were established. Polygyny was the norm. The more wives a man had, the more land could be cultivated, the more children he could father, and the more status and social value he acquired. Marriage had three significant stages. The first stage of courtship *ekeri-boki* was the stage of negotiation in which a go-between called *esigani* and the parents of the girl began to discuss the issue, with or without the knowledge of the couple. Sometimes a young man would identify the girl he wanted for marriage, and the parents or elder brothers would pursue the matter on his behalf. Once the prospective couple had agreed to marry, then the second stage, bridewealth negotiation, was embarked upon. Both parents of the couple began to assume a more important role in the contract through arranged visits. Finally the third stage, called *ekekobo* or the wedding ceremony, was arranged. Before the wedding ceremony, but after the bridewealth had been paid, the bride and the bridegroom were allowed to live together for a period of two months. This period of trial marriage was very important because it enabled the couple to get to know one another and make a final agreement on whether to continue the marriage or not. Once the couple had agreed to live as husband and wife, then the wedding ceremony, *egekobo*, was arranged. After the ceremony the bride was given a traditional name by the older women in the bridegroom's household, and later she was fitted with ankle rings *ebitenge* to signify that she was somebody's wife. Then she becomes a respectable member of that family (Were and Nyamwaya, 1986:146–48).

Cattle as bridewealth was transferred in exchange for a woman's productive and childbearing capacity. If she died prematurely, the number of cattle reclaimed was reduced proportionally to the number of children she had born. If she did not become pregnant within a reasonable time it was legitimate, in theory, to divorce her, send her home and reclaim bridewealth. Pregnancy before marriage was not severely disapproved of, even if the prospective husband was not the biological father: "the child goes with the cattle" it was claimed.

In practice, divorce was almost non-existent. Men would be reluctant to return the bridewealth, and if they were not satisfied with a wife, if for example she was infertile or a lazy house-keeper, they would rather take another wife. Women were reluctant to leave husbands, as this also entailed leaving their children in the custody of the husband (LeVine, R. and B., 1966/77).

The main body of law dealing with marriage, matrimony and compensation had bridewealth as its central institution. Its purpose was to regulate claims between people related by marriage (who because of clan exogamy necessarily belonged to different political entities) but also between male descendants competing for shares of their patrimonial cattle. Indigenous judicial experts used to be consulted on the application of the law, but until the colonial power introduced new authorities there was no truly ascribed authority except that which lay with fathers and grandfathers as patriarchs of their own families (Mayer, I., 1965).

There was a clear interdependence between men and women. Men were dependent on women for status, as cultivators and food producers, to bear their children and to create relations to other tribes. Women were dependent on men for land (the means of production), status, children, protection etc. Just as a man had no status and social value without at least one wife, a prerequisite for full female status and social value was to be married. Consequently, marriage was the bond between men and women that gave status.

Marriage was governed by the following three basic principles:

- A woman should begin to bear children almost as soon as she was able and continue as long as she was able.

- every man (even if old, married and father many times over) should invest almost all available wealth (cattle, goats, surplus grains etc.) to procure childbearing wives for himself or his sons by way of bridewealth payment.

- children born 'irregularly' or 'out of wedlock' would always find a man willing to claim them as legal father. Plurality of wives and offspring was a major ambition of men, and men were supposed to honour each woman's desire to have children at regular intervals, regardless of his preference (LeVine, R. and B., 1966/77:21).

When girls had been initiated at the age of 14–16, they became marriageable. Parents wanted their daughters to get married as soon as possible and for as much bridewealth as possible. This was to enable the father or the brothers to get married in turn, by using the bridewealth of the daughters. There was no culturally prescribed alternative available for women other than getting married. Marriage was a social necessity, not a choice. Through bridewealth the wife gained managerial and use rights in land, the right of maintenance for herself and her children, and the right of her sons to become the legal heirs to the land allocated to her. The husband gained sexual rights, rights to a wife's labour capacity and rights in children. These rights were also fundamental to his status as husband.

Married women were expected to obey their husbands, be deferential to them, accept their allocations of land and consult their husbands before taking any action. They were also expected to respond quickly to the husband's demands and be hospitable to his guests. On minor issues and family matters, women were allowed to give their opinions but these opinions might well be ignored by the husband. Husbands would sometimes refrain from exercising their authority, or not pay attention to their wives until they felt that the wife needed correction i.e. punishment (LeVine, R. and B., 1966/77). The punishment of women who did not fulfil their obligations was beating. Wife-beating was a common and socially accepted practice and form of chastisement. But according to interviews with old people, the level of violence against women found in contemporary Kisii was relatively new.

Should husbands not meet their obligations, women also had certain sanctions available. The most common of these were withdrawal of labour, refusal of conjugal rights and failure to make food. The ultimate sanction was for the woman to return to her parental home and wait for her husband to arrive with a goat as apology and recompense to her parents. Since polygamy was the norm it can be questioned whether these retaliatory measures had much effect given that the other wives 'helped out'. However, what is important to note is that these sanctions were there and fully acknowledged by society.

Changing marriage patterns

Today the marriage system is still characterized by clan exogamy, patrilocal residence and bridewealth, and marriage is still guided by all the above rules. Even if men no longer need to make marriages in order to make peace among themselves, marriage between clan members is not allowed. When a woman marries she must leave the homestead of her birth and settle in that of her husband. A respectable marriage—ideally—still requires at least a down payment of a brideprice to the bride's father. Marriage for a man—as well as for a woman—is still a prerequisite to adult autonomy and status. Polygyny, however, is disappearing—at least officially—and, most importantly, so is the transfer of bridewealth. In about half of the unions formed between 1975 and 1979, no bridewealth at all had been paid in 1983. In the period 1981–83 only 14% of women entered unions preceded or accompanied by bridewealth payment (Håkansson 1988:178).

In my quantitative sample of 720 women, bridewealth turned out to be a most sensitive issue. Most women said that they had been paid for. However, when I returned to a woman and interviewed her in more detail, it often turned out that bridewealth had not been paid at all. In the few cases where bridewealth was in the process of being paid/or had been paid, it was after a very long delay.

In spite of the fact that youngsters elope with no previous bridewealth negotiations, bridewealth is far from outdated. Or—to be more precise—the *notion* of bridewealth is not outdated. It is still a viable, persistent, sensitive and much discussed issue, though in reality bridewealth transfers only take place rarely, and if so, only when a woman has proven her fertility. As an institution, however, it is an integral part of Gusii social life with respect to family organization, property relations, cultural and social relations and interaction. My interviews with both women and men clearly indicate that transfer of bridewealth is fundamental for male and in particular female existential identity, social value and closely linked to perceptions of self-esteem.

Bridewealth is still referred to in terms of the number of cows. However, with no grazing land available and only a few cattle around, cash is increasingly substituted for cows—if a transfer of bridewealth takes place at all. A good dairy cow would easily cost between 5–10,000 shillings, while a more meagre head of cattle would cost 2,000 shillings. In terms of the amount to be paid in money, bridewealth in Kisii today ranges from 10,000–50,000 shillings. Comparing this amount with the current salary of a local agricultural contract worker of 800 shillings per month, a garment factory worker of 1200 shillings per month or a sugar cane cutter of 1800 shillings (in 1992) bridewealth is an unattainable amount of money to most men.

Everybody in Kisii, though, men and women, young and old, are very well aware that a union between husband and wife is not legal unless bridewealth has been transferred to the woman's parents. It establishes binding rights and obligations between husband and wife and towards the rest of the society. It establishes a husband's rights to his children, and to his wife's productive power (rights in uxorem) as well as a wife's right in relation to her husband, such as his obligations to provide her with access to land, adequate housing and proper clothing (Håkansson, 1988). As such, bridewealth constitutes payment from the husband to the family of his bride for his wife's services and for rights in her children. Bridewealth is thus instrumental in affiliating children to a husband and his patrilineage. Through transfer of bridewealth, the woman becomes the socially defined mother, and she gains managerial and use rights in land, the right of maintenance for herself and her children as well as the right for her sons to become legal heirs to the land allocated to her.

'Unofficial' polygynous unions

According to census estimates in the 1970s, 33% of household heads in Kisii are polygamous (*Population and Development in Kenya*. 1980:81). Findings from my survey indicate that among the 723 women interviewed only 10% were second wives while 2% were third and fourth wives (Silberschmidt, 1991a). Census estimates as well as my own survey data are problematic. Census data are dubitable because they do not deal with unofficial polygyny—particularly among the better off. The validity of our survey data on women is also dubitable because the women interviewed were reticent about their real position in the household. Most tended to say that they were first wives even when they were not—a fact which is supported by the qualitative interviews.

Men deplore the fact that land pressure has made it impossible for most of them to accommodate more than one wife. As in many other African contexts, the belief still exists among men as well as women in Kisii that women are in surplus, that there are fewer men than women. Linked to this, there is not much doubt in the minds of most men that a great number of women are available and 'a man needs at least three wives: one to work his land, one to give birth to his children—and one for pleasure'. Besides, 'a man who cannot handle several wives is not a real man'. Plurality of wives and offspring is a major ambition of men (LeVine, R. and B., 1966/77:21). This, I shall argue, is still a major ambition of the majority of men.

Traditionally, a polygynist had several sanctions against a wife who was disobedient. Refusing to sleep with his wife was not only a sign of his displeasure, but it could become very serious—if it lasted long enough. It meant a withdrawal of her only means of achieving status and prestige, namely her capacity to bear children. With only one 'wife' these sanctions have lost their original force. Today most women are not interested in having co-wives or that their husbands have girlfriends for that matter. In polygynous unions (whether or not bridewealth has been transferred) there is a lively—and often very harsh—competition between wives who want to reserve a greater share of the small land plots for themselves and their own children—or there is competition over access to other resources. Each wife wants to be her husband's favourite and to have her children favoured by him, rather than the children of other wives. Women are also jealous, but the jealousy that they revealed to me was rather attached to the fear that their husband would spend money on other wives or girlfriends.

Polygyny makes a great difference in terms of the power relationships within the homestead:

> The monogamous male is dependent on his wife for sexual satisfaction, food preparation and other domestic tasks, and a large proportion of the homestead's agricultural activities. When they have a quarrel, she may run back to her parents' homestead for a week, leaving him a bachelor with the responsibilities of a married man. Once he has a second wife, however, he can do without one of his wives more easily, and the wife is hesitant to run away for fear of diminishing her relative standing in the homestead. The rivalry among the co-wives, although potentially dangerous, works to augment the power of the husband whose favour is a scarce commodity desired by both wives. First wives often foresee this and oppose the second marriages of their husbands; those who are successful in this effort appear to retain a permanent power advantage in the family (LeVine, R., 1964:75–76).

According to Håkansson, although the rural elite is still rather young, it seems likely that they will not find it necessary to set themselves up as polygynists with many wives in future. Instead of gaining prestige in the eyes of the ordinary Gusii, they are likely to lose it among their fellow members. They may still do so, though, if they think that a second highly educated wife may be an advantage, but those who have already married a well educated wife are unlikely to do so. These women are even more opposed to sharing their husband with an additional wife than an uneducated one. They can also stand on their own feet, because a job gives economic independence. Elite members too would certainly suffer a great loss of prestige if they were to neglect the education of their own children. Polygyny soon makes the burden of school fees too tough.

My discussions with men from the rural elite do not correspond with the observations of Håkansson. Perhaps men from the rural elite tend not set themselves up as official polygynists. However, the more wives or 'unofficial' relations with (preferably young) women, the more esteem a man gets from his peers. It is a clear sign of power and wealth, potency, virility and masculinity—and most men's dream. Most businessmen, politicians and wealthy men have more than one wife. As noted by Ortner and Whitehead, and in line with my findings, there is a close correspondence between male status and sexual activity that is the inverse of the female system. Female sexual activity, as will be discussed below, is certainly not status-giving whereas male sexual activity is. However, men were also aware of the problems of competition between wives. Confronted with the question, 'what would your wife say if you take another wife', most men would reveal that 'I have not yet discussed it with my wife because she wouldn't like it'. Therefore they stressed that 'today a man with many wives prefers not to have all of them living closely together. Then they will fight. They should be set up in different places, (always one of them in Kisii town) and the husband should buy a piece of land for each wife'.

Surprisingly many young women are very willing to become second wives—or just girlfriends. This was a matter of animated discussion among my female assistants—particularly those with a husband who had taken a second or third wife. They were very upset: 'men can't get enough wives, and so many women are willing to become second ones'. My assistants distinguished between two types of women: the 'lazy ones' and those with no other choice. The lazy ones, they argued 'even if they have the choice of becoming the first wife—they are not interested if the husband is poor. Life with a poor husband is too tough. It gives too much hardship and too much work in the shamba'. Therefore 'the lazy ones prefer to become a second wife of a wealthy man rather than to marry a young and poor bachelor—then they don't have to work so hard'. 'Lazy women prefer men who can buy them presents and nice dresses'.

The second category—and by far the most common in Kisii—consists of young women who have given birth (at their parents home) without the man feeling responsible for her pregnancy. Her social value has dropped significantly—even if she has proven to be fertile. Most of these women have no other choice than to become a second 'wife' of a poor man: just to get some food. Adult 'unmarried' daughters with children are considered a great burden—and a disgrace—and parents complain if they have to support them. The other alternative for such women is prostitution.

Premarital relationships

Returning to the institution of marriage, it has become a very ambiguous 'enterprise'—filled with contradictions. It is no exaggeration to say that courtship and marriage are misnomers (Were and Nyamwaya, 1986). In fact, cohabitation or union are more appropriate terms than marriage in contemporary Kisii.

Youngsters often elope even before their parents have heard about their relationship. This means that today most young boys and girls engage in sexual activity long before 'marriage age'. In the past, although premarital liaisons were not really approved of by parents, they were not prohibited either. But they had to be carried out discretely. The traditional and socially approved permissiveness where initiated youngsters were allowed to 'play sex' with each other discretely (that is, boys were not supposed to carry out penetration as long as they were not married) is not approved of today. Parents are extremely concerned about their unmarried daughters becoming pregnant. On the other hand, if premarital sex is not accepted, it is certainly expected. 'Young boys are not behaving responsibly. They just don't care', parents complain. While mothers want their daughters to attend school, many argue that 'when boys and girls meet at school, they do not learn to respect each other'. 'But what can we do? Our children need education'. Thus, parents often feel that attending school puts their daughters at risk. When LeVine and LeVine did their fieldwork parents had difficulties in controlling the behaviour of adolescent girls:

> The basis of the difficulty is that the girl is oriented toward young men who give her gifts and flatter her, expecting in return that she will yield sexually or even elope with one of them. Parents .. view an adolescent girl as a family member who must of necessity leave home for marriage and who can at least reimburse the parents who took the trouble to raise her with a handsome bridewealth in cattle. What they fear most is her running off with a reckless young man who has no cattle and, secondly, her becoming pregnant or gaining a reputation as a 'slut' (LeVine, R. and B., 1966/77:175).

Premarital births, though, have become the norm rather than the exception—along with more or less successful attempts to provoke an abortion. Once a girl is pregnant her parents will try to find out who is responsible, and the girl is likely to be sent to the home of the suspected father. If the parents are very lucky they may receive a cow, which establishes a man's right to his child. Or they may receive nothing—which is the most common. If the young father downright refuses to marry or, as is commonly the case, pays little or no bridewealth, parents may go to court and try to claim damages—but most often unsuccessfully.

Helen, my assistant, was very ambitious on behalf of her three teenage daughters. She watched over them like a hawk. She certainly expected brideprice for them. She had worked hard in the local dispensary for the past l6 years, in addition to cultivating her husband's land, and thus financing their education, mainly on her own. She kept telling her daughters to come straight back from school and not to play around with the boys. Her repeated remark to her daughters was 'no first rate boy would ever take a second rate girl as his wife'. Should a girl become pregnant, she would immediately become a second rate person. Helen was determined that her daughters were not going to be second rate women or end up with second rate husbands. 'A man who takes a woman with a child as his wife has no voice among other men'. But increasingly this is precisely what happens. And—as I slowly found out—in a majority of households the first child was not fathered by the current husband.

'Illegal' unions

As a result of premarital relationships, traditional marriage negotiations over bridewealth, where parents and relatives of the respective bridegroom and bride played an important role, have almost disappeared. Traditionally, bridewealth negotiations were an important source of prestige for the elders of both sexes, and it gave them a measure of control not only over the women but also over the younger men. Today, if bridewealth is not paid, the union has no legal status whatsoever. In principle, it can break up at any time without mediation by third parties. This creates an extremely insecure situation for a 'married' woman. She and her children can be chased away at any time by her husband. Her access to the means of production (husband's land) which constitutes the basis for the survival of herself and her children is not secured. A major preoccupation of 'unpaid' women—a fact which women referred to again and again—is that 'a woman needs to know where she will be buried'. With no transfer of brideprice, a woman cannot be buried in her husband's compound which is the proper place for a woman to be buried. Only young 'unmarried' girls can be buried at their parents' homestead.

With no transfer of bridewealth the most apparent and negative effect on women is that women's and their male offspring's access to land is not secured. This means that as long as no attempts or negotiations to settle the brideprice or just part of it have been made, 'eloped' women can be sent back by their husbands at any time. The same applies to their children as their affiliation to their father's lineage is not legitimate when no bridewealth has been transferred. Women thereby lose their right to land, their right to cultivate it, and they are without the means to produce food for themselves and their children. Such women end up as single mothers, a phenomenon not known in earlier times, unable to provide for their children and themselves, and with sons who are not entitled to land. Unless these women find another man, (or marry a childless widow—a custom which is still practised) through whom they can get access to land they are at the mercy of their parents. Parents are often unwilling or unable to receive a returning daughter and her offspring since they have no surplus land on which to feed her. The only way for many such women to survive with their children is, as mentioned above, to become second or third wives—or prostitutes. What should not be overlooked is the fact that men who have not paid bridewealth also lose their rights to their own children.

When brideprice has not been paid, it is common knowledge that a woman is not really committed either to her husband or to her in-laws. And this is reflected in her behaviour: 'If a husband does not see to it that he pays brideprice, he does not respect his wife. Therefore, the wife does not make any effort to please either her husband or her in-laws'. In that case, 'a man is not responsible for his 'wife's' behaviour'. Moreover, he is not dependent on her for social value to the same extent as if he had paid for her.

Precisely the opposite may also be the case. Many women make great efforts to please their in-laws. They try to behave their best to be accepted and in order to put pressure on their husbands to pay bridewealth. Lack of brideprice transfer seriously weakens the woman's position in negotiating. If, for example, her husband beats her, she cannot go back to her parents and wait for the husband to return with a goat by way of apology—a traditional practice. And the economic vulnerability of women often compels them to accept male callousness or irresponsibility because they have no alternative sources of economic security.

In her psychological portraits of Gusii women Sarah LeVine notes:

> Suzanna and Trufena, both mothers of sons, had not yet been paid for, and this it emerged, was the main focus of their thoughts and fantasies. The enduring illegitimacy of their positions confronted them at every turn. Like most of their contemporaries, they had eloped with men of their own choosing with the expectation that in due course their husbands would produce the bridewealth required to ratify their marriages. Both these young women were preoccupied with the anomaly that, having provided their husbands with sons, their bridewealth was still not forthcoming. Thus their status was not only subordinate and dependent but marginal as well (LeVine, S., 1979:365).

LeVine's observations are very similar to mine: 'unpaid' women are in a peculiar situation. They are not legitimate members of their current families, nor legitimate members of their natal families. They constitute a new phenomenon of unmarried singles in a society where marriage is the social norm and necessary to gain social acceptance (Silberschmidt, 1991a). An unmarried, single Gusii woman has no culturally accepted identity (Håkansson, 1985:113). Consequently, the fact that women often make statements to the effect that they are better off without a husband does not mean that they would actually prefer not to have a husband—on the contrary.

Neither Sarah LeVine nor Håkansson, though, call into question men's identity—or social value—when they are not able to pay bridewealth. They do not deal with men's preoccupations in not being able to produce the expected bridewealth. My data clearly indicate that it is also an extremely sensitive issue for the majority of men—just as it is for women. When I asked men if they had paid bridewealth their immediate answer was always that of course they had. Checking with their wives, they had not. When confronted with the question again, men would maintain that they were making efforts to scrape together a bridewealth, but lack of cash was a major problem.

If a husband dies and no bridewealth has been paid his 'wife' has certain sanctions. She can refuse to follow burial rituals i.e. she can refuse to turn her clothes inside out so that the husband cannot be buried. Or she can refuse until his family has paid bridewealth.

Felix was killed in a car accident during my fieldwork in 1992. His brothers had to scrape together a compensation to his 'wife's' brothers. His wife Ester (27 years) was now left alone with 5 children, of whom the first born was 9 years old. During the time that Felix and Ester lived together brideprice was never paid. This was not really a problem for Ester because her parents died shortly after she went to live with Felix. Consequently, there was nobody to put pressure on Felix to pay. However, now that Felix had died, Ester's brothers refused to let him be buried until they had received bridewealth. Felix' brothers then offered three cows to Ester's brothers. The matter was settled and Felix was buried.

Ester's brothers, though, never turned up to collect the cows. Instead, they insisted on getting another two cows and on top of that two thousand shillings. Felix' brothers then got very upset and refused to pay anything at all. As a result, Ester's situation became very insecure. She and her children risked being chased off the land. However, when I last saw her she hoped that other relatives would step in and provide the extra cows and the two thousand shillings. As to the future of Ester, if the right amount of brideprice is paid, Ester and her children can stay on Felix's land and her sons inherit the land. In order for her to get somebody to 'share the bed with her', one of the late husband's brothers will normally be more than willing or even see it as a right. However, she may also find a man with no land from a different clan, who is willing to move in with her—and work under her command. This is an accepted practice not uncommon in Kisii. I met three women who had made use of this practice. One of them was now living with a third man. The two others had been thrown out 'because they were not good labourers'.

In sum, both men and women are perfectly aware of the fundamental transformations of marriage transaction that have taken place. 'If there is no brideprice it is no good', both women and men agree: 'the husband has no say over the wife, and the wife has no say over the husband'. Nevertheless, favourite phrases by women are 'we are bought like cattle' and 'our husbands are our owners', phrases probably 'taken over' from colonialists who did not grasp the meaning of bridewealth. Women often said this in a mocking tone of voice (for my benefit?) as if it were extremely humiliating to them. However, women know perfectly well that husbands have great difficulties in procuring bridewealth. They also know that most women are not paid for, and consequently, that most husbands are not the 'owners' of their wives. But women would love to have an 'owner'. I never met a woman who did not yearn to be bought, like cattle. To get a husband who is capable of paying a brideprice means that he is well off. To get such a husband is the dream of all women: 'It shows that he values and respects his bride so much that he pays for her'. That is the real triumph of any Gusii woman. And for the man as well.

Despite the major socio-economic changes that have altered the context in which Gusii women live their lives, the normative centre of those lives remains in place. Each woman must find a husband whose home affiliations and resources become her own. She must leave her parents and go to live with a man who at least promises to pay bridewealth for her. She is given her own house and fields at his homestead, raises her food and children there, and is expected to serve, obey, and be faithful to her husband, respect and help his mother, and cooperate with his brothers' wives. The norms and obligations of women's kinship and economic roles are largely intact within a restructured socio-economic environment (LeVine, S., 1979:17).

Given education, expanded employment opportunities, cash availability and the deterioration of parental control and traditional marriage, Håkansson asks: why do Gusii women get married? What are the reasons for conservatism in the economic and domestic careers of Gusii females? He arrives at the conclusion that for women there is no other status outside marriage (Håkansson, 1985:113). However, he also emphasizes that only the transfer of bridewealth can make a woman a respectable in the eyes of both men and women (Håkansson, 1994:524).

Bridewealth, identity and social value

In East Africa the institution of bridewealth has attracted the attention of many researchers over time.[17] A basic hypothesis is that societies where females were strongly controlled were those where men identified most strongly with cattle and where cattle formed the most important part of a high bridewealth payment. According to Håkansson in his study of bridewealth in Kisii, bridewealth has three dimensions:

1.   the communicative dimension, i.e. its meaning in relation to the culturally constructed social universe.
2.   the structural aspect i.e. the norms concerning expected and binding rights adhering to transactions; and

---

[17] Gluckman, 1950; Kuper, 1982; Håkansson, 1988 and many more.

3. The social form i.e. how individuals use bridewealth to reach certain goals (Håkansson 1988:20).

A study of economic conditions in Kenya suggests that changes in bridewealth payment are linked to the market economy and the introduction of money in bridewealth during the period of colonialism (Kitching, 1980). The increased importance of agriculture for cash crop production reduced the importance of cattle and caused livestock to be replaced by money in the payment of bridewealth. This then became a source of capital which the male head of the household could use for investments other than marriages. In this process women's labour became more and more important for the production of ash crops, and brideprice increased in value as a result. Under these altered economic conditions, parents could pursue a strategy of offering their daughters to the highest bidder, and those forming large polygynous families would enter into open competition and outbid each other. But the money economy did not change the men's goal of investment, which continued to be cows and wives, the two measures of wealth and prestige (Håkansson, 1988:20). As a result, women's position in the household was weakened and their rights in resources and income declined vis-à-vis men. Women's labour began to be used for the production of cash crops, the income from which was appropriated by men. From this point of view commodity production and money influenced bridewealth which then became payment for women's labour resources. This again created a change in the norms governing husband and wife relationships with respect to the control of resources (Kitching, 1980).

In addition to these immediate and visible effects, my study clearly reveals some less visible effects. While bridewealth increased and with it women's value, the payment of bridewealth decreased. When interviewed, women often expressed shame and felt that they were not much valued when their husbands made no attempts to pay for them. They felt neither accepted nor respected by their in-law relatives: 'they do not make me feel at home'; 'I have been given a very bad piece of land'. In terms of a woman's relations to her own parents, they would be very tense and she would feel under constant pressure from them. Moreover, they would not respect her husband. Women would often argue 'how can I go home and face my parents, when they have received nothing for me?'; 'my mother has a bag of maize for me, but how can I collect it when my husband neglects his duty?'; 'I have not seen my mother for some years, and I miss her so much. But I am too ashamed to go home'; 'once I ran into my mother at the market in Kisii town but I had to leave her right away because I cried so much'. A woman's link to her natal home depends on her bridewealth being paid and upon which family member got the money and the use it. A special link is forged between a woman and the brother who used her bridewealth to marry. Such a bond also exists with the brothers whose school fees were paid with her bridewealth (Håkansson, 1988:151–152).

Apart from trying to put pressure on their husbands to pay at least one instalment, women seemed to have two main strategies in order to stabilize their position:

1. to make use of their fertility and produce many children, preferably sons; or
2. to try themselves to pay part of or even the whole brideprice to their parents.

Linked to the first strategy is the fact that public opinion and sometimes the husband's own parents would blame him for being irresponsible if he tried to get rid of a wife who had given birth to several children (at least two sons). Moreover, our quantitative survey reveals a relationship between payment of brideprice and family planning use in that there is a marked difference between family planning users and non-users when brideprice is paid:

	Bridewealth paid	Bridewealth paid only in part	Bridewealth not paid
FP-users	55%	29%	16%
Non-users	33.6%	35.3%	30.4%

These figures could lead to the assumption that there is a connection between payment of bridewealth and women's use of a family planning method.[18]

As far as the second strategy is concerned, many women mentioned that they had given up hoping that their husband would ever scrape together a bridewealth, and now they were trying themselves. Women who do succeed in raising funds to cover their bridewealth are few, though, and the majority of them have an income of their own (Håkansson, 1988).

While it can be argued that, from the point of view of the husband, his position is not nearly as vulnerable as that of a wife, not paying the expected brideprice has repercussions for him too. As already mentioned, men were reluctant to admit that they had not paid brideprice. A man's right to his wife's labour and produce is not legalized when brideprice is not paid. He is not the 'proprietor' of his wife in the traditional sense. However, as long as he supplies her with land he is entitled to appropriate both her labour and

---

[18] Factors such as women's access to economic resources (Safilios-Rothchild, 1983 and many more) and education are normally correlated with women's use of family planning. However, these explanations are increasingly questioned (Egerö and Hammarskjöld, 1994; Kirumira 1995). In our survey there is no convincing correlation these factors and women's use or non-use of a family planning method (Silberschmidt, 1991a).

her produce.[19] Most importantly, lack of bridewealth deprives a man of his paternal right to his children, and that is a serious threat. Moreover, his kin group and the community will doubt his respectability if he makes no attempt to settle the bridewealth. Consequently, there is no doubt that it gives social value and respect to pay the bridewealth. My findings are in agreement with those of Håkansson:

> A man knows, as does the community, that according to the cultural definition of fatherhood, his biological children can never be his unless he pays bridewealth. To die childless is considered a horrible fate by the Gusii. Rights in children have an almost mystical aspect. There is a belief that if a man continues to elope with women, but never marries, he will become a *ribaki* or a *riochi*, a wanderer, a vagrant. It is believed that he will not be able to win a woman because everyone knows of his behaviour. If, however, he pays bridewealth for a woman and has sons with her, Gusii say that "wherever he is when he dies, he will at least not die naked" (1988:141).

Traditional marital stability in Kisii was closely linked to the fact that custody of children was vested in the husband who had paid bridewealth. This means that if a wife wanted to leave her husband she had to leave her (male) children behind, regardless of age. For a woman, then, it would be almost impossible to leave her husband because it would virtually mean that she would have to abandon her children. Moreover, she had no automatic right to return to her home of origin. Her parents would fear this because it meant that they might have to return the bridewealth. This would hardly be possible, having used the cattle to marry their sons. In short, a separation or divorce would damage a woman's character in the eyes of the society. She would constitute a threat to other women in the society because her only option was to find another husband (or become a second or third wife) as soon as possible.

Scrutinizing the changing institution of marriage in Kisii many paradoxes emerge. On the one hand, it can be argued that women and men have been 'freed' from traditional bonds that link the couple tightly together, bonds which make it virtually impossible for a woman to divorce her husband and vice versa. A man who has paid brideprice can never count on getting his payment back from the in-laws if he wants to rid himself of his wife. With no bridewealth transfer, the spouses have become independent individuals who do not need to stick to each other the rest of their lives, if their 'union' is unsuccessful. The woman can take her children with her when she leaves, and the husband has no claim on them unless at least a part of the brideprice is paid. The wife has a new won freedom. If she does not want to stay with her husband, she is free to leave him. But this is only in theory. With no transfer of bridewealth the whole foundation for her sub-

---

[19] cf. Kitching's argument above

sistence is jeopardized. Consequently, women will try to influence husbands to pay and stabilize the unions—even to the extent of contributing to their own bridewealth—as mentioned above. A woman in a nonpaid union has no attractive alternatives. Leaving the man will expose her both to gossip and ostracism for being a loose woman and to economic insecurity and poverty (Håkansson, 1994). On the other hand, if an 'unpaid' wife does not behave properly, the man cannot be blamed. 'This is to be expected', both women and men argue.

In sum, transfer of bridewealth is fundamental for male and female identity, self-esteem and social value. Women lose social value if they are not paid for. Men lose social value if they cannot pay brideprice. Somehow, though, transfer of bridewealth seems to be given less priority by men than by women, even if many men when interviewed said they feared that their wives might leave them. They were perfectly aware that they need to make a transfer of bridewealth in order to have rights over their children. This raised the question of why there is this difference in priorities.

Cross-sex bonds, identity and social value

As wives are normally sexual partners, and mothers and sisters are not, an emphasis on wives tends to give more ideological prominence to the sexual aspects of women in general. This point is expanded by Ortner, who argues that women in roles with a major sexual component are more easily considered simply as different kinds of 'natural' beings than men, whereas kinswomen are more easily seen as different social actors. Consequently, cultures in which kinship definitions of womanhood are more important than sexual and marital definitions appear to be both more sex-egalitarian and less sex-antagonistic than cultures in which the opposite is the case (Ortner and Whitehead, 1981/89:23).

This tendency to define women by relationship is seen as a reflection of their exclusion from the world of male prestige. It is not a matter of two parallel value-equivalent domains: domestic/public or male/female. The category of femaleness is not generated in terms of some sort of abstract symmetry with masculinity, but in terms of women's relationships with men and the relevance of those relationships to male prestige (1981/89:19). This has consequences for cultural notions of the sexes way beyond this tendency to designate a man in terms of social position and a woman in terms of her menfolk. Few empirical studies have addressed the issue of how specific variations in kinship and marriage organization interact with and influence the relations between genders as well as male and female identities. In his latest work, though, this is precisely what Håkansson does, arguing that the variations in kinship and marriage organization depend on the content of women's relationships with their natal kin and on the role of marriage in defining the character of women's social identities. Where women retain their natal lineage identity upon marriage and where they can utilize these natal kinship links, women's position is more secure. This is not the case in Kisii, and the marriage organization interacts negatively with female identity (Håkansson, 1994:516).

Given the existential and non-negotiable identities and the role-based identities, Håkansson argues that the specific character of a woman's identity in any society may constrain or facilitate negotiation of their socially approved roles. In contrast, features of role-based identities may be negotiated and the identities themselves relinquished without sanctions (1994:517). Håkansson distinguishes between two different patrilineal gender and kinship systems in East African societies:

> 1. Systems where women, irrespective of marital status, maintain socially sanctioned identities and jural, ritual and economic rights and obligations in their natal family and lineage throughout life. The statuses of sister and daughter in this system are immanent features of a woman's existential identity, and these statuses, in turn, entail certain constitutive rights. Although the status of wife entails rights and obligations vis-à-vis the husband and his family, the latter status is a negotiable feature of a woman's identity.

> 2. 'Systems where females from the time of birth hold an ambiguous position in their natal family and lineage, and where they attain ritual, economic, and jural rights and obligations predominantly through the statuses of wife and mother. Thus, the status of wife in this system is an immanent feature of a woman's existential identity, entailing stronger constitutive rights than either of the two statuses of sister or daughter. Rather, in these systems, the latter are deemphasized and contingent, and do not in and of themselves entail rights as strong as those entailed by marriage (1994:517).

While the second system corresponds to that in Kisii the first system can be found, for example, among the neighbouring Luyia tribe. The kinship identity of a Gusii woman is immediately revealed when she is asked about clan affiliation. She always answers with the name of her husband's clan or sub-clan, whereas a Luyia woman would refer to her father's clan. According to Håkansson, bridewealth transactions offer an analytical datum line because, in changing societies like Kisii, they constitute processes through which the content of gender and kinship relationships are continuously being redefined (1994:516).

The implications of different patrilineal systems for women's kinship and gender status (and subsequently for their economic and social strategies) were first pointed out by Southall (1960). One system was characterized by women's reproductive powers and rights in their own persons being transferred to the husband and his lineage at marriage. All children subsequently born to a wife were considered members of the husband's descent group, irrespective of their biological paternity. This system was accompanied by high bridewealth, rare divorce, a strong identification of a wife with her husband's group, and a weak relationship with her natal lineage. Men of the same descent tended to live as neighbours in the same locality. Thus, clans and lineages corresponded largely to territorial settlements. The other system had precisely the opposite characteristics.

Sacks stresses that women's social identities, access to resources and socio-political power are dependent on whether or not they maintain a social identity as sisters (Sacks, 1982). But Parkin argues that women's kinship identities are rather defined by the structural character of patrilineal ideology—as symbolically expressed in bridewealth transactions (Parkin, 1978, 1980). Consequently, in terms of women's future changes in status, it is important whether women are primarily identified as daughters/sisters or as wives/mothers (1980:219). Parkin also distinguishes between two types of bridewealth. In some groups (like the Gusii) bridewealth is undifferentiated with respect to payment for rights in children and rights in a wife. In other groups (for example Kikuyu) bridewealth is a composite of several payments. When rights in wife and children are distinguished the role of the woman is ambiguous, because she is culturally recognized as a producer of children for both her natal and her husband's lineage. When such a distinction is absent—as in Kisii—there is a total and clear transfer of a woman both as mother and wife to her husband's group. Similar observations have been made in a study from New Guinea: where the lineage and clan are seen as growing only through male kinship links, women must be symbolically 'detachable' from their natal kin in order to allow unambiguous patrifiliation; and the woman becomes incorporated in her husband's lineage as a whole person (Strathern, 1987).

Håkansson concludes that 'the trajectories of change in women's and men's relative control over and access to resources depend upon the flexibility of the rules for group affiliation and perpetuation'. And he proposes that 'these rules for group affiliation and perpetuation, and the symbolic content of transactions effectuating affiliation, define the transformational potentials of gender and kinship relationships in contexts of rapid social change' (Håkansson, 1994:520). Consequently, with the increase of elopements, broken unions and landless women in Kisii, women are both being barred from their 'husband's' farm and also being estranged from their natal kin:

> ... a Gusii woman's rights and proper identity as a daughter and sister are contingent upon marriage. Thus, the payment of bridewealth has a double significance. It establishes her legitimate relationship with her natal family as a married daughter who, by virtue of her bridewealth, has contributed to the growth of her own family. In discussing marriage, women emphasize the importance they place on pleasing parents through the transfer of bridewealth, and the special prestige and status they are accorded at home by virtue of its payment:' When bridewealth is paid, there is respect to your parents. Even if you are mistreated, you cannot become 'a woman who moves from place to place' because bridewealth was paid'. And, 'if bridewealth is paid, you can go and ask your father for money because you know he was given something for you' ... .

Through marriage, an adult woman attains a position as mother and wife, while at the same time contributing to her natal family's growth and well-being through the bridewealth that was transferred for her. *Without marriage, she remains 'detached' and outside a proper social identity* (1994:524 [my emphasis]).

Thus Håkansson argues that Gusii women's position in their natal families and lineages is ambiguous and peripheral. Through their status as sisters/ daughters, they have few rights to resources. Instead, through marriage they are included as members of their husband's families, and as married women they verbally identify themselves with their husbands' clan names:

> The spontaneous elicitation of a woman's clan membership is more than a label and a badge: it is a gloss for a number of unstated cultural assumptions about her existential identity and its constitutive rights' ... . 'The status of wife is an immanent feature of a Gusii woman's gender identity. Unmarried, she is considered deviant and anomalous, and her socially sanctioned rights as a daughter/sister alone are few and attenuated. In other patrilineal societies ... women retain natal lineage and family membership throughout life and thus have an accepted alternative identity to that of wife. A woman's proper social identity, of daughter and sister and the rights adhering to these statuses, are independent of marriage and, therefore, can be used separately to negotiate kinship claims (1994:533).

I agree with Håkansson that the status of wife is a feature of a Gusii woman's existential identity and without proper marriage she remains outside a proper social identity. However, having said that, I end up asking: what about all those Gusii women who live in unions where no attempt has been made to pay bridewealth? What about the social identities of these women? Have they become passive victims with no proper social identity? As I read Håkansson, women are structurally trapped. Consequently, Håkansson ends up with a somewhat categorical and static view. He is not able to identify female strategies: to see how women are actively manoeuvring and manipulating in their daily lives—to 'stabilize' their existential identity or perhaps create a new social identity—in spite of their difficult situation.

My discussions with Gusii women clearly reveal that they have developed a number of such strategies. Linked to this, I shall argue that women have learnt the language of subordination in order to manipulate it while at the same time subverting the very ideology of it. Although the structural organization favours men, men are increasingly preoccupied with the fact that women have become more and more uncontrollable and 'disruptive'. Men blame women for 'breaking the home'. In spite of their structurally unfavourable position, women, I shall argue, have always had the 'powers' to undermine male authority and to manipulate men—if not structurally—then in practice and often with very subtle means. Women are using 'women's weapons' not only in order to survive in deep water but also to move the boat in the direction they want—and many seem to have brought the boat in their direction—against all odds.

Social change in Gusiiland presented a number of challenges to paternal authority. Patriarchal authority was already being questioned in the 1950s (LeVine, R., 1964:81). With his focus on women, Håkansson is not concerned with the impact on men's identities or patriarchal authority, although he recognizes that bridewealth is crucial for men to secure descendants:

> What remains to be transferred for men are rights in children, and since the socially recognized descent of children from men is intimately connected with cattle, transfer of a few beasts is mandatory'.. 'among the peasants where the traditional social structure is still reproduced, cattle must still be transferred in order to validate patrilineal descent ... (Håkansson, 1994:218–19).

Men, therefore, are faced with a contradictory situation. It can perhaps be argued that it is the patrilocal position of men that constitutes the basis of male superiority, and is also the reason why payment of bridewealth is not as crucial for male existential identity as it is for female identity. Nevertheless, not paying bridewealth has a very negative effect on male self-esteem. Male identity and male prestige are also deeply involved in cross-sex relations. Cross-sex relations impinge upon male prestige-oriented action:

> In perhaps the majority of societies, the cross-sex bond most critical to a man's social standing is marriage. The frequency with which marriage is in fact the most prestige-relevant cross-sex relationship, relates to the extra-ordinary versality, both functional and symbolic, of this institution. In many societies, production for both use and exchange is based on the domestic unit. A wife is thus often a productive asset, and particularly a producer of goods ... . Wives also bear children ... who may also represent the continuity of a man's line or name...A consideration of which cross-sex relations are of greatest consequence for male prestige is thus only the beginning of the analysis. One must then proceed to consider the specific ways in which ... the marital bond affects prestige and hence why wives are seen as disruptive ... a deeper investigation may uncover the importance to a man's position of wifely productive labour, or female kin links to trading partners, or property rights in women and children; and these factors in turn can be shown to motivate particular images of women, procreation, or sexual activity (Ortner and Whitehead, 1981/89:16–24).

In sum, the decline of bridewealth payments seems to have had at least two serious effects on men: 1) male loss of control over females, and 2) weakening their rights as fathers. When men have no 'legal' control over women and their offspring, their role as heads of household crumbles and their daily performance is questioned. Male self-esteem, social value and social identity are also at stake. Men from poor families have no hope of obtaining patrimony and have entered an emerging landless proletariat working as casual labourers. They do not have the means to make bridewealth payments, and even if they had it would be meaningless outside the context of property and lineage relationships (Håkansson, 1994:535). The position of women is ambiguous. On the one hand, the absence of bridewealth bars them from legal access to their husbands' land and estranges them from their natal kin. On the other hand, the absence of bridewealth increases their lack of respect for their husbands and exacerbates gender antagonisms.

While Ortner and Whitehead focus on the importance of the cross-sex bond for the social value of both genders they are not concerned with what happens to the relations between genders when the marital bond is redefined or broken. Håkansson argues that bridewealth transactions is the analytical crux for examining processes through which the content of gender and kinship relationships are continuously being redefined (1994:533). But he does not develop his argument to encompass the effects of these redefinitions on the relations between genders. Based on my own data which suggests that all features of marriage are undergoing redefinition and renegotiation, with male authority under threat etc. this seems to contribute significantly to the underlying reasons for the escalating gender antagonism in contemporary Kisii.

In order to explore in more depth the intensifying contest between genders in the domestic arena, the household, that is the circuits of economic, symbolic and cultural capital that lie inside, needs further scrutiny (Carney and Watts, 1991:678). But first, I shall briefly look at the relationships between women and men within the household—mostly as Gusii men and women themselves see it.

Antagonism, the cornerstone of 'marriage'?

'Love is when husband and wife go to the mass together' (an eighty year old woman, 1990).

It is a widespread ethnocentric myth that love and romance is a product of medieval Europe and that it has only recently spread to other cultures with modernization and individualism (Fuglesang, 1994). This said, I shall also argue that emotions, love and sexuality are socially and culturally constructed and moulded by custom and socialization. Culture prescribes the situation which provokes emotions such as love, hate, grief, etc. for how long and how intensely they are to be felt, and how they are expressed (1994). Emotions take on different forms in different contexts.

In Kisii, love, affection and tenderness are not the most obvious characteristics of the upbringing of children. Already in infancy, Gusii children are trained in emotional restraint and mothers do little to stimulate their positive response to other persons (LeVine, R. and B., 1966/77:194). This is in line with my general observations. While I have seen a few Gusii mothers in situations where they expressed an amount of love and tenderness towards their children that I have seldom seen in western cultures.

According to LeVine and LeVine, husband-wife relations lack tenderness and affection, and a young child is likely to hear the mother's cries and protests during sex. It is likely that each child has the opportunity to observe the aggressive idiom of sexual intercourse between his parents. This may make a deep impression on his own conception of what sexual behaviour is and should be (1966/77:198–199). Tenderness and affection between spouses are never shown in public. The majority of Gusii women survive almost on a starvation diet, in so far as marital relationships of trust are concerned. Companionship and emotional reciprocity, as we know them in our own society, are neither expected nor sought (LeVine, S., 1979:368).

'If you can't sleep in the same bed all night there is no love', one of my newly-wed informants told me. However, most couples don't. As a 24 year old woman with four children, pregnant with her fifth child, told me 'my husband always tells me to leave the bed when he is satisfied. I don't mind. I prefer to sleep on the ground with my children'. When I asked if a woman 'marries' for love, most of the times I would get the same answer: 'a Gusii woman does not marry for love; she marries to have somebody to plan with'. While physical attraction is important for sexual liaisons, informants' discussions about marriage and elopement always revolve around what westerners would consider economic and social criteria. What a westerner would call romantic attraction is seldom heard of in the context of elopement and marriage (Håkansson, 1994:535).

But whatever type of 'marital' union men and women enter, the belief in male superiority and female inferiority exercise a powerful effect on both male and female ideas of their relations. Regardless of the socio-economic circumstances in which they find themselves, men are consciously and constantly preoccupied with the fact that they are men, and that this condition differentiates them radically from women. At the same time, and paradoxically, a general feature emerging from my interviews with men was their feeling of being pressured and ordered about by women. 'Women are so difficult nowadays'. 'They know their rights'. 'They say that they are equal to men'. 'They don't apologize any more'. 'They complain all the time'. 'They criticize you if you do not do the right thing'. 'Before they were to be seen, not to be heard. Nowadays they sure make themselves heard'. 'They feel that their needs are not satisfied'. 'Women are not like before. They abuse men and speak rudely'. 'They beat men and speak with no respect'. 'Women have become the decision-makers at home'. 'They complain when men go to meet their friends'. 'They want their husbands to stay with them. If they don't, they will get involved with other men'.' Today, women misbehave'. 'If you do not give them money, they sell themselves to other men', and 'so many women roam about'. 'Nowadays, women have their own ways with men friends', and 'some women have even started to take alcohol'. Moreover, 'women are not trustworthy; 'they do not speak the truth to us', they even 'tell their home secrets to others outside their home'. 'If they do not get their own ways, they refuse to cook for their husbands'; 'some women refuse to let their husbands in at night if they are late, and they have to sleep outside'; 'women put a lot of pressure on their husbands'; 'they forget that we are the masters'; 'women are pursuing husbands'; 'women are bothering husbands with trivialities'.

Women 'overpowering' men is a very central and much discussed issue in Kisii. All men questioned said unanimously that they know many men who have been 'overpowered' by their wives i.e. the wife had the upper hand in the household. A few men admitted to me 'I am such a man'. The reasons for being overpowered by a woman were mainly attributed to men's lack of contribution to the upkeep of the household. 'When a wife then had taken over the responsibility'; 'when a husband cannot keep wife and children in clothes, food and other necessities'; 'when the husband is not able to contribute to the school fees'; 'when a woman has to find school fees, when she has to clothe herself, the children and also the husband, and when she is the one answering difficult questions from the neighbours'. 'When he is irresponsible', or 'when he does not care whether there is food or not for his children'. 'A man has been overpowered when his wife dares raise her voice in public'; 'when she dares complain about her husband's behaviour'; 'when she questions his whereabouts'; 'when she puts demands on her husband'; 'if he gives her all his salary'. Or 'when the woman is the one to say what should be done or not—and the man follows the instructions because he fears that she might run away and find another husband'.

Other reasons for being 'overpowered' were 'when the husband has become a drunkard'; 'when a man is born stupid' or 'when he is a coward'. 'When there is quarrel between couples and a man keeps quiet before his wife and does not beat her'. 'When the husband has no say over payment from cash crops'. 'When the wife does not inform her husband about her whereabouts'. 'A man is too kind if he does what he is told by his wife, for example, to go to the shamba, to fetch water, and if he grazes the cattle'.

According to women 'husbands say that they own us—but most of them do not bother to pay brideprice. If they get some money they spend it right away on *busaa* or *changaa*'. 'They get angry when the children are not in school—but they do not contribute with school fees'. Bitter women ironically commented that 'men are so delicate, how can we ask them to go in the shamba', and also 'men are overprotected. They expect everything to be done by the wife'. Both men and women agree that quarrelling and fighting were 'a lot'—often the only type of communication. As one woman put it 'women and men have agreed to disagree'. From the point of view of women, the main reasons for the quarrelling were husbands' economic neglect and their lack of concern; their little interest in the upbringing and education of their children; their 'laziness'; 'they can sit around a whole day doing nothing', and 'if men help in the shamba they get exhausted right away'; their drinking (money used on personal consumption), and their infidelity including money spent on girlfriends.

Both genders agree that 'women do not trust their husbands, and husbands do not trust their wives'. In particular women are disappointed,

angry and disillusioned. 'Men are irresponsible, selfish and cannot be trusted'. On the one hand, women seem to accept their husbands' 'bad' behaviour. On the other, they don't. Francis, one of my informants, who had
the reputation of being able to give good advice and to solve problems said
that it was mainly women who brought their 'cases' to him.

Both men and women knew about cases in which wives had used magic
and herbs on their husbands. Some are said to have used so much that their
husbands have become like frightened children, who hide when visitors
come. A majority of men know about other men having been given herbs by
their wife to 'weaken their thinking' in order for the wife 'to command and
direct the husband so that he would do what was not his responsibility' (i.e.
weed the shamba or help preparing the food). Rumours were constantly circulating of husbands having been killed or made completely apathetic with
poison that their wives had obtained from 'secret sources'. When I asked to
meet such men, I was always told it was impossible, because they would
hide from fear of any stranger.

Thus antagonism seems to be the cornerstone of 'marriage'. Marital con-
tacts, sexual and otherwise, are not expected to involve tenderness or physical demonstration of affection, and the family atmosphere is certainly not
one of easy going solidarity and mutual dependence. There is a lack of positive emotional display within the family homestead—in spite of expected
loyalty:

> ... that the financial aid and store-bought items that the men give to family
> members are also important nowadays. Other than this giving of material ob-
> jects to which great symbolic value is attached, there is little nurturance of a
> purely affectionate variety (LeVine, R. and B., 1966/77:188).

Why is there this tension, anxiety, ambivalence and opposition in intersex
attitudes and behaviour—and why do women show such contempt of their
husbands? Listening to the voices of both women and men, neither gender
lives up to the expectations of the other. Men, in particular, do not perform
their role as heads of household, as protector, as caretaker—and certainly
not as providers (in the sense of 'breadwinners'). Consequently, the authority they used to exercise is being questioned—to the extent that women now
criticize men's behaviour in areas which were formerly unquestioned male
prerogatives. Emotional warmth and affection between spouses is an exception to the rule (just as expressions of community solidarity are rare)
whereas interpersonal hostility flourishes. As observed above, it is extremely
important that men provide material objects. They have acquired a symbolic
value (of love and affection)—not to say a practical one. But 'husbands do
not even bring sugar and tea', women complain. And both women and men
know that 'when you see a man and a woman talking, laughing together,
chances are that the couple is not a husband and wife, but a man and his
mistress'.

As noted above, words are not always reliable—and sometimes people do not say what they mean. In order to explore in more detail what is actually going on inside the household, in the following chapter I shall look at the division of labour, financial contributions, responsibilities etc. and whether women and men in Kisii have identical perceptions of what is actually taking place.

Chapter 5

The Contemporary Kisii Household—Gender Roles, Identity and Social Value in Every Day Life

Introduction

> 'When poverty comes in through the door, love goes out through the window' (poster sold at Kisii municipal market, 1992).

Between 1985/86 and 1992, when I returned to do my last collection of field data, according to my informants, killings within households had increased tremendously . Husbands killed their wives, wives killed their husbands.

In early anthropological studies the 'African' household was often described as an unchanging unity of loyalty, protection and production with a fixed division of labour. Today such households are the exception to the rule. While households are places where survival and reproduction are concentrated:

> It is abundantly clear ... husbands and wives seldom form a unified production unit ... . Of course this is not to deny that there is much mutual dependence and complementarity within the household (Hill, 1975:123).

In Kisii, husbands and wives never formed a unified production unit. However, traditionally, there was both mutual dependence and complementarity between spouses. Today, while in principle for households to survive mutual dependence has increased, such dependence and traditional complementarity have become issues of negotiation.

The gender division of labour demonstrates an 'operationalisation' of gender relations which makes them visible as an organizing principle of society and everyday life. During periods of relative stability, the gender division of labour tends to express, embody and perpetuate relations of gender. In situations of rapid transformation they become dislocated. New processes and struggles are generated at the level of the household and within more fundamental relations of gender. Most importantly, the sexual division of labour cannot be analyzed in strictly economic terms. This is because task allocations are mediated by a particularly powerful ideological operator: the social construction of gender identity (Harris, 1981:117).

In Kisii, the division of labour has certainly been dislocated, and linked to this, Kisii households have increasingly become the site of gender struggle, negotiation and expression of various features of gender relations. Discussions of gender divisions of labour within households involve the kinds of activities associated with women and men. But they also involve how 'trade-offs' are negotiated in response to the many pressures that derive from 'internal' changes in the domestic cycle and from 'external' changes in the socio-economic context in which households are located. The way in which land, labour and incomes are controlled involves complexes of rights and duties, sanctions and consequences. Whether women can or cannot own land, manage their own incomes, absent themselves from the husband's home, be received in their natal home in case of divorce etc. all form the framework of more general cultural designations of women's and men's work. Of course these change as conditions change, but they do not change imperceptibly through gradual cultural transformation, nor rapidly through rational choice; they seem typically to be the results of protracted struggle, sometimes with painful and contradictory results (Guyer, 1981).

In the Kisii household there is an ongoing competition for and control over scarce resources and struggles between genders over new roles and obligations. Sometimes women's and men's interests are mutual, sometimes complementary but most often conflicting. This is because 'The phenomena we are trying to understand still include the 'tenacity of old social and cultural forms' in a situation where 'a number of influences are simultaneously at work in opposite directions' (Hart 1974/78 cited in Guyer, 1981:88). So an understanding of women's and men's different interests and opportunities extends far beyond a cataloguing of their current roles and responsibilities. As rightly noted by Moore, though,

> ... the conflict between men and women ... stands in marked contrast to their interdependence within the joint project of marriage (Moore, 1986:113).

There is a close interaction between gender roles, identity and social value. Social value is fundamental to women's and men's identity, self-esteem and gender relations (Ortner and Whitehead, 1981/89:16). This chapter comes to grips with the extent to which the emergence of a new economic situation, a changing sexual division of labour, new demands and new roles leave social values intact or create new or contradictory norms and values. Linked to this, it becomes important to investigate 1) what type of new social roles and new social value systems have emerged for men and women respectively, and 2) how new social values interact with male and female identity and gender relations.

I shall continue to use, as far as possible, the words of the actors themselves. I shall complement this with my own interpretation of the situation, intertwined as it is with the versions the actors themselves portrayed for my benefit. In order to put the present Kisii household and changing value systems into perspective I shall briefly recall the precolonial household as well as traditional male and female roles, responsibilities and values.

The household today—Gender roles, responsibilities and notions of social value

Today the social and economic organisation of the household, its institutional forms and morality have altered profoundly. Earlier functions, including the traditional division of labour, have been upset and existing norms and values are challenged.

The household

In the 1950s, the people of Nyansongo were still fairly prosperous agriculturalists who supplemented their subsistence and cash crop cultivation with employment and market trade. Pastoralism had been retained largely for prestige and ceremonial purpose (LeVine, R. and B., 1966/77:17). According to Orvis, who undertook major fieldwork in Kisii in the mid 1980s, the former peasantry has been destroyed by pressure on land, which is no longer the main basis for family reproduction or accumulation of capital. The District cannot feed itself and has to rely on food from other areas. Households often invest their limited resources in rather uneconomical ways in order to avoid the insecurity they face as a result of integration into the market economy and the concomitant breaking down of the extended family system (Orvis, 1985 a and b).

With a general decrease in the amount of land possessed, production as well as income accruing from it, is becoming increasingly limited. At the same time, the demand for better food, better clothing, housing and schooling is increasing. Thus cash is needed for buying food when stocks are exhausted, for clothing, for health—not to mention school fees. Women as well as men agreed that the major burden was school fees. With the majority of households growing both food and cash crops,[20] it goes without saying that cash from sale of crops is limited, though for many households this is the major if not the only source of income. Linked to this, the vast majority of men interviewed said that their wives cannot run the household and pay school fees without a contribution from their husbands. Women agreed, adding that they could not rely on husbands' contributions; they varied considerably both in terms of amount and also in terms of frequency: 'You cannot rely on husbands today. Sometimes they even steal money from you'.

Men's roles

By 1940, as mentioned above, Kisii was a society of predominantly women, children and old men (Hay and Stichter, 1984). This is far from the case today. Men are still migrating out of Kisii, but to a far lesser extent than before and mainly on a seasonal basis. Given the high population density, the rate

---

[20] Average household size = 8 persons with access to 1ha = 2.50 acres.

of out migration is surprisingly low. Data from population census pyramids (1969) indicate that men from Kisii out-migrated in their early twenties, but stayed away for shorter periods than men from high out-migration districts (Ominde, 1984). In 1961, out migration rates for Kisii were only 7% for men, compared with 17% for Luhya and 17% for Luo (1984). A local study in the early 1980s claims that the reason for the low out-migration is homesickness, from which Gusii men, in particular, seem to suffer (Njonjo, 1983). When I asked why so few men migrated, the usual answer I got was that 'Kisii is home, and one should stay at home'. According to another study 'people say that they miss that special something which only 'home' can provide and the sorts of conversation which are only possible when all involved speak Ekegusii and know the social conventions, rules and evocations that go with a mother tongue' (Raikes, P., 1990).

While this is certainly true, one should set these comments in a broader context. Unemployment is now a major problem in Kenya. Employment opportunities have become increasingly scarce due to intensified population growth:

> The District's population growth rate not only generates a work force too large for foreseeable job opportunities, but also drains potential savings from job-creating investments into consumption and rudimentary basic needs (*Kisii District Development Plan for 1989–93*, 1992:31).

The problem of finding work even applies to many well-educated Gusii youngsters. Tea-picking on plantations in Kericho does offer employment opportunities but is considered a very tough and not well paid job. It certainly does not appeal to the young and well-educated. A few have tried their luck in Nairobi, but only a fraction have succeeded in obtaining a permanent job. Some have become night watchmen, a dangerous and badly paid job. The competition is tough, and the majority have searched for jobs with no result. Many have ended up staying in the slums of Nairobi. Those who did not end up with a new 'wife' and children in the big city have returned, eventually. Some have left crestfallen, often leaving their new Nairobi family behind. 'City life did not agree with me', or 'my wife in Kisii stopped sending maize and other food stuff'. Not wanting to reveal their struggles and defeat, homesickness constitutes a good reason for returning. Another reason often given by men interviewed was that 'if men work in the towns, their wives will start roaming with other men'.

Martha's husband left her and their three daughters in 1986. John had always dreamt of going to Nairobi. Besides, he wanted sons, but Martha (who worked in a Catholic health centre) was not willing to give it another try. John soon got involved with a woman in Nairobi, and she got pregnant. Martha was furious. After two years, when the town wife was pregnant with her second child, John wanted to return to Kisii with her and their children (one girl and one boy). Martha refused. 'Never, ever' would she have another woman on the compound. Another two years passed by. Then town life became too much for John, and he returned leaving his second wife and the children behind. 'What about the woman and the children?' I asked. Martha couldn't care less.

With hardly any migration out of Kisii and with few possibilities for employment, what do men do? A few work as local contract workers on a seasonal basis, as government employees, artisans, matatu drivers etc. Some are involved in small scale business activities of a more or less formal character. The fact that most men leave the farming to their wives does not prevent them from considering themselves as farmers, whereas women are considered as housewives both by their husbands and themselves. 'We are all farmers', men say. This, however, does not mean that they do any farming themselves, though some did a little digging in the shamba a couple of hours in the early morning. A man is a farmer when he owns land, and land ownership is essential. If he has only 1/2 acre, he would still also call himself a farmer: 'a man with no land has no home'. In a few areas close to neighbouring Luo land, where men used to be farmers in earlier times as well as in 'settlement' areas close to Kericho District, men are more involved in farming activities, though mainly in relation to cash crops such as coffee and tea. The only type of work that absolutely has to be performed by men is the building and construction of the basic body of the houses (the mounting of the wooden poles) and, in particular, the thatching of the roof. If the husband does not carry out this task, hired labour has to do it.

Steven Orvis' study undertaken in Kisii in 1985 is revealing. In his selected sample of only 'full time' male farmers, total labour time for farm activities shows that women contribute 54%, men 38% and children 8% (1985a:14). Orvis concludes that male labour is in surplus whereas women's labour is not. Because of illness (including reduced working ability because of pregnancy and child birth), women lost 21% of their 10-hour working day. Comparing this figure with women's 54% labour investment, women in his sample seem to be under a tremendous labour strain compared to their husbands.

In sum, and contrary to other neighbouring tribes, there is no tradition among men in Kisii of doing agricultural work, except for clearing the ground. 'If a man goes to the shamba, he has become inferior'; 'shamba work is for women—not for men', both women and men agree, although women also agree that they need help from their spouses. Work on somebody else's farm as paid labourer is somewhat different—and therefore more acceptable—though still not really giving social value—except that the man earns some money which he can either invest in the household—or more likely—on drinks for himself and his friends (Cohen and Odhiambo, 1989).

Men assisting each other in reparing a thatched roof and preventing the heavy rain from coming through the holes in the roof.

Men gathered in a local bar. The background is decorated by the owner, a woman who has also produced the local beer, *pombe*, herself.

The local family health field worker tries to convince men in the local bar that they should rather spend their money on their families' needs than on beer.

> Many men in Kisii regard the hard slog of agricultural labour on their own farms as "women's work" and demeaning and use this as a successful excuse for evading it—though some of these will undertake it for wages on the farms of others, which apparently reduces the stigma (Raikes, P., 1992:11).

The Kisii District Development Plan for 1984–88 stresses that, in Kisii, men are the breadwinners. There is no definition of a 'bread-winner', and women are not mentioned at all. In Webster's and Oxford's dictionaries, respectively, a breadwinner is defined as 'one who earns a livelihood for himself and those dependent upon him' (1989) and 'the person whose work supports a family'(1993). In Kisii there are of course men who are breadwinners and who fit these definitions. However, they are the exception to the rule. With untapped farming potential and the available labour of unemployed husbands, current agricultural production could be intensified. The primary objective is to provide basic needs and alleviate poverty through growth in agricultural output. Linked to this, it is noted that:

> It is, however, known that a significant number of the potential workers live within the agricultural sector *doing no gainful work*. This reality gives a higher dependency ratio than what is calculated (*Kisii District Development Plan for 1989–1993*, 1992:29).

These observations are interesting in that there is no reference to which sex 'the potential workers' belong. My data clearly indicate that this significant number consists of men. What can be concluded from these observations? First, that the notion of men as breadwinners needs reconsidering. Second, there is an urgent need to increase productivity and output, in particular from small-scale farmers.

Men are not unaware of this fact. However, the repeated argument is 'we were never shamba people', 'shamba work is women's work', 'if a man goes to the shamba, he is not a real man', 'such a man has been overpowered by his wife'. On the one hand, shamba work is certainly not prestigious. On the other hand, land could perhaps be utilized more efficiently, if labour (and money) were invested. Many men, particularly those living in poor households and with no regular income, are caught in a dilemma. How can they be respected if they do not fulfil their male obligations towards the household? But can they be respected if they do shamba work? Women would tell me over and over that 'young boys grow up with the mentality that there is no suitable job for them. Women are more flexible'.

Jeremiah, 28 years old, was an exception to the rule. He worked side by side with his wife in the shamba. Both were hard working. Maize was their main produce, and they were able to produce a considerable surplus from a relatively small acreage. They even expected to hire some additional labour. Jeremiah, however, was ostracized in male circles. He was laughed at by other men (and even by some of the women). No men in his neighbourhood would socialize with him. As a good Christian (one of the very few), he did

Women working in groups and weeding a shamba.

not take alcohol, which was an additional 'alienating' factor. Helen, my informant, who was very familiar with Jeremiah's household, as well as the reaction of other men, was worried on his behalf. She knew that many were jealous because Jeremiah did well, and feared that somebody would 'bewitch' his family 'so that something bad would happen'.

Women's roles

Comparing the traditional agricultural cycle with the present cycle, farm activities have increased considerably. The labour of Gusii women has changed little since the colonial era, except that it has intensified. It has become part of 'the ongoing process of bargaining about the organization of interpersonal transfers and responsibilities under shifting conditions' (Guyer, 1988:171). Dwindling supplies of land have to provide for both home consumption and cash (from sale of food crops at the local market). New types of maize can be harvested twice a year, and the traditional times for clearing, sowing etc. are now replaced by a continuous cycle of preparation of land, seeding, fertilizing, weeding and harvesting. With the possibility of prolonged harvesting periods, and two harvests a year instead of one, the level of labour input for women has increased enormously. The sowing of maize can be performed with little additional preparation of the soil and weeding is simple because it can be done with a hoe. Other crops, such as finger millet, demand a finely pulverized soil, carefully weeded. This is a painstaking and time-consuming task performed by women only.

A woman selling her grinded maize in the local market.

The majority of women work on increasingly smaller plots, still using mainly a simple hoe (a jembe) and a panga. They also fetch water, firewood, dry, shell, store, cook the food from their shamba. One or two afternoons a week are spent in the local market place, where basic necessities such as salt, sugar, soap and matches are bought or exchanged for surplus produce. Transport to the market (maize or vegetables) or to the factory (tea or coffee) is mostly done by women alone. Out of 711 valid cases in the survey, only 18 women said that their husbands were involved in transport of their produce.

In sum, the structural pattern developed in the colonial period, where women's productive role in agriculture was intensified and men became increasingly alienated from their traditional tasks, continues to predominate. The general picture that emerges is that the majority of women cannot rely on any regular assistance on the part of their husbands. The fact that male migration has almost stopped has not had any effect on women's labour input on the farm. When questioned about who had the heaviest work load in agriculture, 707 of our female respondents answered women; 4 answered men (11 cases missing). Counterchecking this in the male interviews, the vast majority agreed that of course women did most of the work. Thus, with men feeling 'alienated' from shamba work, there are increased demands on women's labour in order to make ends meet. In her subservient role as wife, no work seems to be too hard for a woman. She continues to be socially defined as a housewife (except for a very few) but has the full responsibility of the majority of working tasks within the household.

Access to and control over resources

'Men have not yet realized that their kingdom has shrunk'
(observed by Joseph—one of my male interviewers).

Men still own the land and the cattle and monopolize cash crops. Returns on coffee and tea, delivered to the respective factories or cooperatives, are issued to the head of the household, the husband. Sons inherit land from their fathers, and women's access to resources is via men. In the case of the husband's death, the widow administers his land until it is divided and taken over by the sons. The male prerogative of controlling all significant forms of wealth and the female claim to certain resources, including land, are now in conflict as land has increased in cash-generating value. The right to sell land allows the head of household to engage in gross irresponsibility towards the family: to sell land and use the profits for his own pursuits, whether beneficial to the household as a whole or not. This is not a common pattern but it happens increasingly. Women's access to resources is certainly controlled by men, and the ideology legitimizing it makes it difficult for women to move into existing male preserves.

This being said, I shall argue that, in current Kisii reality, male monopoly on and control over resources and women's dependence on men is not as simple as it appears. Considering that the majority of men in Kisii are poor small scale farmers with an average size of land of 2 1/2 acres, with hardly any cattle left, with no regular employment or income I suggest that male control over resources needs reconsidering. What resources are we actually speaking about in the Kisii context? Even in the 1950s there were major struggles over resources:

> ... land, once abundant, now is fought over. The system of land tenure and land inheritance, understandably vague in the past, has in the modern era pitted brother against brother, neighbour against neighbour, and kin group against kin group in a struggle over land rights and ownership ... . Since employment and trade are regarded as supplements rather than substitutes for the life of the field and pastures, it appeared to many that the economic basis of their existence is gradually slipping away (LeVine, R. and B., 1966/77:10–11).

Today, these struggles are even greater. Considering, on the one hand, male marginalization in the household reproduction process and their 'alienation' in terms of shamba work, and, on the other, women's role as daily managers of the household, including their husbands' land, there seem to be some contradictions and discrepancies. While women are subordinate to men, women also have a considerable degree of both actual and potential power—a power which derives from their control over production, reproduction and consumption:

> ... it is therefore the case that the ideology of complete male control over the productive and reproductive potential of the household has to be understood in

the context of an actual reality of male and female interdependence. Men not only depend on their wives for labour to produce the crops which feed their children and provide the grain for beer, but in addition are crucially dependent on women as reproducers, reproducing both clan and labour force (Moore, 1986:112–113).

Men's frequent absence from the homestead gives women control over season to season land use, managerial control over agriculture on a day-to-day basis as well as control over income from cash crops that require large local investments of marketing time for relatively small amounts of income. Moreover, women have developed various 'coping' strategies such as selling part of these crops through middlemen, though at lower prices. Beer brewing and the production of *changaa* often constitute substantial means for women to get access to an income of their own. In fact, many women in my sample financed school education through the production of alcohol. It is an illegal activity, and is rejected by women's organizations. However, it is a sensitive and complicated issue because it creates an income for women while, at the same time, it facilitates men's access to cheap alcohol.

In sum, women's access to and control over resources is usually limited by men's ultimate control over land. However, women's position as important managers of both food and cash crops, and often as sole managers of the farm, makes them crucial to the success or failure of the outcome of household production. Linked to this, there is no doubt that many women have become more autonomous, and they increasingly make decisions without involving and consulting their husbands, present or absent. When it comes to weapons against their husbands, it can be argued that women's ultimate weapon is withdrawal of their direct labour and reproductive labour-producing capacity by leaving their husbands. For women to be able to make use of this weapon, they must have somewhere to go, and perhaps it depends even more on whether the bridewealth has been paid or not. However, women's power in other domains of life cannot be ignored. In addition, it seems to be a gross oversimplification to speak about male "ownership" of any part of the family estate. There is no doubt that wives (at least when bridewealth or part of it has been transferred) also have rights in family land. This they actively defend if they are threatened. Some categories of women, such as widows, can be fully economically autonomous in spite of the fact that they—in principle—only administer the land until the sons take over.

The law does not prohibit women from owning land. And 'if a husband agrees with his wife he can register land in her name'. In some cases, women have been able to buy land of their own. But 'if a woman wants to buy land on her own it is a sign of separation', people say. According to research carried out by Achola Pala (1975), 4–5% of farm land in Kisii was registered in the name of women in 1975. By 1992, close to 10% was registered in the name of women (personal communication with Ministry of Land in Kisii). It is now being debated, at government level, whether women should also be entitled to inherit land from their fathers. In spite of the fact that women are expected only to control enough money necessary for home consumption, an increasing number of women have their own bank accounts. However, they are certainly not supposed to reinvest profits—according to men. Informally—and in rare cases even formally—women do exercise varying and sometimes extensive degrees of autonomy and control in areas where the control of men cannot reach. Moreover, 'women can refuse: 'say, there is a cow at home that the husband may want to sell. If the wife doesn't want it sold, it will never be sold'; or 'a husband may want to rent out his shamba. If the wife feels that he should not she can refuse and nothing can be done'; 'if a woman is married to a teacher, and he misuses the money, she can report him to the chief and get half of his salary from the Government'; 'if a man sells a piece of his land, his wife can even take him to court'. Local informants recounted several disputes between husbands and wives over land. In one case, land had already been sold by a man. His wife, though, went to court along with her adolescent sons. The wife won the case on the grounds that her husband was irresponsible, and the land had to be returned. Men expect solidarity from wives—but as mentioned above 'women tell home secrets to other people'.

Based on the above, I agree with Moore that the notion of male control over resources needs to be modified and discussed in the particular context. This said, the situation is filled with contradictions. With an ideology based on male superiority, and male entitlement to control all essential resources, including those derived from the labour of their wives, women are certainly in a dependent situation.

Male and female contributions to the household

There was consensus (even by men who admitted that they did not contribute financially) that wives cannot run the household and pay school fees without some contribution from their husbands. All men agreed that 'a man should be the head of his family'. A man should be its protector, councillor, decision-maker and breadwinner. 'A man who fulfils these obligations is a respected man'. Men also agreed that 'women are second to the head of the family' with the afterthought—'though some have become the head by planning and taking care of the family'.

Ideas as to men's areas of responsibility are for the most part not in agreement with what happens in practice. According to women, the majority could not rely on regular financial assistance whether or not their husbands were living permanently on the farm.

Men with a regular income claim that they take care of all major expenses, including school fees, a sum that can reach several thousand shillings. The financial assistance indicated by the majority of men inter viewed is from 100–200 shillings a month. It can be argued that, because it depends on size of land, family members, the amount of school fees needed etc., such amounts are derisory. However, a monthly contribution of 100–200 shillings is extremely modest, as land is scarce and living costs are high. The majority of men claim that they contribute quite regularly (monthly). As most men did not have regular incomes, this claim is questionable. Checking with wives, many claim that they have never received any contributions from their husbands. Quite a few men, in fact, admitted that they never contributed to the upkeep of the household but used whatever income they may have on investment for their own purposes and on 'social activities'.

While fertility—and children—are highly valued by both genders, and while men and women often share the same values linked to fertility, the two genders have what seem to be different and contradictory priorities. Men, for example, often tend to leave their wives with the responsibility for the children. According to Frank (1987), the childbearing family structure creates a cleavage of domains of family responsibility such that economic and demographic systems are truly separate. Although women shoulder the costs of childbearing, the marriage contract ensures that they ignore those costs in their childbearing behaviour (see next chapter). Moreover, mutual obligations of spouses almost invariably come second to those which a husband has to his own family. When a man has a regular or even occasional income he will immediately be pursued and pestered by other relatives. Particularly when the education of younger brothers is concerned. It has not been possible to establish to what extent this assertion holds true. When asked directly, only a few admitted to financing the education of their younger brothers. I suspect that men rather relate to the norm that older brothers 'traditionally' are responsible for educating the younger (which nowadays is equivalent to paying school fees). When counterchecking with younger family members, they reported that they never received help from older brothers.

Few households could survive on subsistence production alone and virtually none do. For most households, the most important single investment which can be made is in the education of children, to give them a chance to get jobs at higher wage levels and with greater permanence than the casual labour which is about all that is available to uneducated young people (Raikes, P., 1988). Lack of jobs is in turn, and in contradiction to the investment in education, a major incentive to investment in off farm enterprises of varying sorts. They range from quite substantial trading, transport and processing, down to the sale of a few bunches of bananas by the roadside (1988). As mentioned above, the limited household resources are diversified in rather uneconomical ways. This does not clarify precisely 'who' is investing in uneconomical ways, though I strongly suspect that it refers to men's investments, which would be in line with my own findings.

... for a husband to contribute to family food expenditures seems exceptional, though probably the incidence rises in cases of serious need ... . The notion of a husband putting a regular amount into the 'housekeeping' is most uncommon. But again, the variation between men, like that of their incomes, tends to be far wider than for women ... . As one goes down the (income) scale less is saved and the wage lasts less long, until one reaches the situation referred to by many men as 'four days of living and twenty-six of survival', that is four days in which disposable income is spent, followed by a period until the following payday, when the man is without money and dependent on food provided by the wife to survive. Right down the bottom end of the scale are those men who contribute nothing at all, or even less since they spend virtually all they earn (usually from casual labour) on drink and then come home drunk and take their wives' savings by force. It is in this light that one has to consider the remark often heard from Gusii men that 'women are our savings (Raikes, P., 1988:34–35).

Nevertheless both women and men agree that husbands should provide wives and children with proper clothing, school uniforms, school books, school funds, not to mention school fees for secondary education. Agricultural implements etc. should be provided by husbands, and if cattle are purchased, it is the husband's duty to pay. As far as the health of the family is concerned, the husband should also take care of such expenses. The provision of food for the family is the obligation of women, though men say that they should contribute with money for food, when their wives cannot manage on their own: 'when the wife has no more left from her own produce the husband should buy food for the family'. 'A good husband takes nice care of his wife and children'. In practice, though, according to women 'good husbands are few'.

Both men and women agree that a man must socialize with other men. In practice, this means getting together with other men in local bars. It also means that large amounts of money are spent outside the household. Men's personal consumption and 'investments' are 'musts', and they are given priority. Women, though, may not have the same priorities as men, and while on one hand they agree that a man must socialize, women certainly do not approve of men spending money on drinking.

... food and beverages accounts for about 60% of the total household monthly consumption expenditure. However, this proportion varies considerably with household size and net income. For example, households in low income categories ... allocate a much higher proportion of their net monthly income to food (*Kisii District Development Plan 1989–93*, 1992:39).

These statements are obscure and misleading. First of all the household is treated as a joint consumption unit, and there is no differentiation made between what is spent on food and what is spent on 'beverages'. As neither women nor children consume beverages (sodas) except on rare occasions, beverages refer to the personal consumption of the husbands. This means that treating the household as an income-pooling unit based on sharing of resources conceals a pronounced asymmetry. A general pattern seems to be that husbands—when they have some income—do not invest in the house-hold but rather outside, and often in uneconomical ventures. Besides, if a man has no money when he goes to the bars, his friends are expected to pay for him, just as he is expected to pay 'rounds' if he has some money. Never-theless, the myth exists that men are the breadwinners. While men believe in this 'myth' they do not seem to identify with this role—a fact which is not really recognized either by men or by women.

Summing up, in terms of contributing to the 'housekeeping', many men, including the economically better off, seem caught in a contradiction. If they made investments outside the household and were doing business (almost everybody interviewed aspired to become a businessman), if they were gen-erous, socialized with other men and attended funerals they were at least fulfilling part of male obligations. However, as heads of households, they did not fulfil either traditional or present norms and ideals. With no more feuds with neighbouring tribes, the ideal of the head of household as its pro-tector and councillor is now closely tied up with men's financial contribu-tions to the 'welfare' of the family.

Men with an income have the option of investing in the household economy or using their profits for their own personal or business endeav-ours. This, combined with greater male access to wage labour during colo-nial time, resulted in members of each household facing the market as indi-viduals rather than jointly as members of a particular household, rendering the household simply a labour-allocating unit. There was no absolute trans-fer of surplus product from men to women, and the mother-child unit be-came the basic unit for reproducing labour. The combination of external wage labour and cash crop production increased the independence of men from the household economy and resulted in the marginalization of men from that economy.[21] At the same time, though, men were dependent on women's labour for the production of cash crops.

Thus, women are involved in all kinds of activities and their income is used for household needs. The threat by women of withdrawing their labour can sometimes push a man to reinvest the rewards of the crop into the household economy more than he might otherwise. In fact, men who do not reinvest in the household put not only their households in an insecure position but also themselves. Given that a significant number of potential workers live within the agricultural sector but do no gainful work gives a higher dependency ratio than what is calculated. And this implies an in-creasing male dependence on women.

Over the past decades, women's groups have mushroomed in Kisii. Many women are actively involved in various group activities from which they are able to get some economic benefits, not to mention psychological support. Men's attitudes to such groups are very ambiguous. On the one

---

[21] Kongstad and Mønsted, 1980. This argument is supported by Orvis, 1985 a and b.

hand, men do not like their wives spending time working with groups and attending group meetings. 'Wives leak home secrets to other women'. Men are certainly right. While the activities of the formalized groups are often questionable and many have stopped their activities, it is also in such groups or informal groups that women discuss their frustrations and their 'home secrets'. And men know that women discuss men's behaviour. This is where women wield power. If men's bad behaviour becomes well known to the public, they lose face. On the other hand, the whole family, including husbands, can benefit from such women's groups. Some men demonstrated a certain jealousy and even expressed the wish that they also become members, or that they could get support from the government to start men's groups. In some women's groups men had been allowed in. However, as one group clearly stressed to me: 'We do not want men in any key positions (chairperson, treasurer or secretary). They cannot be trusted. We only use men for digging and hard work'.

Negotiations between spouses

'Women have to monitor everything. Men just create disturbances'.

Coping with new situations means coping with new problems and dealing with dilemmas in which a number of different issues are intertwined. For example, men, as the formal and acknowledged heads of household, are the decision-makers. Both men and women agree that 'husbands should always be consulted in all important matters', and 'men have the final word'. But this is not what happens in reality. Men's general complaints were that 'women put a lot of pressure on husbands'; 'they forget that we are the masters'; 'women bother husbands with trivialities', 'they complain to other women'. Men are right: women *are* constantly complaining, particularly about the lack of male financial responsibility, and the absence of male solidarity. Male 'sociability' has become the subject of dispute, as have men's increasing visits to local bars—an extremely important part of their sociability.

Men are the acknowledged heads of households and decision-makers. But a general theme among men was that 'it is difficult to get the final word with women'. Moreover, 'women do not do what they are told to do'. 'They need a lot of correction'. 'Correction' is often equivalent to beating—a common and socially accepted practice. Many women end up in Kisii Hospital badly injured after having been 'corrected' (see below). Consequently, women try to avoid open confrontations. Instead 'when a husband makes a decision, and the wife disagrees she keeps quiet'. However, this does not mean that the husband has the final word: on the contrary. Women proceed to act quietly according to their own views. For instance, 'if a husband tells his wife to plant in a particular place, and she disagrees, she does not say so.

But she just plants where she wants. If he finds out later, she will say that the seedlings were not growing properly. In order to save them, she had no other option than to plant them elsewhere'. Thus, most women agree that 'husbands should not be consulted on matters which will lead to fighting'.

Curiously enough, my data indicate that what women consider 'consulting' is often equivalent to what men consider 'complaining', and most often the complaints are related to financial issues: 'My dress is torn and so are the school uniforms of the children; where do I get money for a new dress and uniforms?' 'The children were sent back from school, because of lack of fees; where can I get money?'. According to men, 'women are never satisfied'. 'They never stop asking for money'. 'They are so interested in fashions, it was much easier before when we used animal skins for clothes'. A recurrent complaint made not only by women, but in which men concurred, was that because of serious alcohol problems men could not be counted on, either for work or for financial contributions to the survival of the household (see below). A repeated remark from women was, "A husband is like an extra baby in the house".

From the point of view of women, the main reasons for quarrelling were husbands' economic neglect, lack of concern, lack of interest in contributing to the education of their children and their 'laziness': 'men can sit around a whole day doing nothing', 'they expect wives to do everything', and 'if men help in the shamba they get exhausted right away'. Both genders agree that 'women do not trust their husbands, and husbands do not trust their wives'. In particular women are disappointed, angry and disillusioned. 'Men are irresponsible and selfish. They do not even care if there is food for the children'. On the one hand, women seem to expect and accept 'bad' behaviour from their husbands. On the other, they don't.

Many men are worried about all this. They fear being poisoned by their wives. Rumours were constantly circulating in Kisii of husbands having been killed or made so completely apathetic by poisons that their wives had obtained from secret sources. In fact, in our qualitative interviews with men, much attention was attributed to the love potion called *kababa*, and men frequently mentioned their suspicion about food given to them by their wives or girlfriends. *Kababa* (an extract in powder form from the gall of a crocodile, we were told) is supposed to be a 'wonder drug' prescribed for couples wishing to achieve complete harmony in their relationship. But with one partner dominant. Consequently, it is claimed that when women give their husbands the potion, it makes them loyal to them and they never leave their homes to go socializing. It was even argued that the drug was so potent that it caused men to be totally inactive and afraid of other men. Some men, it was argued, even died from the love potion. When contacting the local prison in Kisii Town, we were told that the three major reasons for women to be imprisoned were: 1) Brewing *changaa* illegally; 2) poisoning their husbands; and 3) physical violence against their husbands. The duration of imprisonment would vary, but it was quite common that a woman would get three months for poisoning her husband (on the condition that it could be proven that he had been a bad one), since she had to return and take care of her children and see to the farming activities. Some women were referred to as "wicked witches"; "wicked witches are invented by frightened men" some would argue. However, certain women (and never men) are thought to possess magical powers which they use to manipulate men. Such women are believed to be able to cast the 'evil eye' and, if crossed, their reprisals are dangerous.

Many women argued that they would be much better off without a husband. Although men complained about their wives and women in general, not a single man interviewed said that he would be better off without a wife. 'Husbands come home and eat the food. They never bring sugar, tea or soap'. However, there is little doubt that a woman needs a man just as much as a man needs a woman. As has been examined above, a woman without a husband has no status (Håkansson, 1988). Exactly the same applies to men. Men need a 'wife' to grow food, to cook and to bear children. Then how to interpret women's comments? Both men and women are deeply frustrated—but their frustrations are different. Women are not only frustrated but also angry because husbands do not contribute economically to the survival of the household; economic pressure has become intolerable, and men's support is needed. Women want husbands that are responsible heads of households as well as 'family providers'. But they are not. On the contrary 'men have become a burden'; 'men are weak'; 'men are incompetent'; 'men expect everything to be done by the wife'.

Men's comments are aggressive as well, and women are blamed for 'breaking homes'. But the nature of men's comments is much more defensive and 'wronged'. This has struck me as very unusual in a society such as Kisii where patriarchy is supposed to be the dominant structure—and where women are structurally subordinated to men, and even considered 'minors' all their lives. Analyzing my data, I shall venture to suggest that men are also structurally trapped: that men—because they are men—have to act out roles that they are no longer equipped for. Along with fundamental socio-economic changes, land shortage, poverty etc., men have been assigned a new (Western/modern) role—that of a breadwinner. At the same time the government harps on the traditional male 'virtues': a 'real man' has lots of land; he can handle many wives, many children and many cattle.[22]

---

[22] The Kenyan Government has recently been giving very confusing signals in terms of large numbers of children. On the one hand great concern is expressed in terms of the population growth. On the other, the member of parliament, Mr. Nicholas Biwott (one of the most powerful politicians in the country) advised the Kalenjin community to forget about family planning and multiply freely. He underlined the interest of smaller communities to multiply as much as possible, since power in Kenya derived from numerical strength. According to Biwott, instruments of development were allocated to communities according to population size and, therefore, larger tribes got larger allocations. 'Those who follow family planning will suffer

Bedroom in disorder.

These demands are overwhelming and unrealistic to most men. Different social roles entail normative prescriptions and proscriptions enforced by positive and negative sanctions. An individual's role behaviour is either in conformity with the normative rules or deviant from them, and he/she receives special rewards and punishments accordingly (LeVine, R., 1982). As most men do not conform either to traditional or to 'modern' roles, a majority of men find themselves between two stools. Though men from different socio-economic backgrounds often had the same views, those with the greatest frustrations generally belong to the lowest stratum of the economic and occupational scale. This stratum contains the great majority of men in Kisii. Higher income levels and greater prestige-giving work makes it easier to meet both traditional and modern expectations.

As also observed by R. LeVine, the scarcity of family resources often creates a competition so intense that only respect for paternal authority, skilfully used by the homestead head, can contain the conflict. There are a number of challenges to paternal authority. First, the authority of the household head is seriously challenged when daughters elope. The fewer bridewealth marriages take place, the less the homestead head has an important resource under his control which will command the respect and obedience of his sons. Moreover, an important paternal power has been lost in that fathers have the traditional right to deny bridewealth to misbehaving sons. Second, open defiance develops when sons for example decide to appropriate some

---

because of their small number while those who multiply will get several benefits', the former minister of energy said (*Weekly Review*, June 3, 1994:17).

of the produce from the father's land for their own use. Fathers report sons to the police for thieving. A final challenge is land fragmentation. The less land the father has to allocate and to leave to his sons at his death, the less will they be dependent on him. Combined with all other 'losses' these challenges are serious threats to adult male authority.

In sum, new gender roles, new values and a new competing 'moral' universe have emerged, creating confusion and conflicting models of behaviour. While women and men do realize the emergence of fundamental changes in their lives, there is a lack of awareness of the incompatibility between past and present norms and values. Everybody is clear though, that wives have become increasingly rude and abusive, husbands have become increasingly irresponsible towards their families, households have become violent battlegrounds and the number of 'broken homes' is on the increase.

Sociability and alcohol consumption

ALCOHOL
My name is alcohol
I am the greatest killer in history.
I have killed more than any one battle
I have turned men into brutes
made millions of homes miserable
transformed many promising youths
into hopeless parasites
destroyed the weak and weakened the strong
made wise men fools and trampled fools into disaster.
The abandoned wives know me well
the hungry children
the unfortunate husbands know me well too.
Under my influence one wishes to take more and more of me
for they cannot resist me.
Therefore I am the "greatest" being.
Three big cheers to me strong alcohol
I am dangerous to your life, so beware.[23]

The intake of beer (*busaa*) was originally an institutionalized activity surrounded by many rituals. It took place in connection with major ceremonies such as marriage, burial and circumcision. In the circumcision ritual, beer drinking was primarily a male activity, associated with masculinity and linked to the establishment of good relations to family and friends. Beer was also served at the end of a working day to groups which had participated in helping on a particular farm. Consequently, the intake of beer was connected with a social event. Wives were the beer brewers but women were not supposed to drink, though older women were allowed to take a little *busaa*. Today a woman is allowed to take a little 'if she cannot help it', but

---

[23] Quote on the wall in the District Commissioners office in Kisii town, 1992.

never if she is pregnant. Alcohol and loose (female) behaviour are closely connected and 'a woman should always be able to control herself'; 'she should not involve herself in forbidden practices; 'she may be tempted to do so if she under the influence of a strong drink'.

From being a social activity on limited occasions, drinking gradually became an activity which took place outside the customary fora and spread with frightening speed after independence. The production of the locally brewed and distilled *changaa*—with an alcohol content of up to 70%—is illegal. But restrictions are not observed, and *changaa* is easily obtainable from early sunrise and throughout the day.

Both men and women place great value on sociability and personal relationships. As is stressed in my interviews a sociable person is respected. A 'real man' must socialize. So must women. Socializing, though, has different meanings for men and women. Men's socializing is closely associated with going to bars and drinking beer or *changaa*. The bar is a man's place. It is unusual for men just to pay for themselves, and men take turns in offering rounds. Respectable women do not frequent bars. Only prostitutes go to bars. Most men say that they meet with their friends daily. Friends constitute important social networks. Men who do not go to bars are looked upon by other men with suspicion: 'he has been overpowered by his wife'; 'he acts like a woman'. Consequently, it is a man's 'entitlement' to go to the bar. It is part of being a man. On the other hand, men—preferably wealthy and of a certain age—who do not drink and behave like real Christians are also respected both by women and by society at large. But young men like Jeremiah are often ridiculed. With the persistence of the high value attributed to male sociability, it can be argued that such values are significant factors inhibiting men's involvement in their nuclear family. Drinking relationships between men tend to take precedence over marital relationships and obligations. There is evidence to suggest that individuals seek positive social identities in their interactions with others, and group membership is very important for self conception. Individuals interact with members of their group in ways that create a positive social identity (Gudykunst and Ting-Toomey, 1988:94–95). Following this line of argument, with networks based on kinship and marriage now dissolving in Kisii, men may be 'thrown upon' networks where their often miserable situation is all they have in common. But with all being in more or less the same situation, this may give the individual a positive social identity.

When men are together in bars they say that they discuss important problems: quarrels over land; how to increase yields; whether other types of crops could give better yields; inflation; lack of money; lack of jobs; insufficient salaries; politics; government taxes; the burden of school fees; health problems etc. Men's conversations on regional and national politics would invariably end with a shrug of the shoulders and resignation. Moreover, the 'level' of discussion varies according to how much alcohol is consumed. The fact that men's sociability is closely linked to the consumption of alcohol has become a paramount problem in Kisii, as elsewhere in Africa (Beckman, 1988), simply because alcohol is addictive, and more and more men seem to depend on alcohol. In our in-depth interviews, quite a number of men admitted that they were not the breadwinners—their wives were. Wives' heavy workload, though, did not worry them. What really did worry many men was their dependence on alcohol. Many expressed the wish to 'be cured'. However, they did not know where to turn to, and as I found out, they had nowhere to go with their problem. The only 'assistance' that was given by the local psychiatrist was: 'You know very well that it is not good for you or your family to take alcohol. So make up your mind to stop'. Wives were disgusted: 'Men turn tail on their responsibilities and indulge in socializing'; 'no-one wants a drunkard in the bed who keeps you awake all night because he has become too weak to fulfil his duties'.

The men interviewed give two major reasons for their drinking. First, men drink for pleasure and to socialize with other men. Second, men drink 'to get away from your wife's reproaches'; 'a man needs to relax, to refresh his mind and to get away from the wife's complaints'; 'this is done best by drinking with one's friends'; 'men drink to drown their problems', 'in order to get a good night's sleep', 'not to feel cold at night', 'to forget that your children do not have any blanket'. When I said 'if you saved the money you could buy a blanket', the answer would invariably be 'yes, but it is impossible; a glass of *changaa* is only one shilling and a blanket is 85 shillings. I would never reach there'.

If a father drinks, the repercussions on the family's welfare are considerable and more severe than if the mother drinks. Mothers—if they drink—seem to confine their drinking to the latter part of the day, and they do not neglect their agricultural tasks to any marked degree. Thus, even if the quality of family life is inevitably impaired, repercussions on the family's welfare may not be felt to the same extent as when men are alcoholics. While excessive drinking is associated with personal depression and discontent, under stress someone who hitherto drank rarely may suddenly begin to drink to excess, a tendency the community has no resources to rectify (LeVine, S. and R., 1981).

The 'absent father syndrome' is discussed increasingly in the Kenyan daily newspapers, and it is argued that children with absent fathers (both emotionally and physically) tend to have certain patterns of behavioural disorders. Juvenile criminality in Kisii—which was an unheard of phenomenon in earlier times—is now very common. Obviously, such criminality is not due solely to an 'absent father syndrome'. However, men's absence in everyday life, the fact that many youngsters have more or less jobless fathers who are seriously addicted to alcohol, who do not seem to care much about their children and are fathers whom they do not respect—may be additional and exacerbating factors.

While over and over again, women expressed concern about their sons having 'nobody to take as a model', men's notions of sons 'who might kill them' reflect the fact that many youngsters in Kisii do not have much respect for their fathers. Some women said that their husbands were afraid of their own sons, and 'men do not dare to beat their wives, when their sons are around'. Both men and women agree, though, that many boys grow up as 'masters'. They believe that there are no suitable jobs for them to do, either in terms of contributing to household activities or in general. 'They grow up overprotected' and 'they never learn to handle responsibilities'. The main reasons given by women were that 'they had never seen their father do anything'—leaving them to the traditional male privilege of 'indulging in leisure' and 'roaming about'.

In their study in Siaya, Cohen and Odhiambo also deal with the phenomenon of 'runaway fathers'. Curious paradoxes developed in these households. Households that had lost their male heads were taken over by women and run for years as if the men were dead. The remaining male kin of the runaway husbands gradually lost their influence over the household. Yet in time, sons of the runaway husbands considered going out in search of their fathers. One of the motives behind this search was that the sons of these fathers had felt at a disadvantage when arranging marriages for themselves (Cohen and Odhiambo, 1989).

Violence against women

As mentioned above, men's excessive drinking often results in serious wife beating. The cases documented from Kisii District hospital are many—and steadily increasing. In a study of gender, feelings and violence in Greenland it is argued that what may strike the anthropologist as violent social actions, such as wife-beating, may well be interpreted differently from the point of view of the indigenous inhabitants (Sørensen, 1990:93). One is tempted to say the same about wife-beating in Kisii. At least this is what is reflected in the daily newspaper:

> Women in Kisii are told to shut up and stop all their noise at night. One could believe that it was something serious such as tribal fights. (*Daily Nation*, March, 1992)

Wife-beating in Kisii is an almost institutionalized phenomenon, and most women have experienced it. The meanings and applications of the term violence are culturally specific, and physical hurt done to others counts as violence only in certain social contexts. Thus violence is a highly contested term, and we need to distinguish between legitimate and illegitimate uses of physical force (Sørensen, 1992:60). In Kisii, as in Nuuk, wife beating is not usually seen as illegitimate. In most cases, and even if the husband is drunk, it is assumed by women and men that the wife asked for it. Moreover, wife beating is considered a very personal matter in which outsiders should not interfere. Many informants told me that if at night screaming would be heard from one of the houses in the village, and the villagers actually knew that it was a drunk husband beating up his wife, no one would react. However, a drunken husband who beats up his wife is not respected by his fellow villagers: 'this man can only control his wife by beating'.

The more ambiguous the boundaries of one's own social group are felt to be, as against another group, the more anxious one becomes to demarcate these boundaries. When boundaries are self-evident, there is no need for demarcation (Jacobson-Widding, 1983:22). Sørensen argues that violence against women can be analyzed in two contrasting ways. First, wife beating is a disciplinary device by which a man 'marks' his spouse in order to expose her to public scorn. Such a model is linked to the necessity of being 'married' and centres on the male role as a family head as well as an agent. The new element in this model is that the legitimacy of the act is increasingly being questioned by women. The other conception is based on the 'victimization' of the male and seems to represent a more recent development, emphasizing the 'problem-laden man' who cannot help beating his wife (Sørensen, 1990:60), and that verbal conflicts often lead to violence (Collier and Rosaldo in Ortner and Whitehead, 1981/89:293). Sørensen suggests that male violence should rather be analyzed (in a third way) as a result of a new reality (in which men are at a loss) where new rules have not yet been created, and outdated traditions are still made use of in order to impose male power (Sørensen, 1992:60–69). My data seem to confirm a combination of all three interpretations. Moreover, as mentioned earlier, it should not be overlooked that there are many cases in Kisii of women 'overpowering' drunken husbands who end up in clinics and hospitals with serious panga injuries.

Men, women and psychological disorders

'Men cannot carry their responsibilities, so they break. Women stay with their problems, but they do not break'. (Male nurse with 25 years' experience in the psychiatric ward at Kisii Hospital.)

Many men in Kisii 'break'. Local explanations for men's frequent 'breaking' are closely connected to male responsibilities as heads of household. It is acknowledged that women are faced with heavy work and responsibilities. Women's responsibilities are generally seen as much less of a burden than men's. As heads of households, men's areas of responsibility are much greater than those of women, and men are seen as carrying much heavier loads. They have the overall responsibility for the household and its well being—in principle—as is emphasized in the initiation ritual. Moreover, it is a male responsibility to ensure that their wives do what is expected of them.

Women, however, are in a more advantageous position; they can 'lean on their husbands for advice'—both men and women would argue—knowing perfectly well that this is not so.

According to the local psychiatrist, Dr. Badia, male and female disorders are very different. Men feel inadequate, incompetent, insecure, inferior and persecuted. They suffer from feelings of guilt, sleeplessness and they wake up perspiring at night. Men complain of being pressured by their wives and relatives. If they have an income, they are constantly pressed to pay school fees for younger brothers and cousins. Female psychological disorders, according to Badia, are more linked to depression because women do not know how to make ends meet. Sarah LeVine's observations on women throw light on the 'fact' that men tend to 'break' more easily than women, or at least they break for different reasons. As mentioned above, women often tend to adopt a 'low profile' strategy towards their husbands. According to LeVine, the low profile strategy sometimes involves minimizing social visibility and avoiding taking initiative if there is any risk that this could be interpreted as self-aggrandizing. Complaining of personal difficulties is consistent with this strategy, because it portrays the self as more acted upon than acting (LeVine, S., 1979:379–80). But very interestingly, and very much in line with my own findings, LeVine concludes that a new consciousness among women has developed as well as a new perception of self. Linked to this, departures from the low profile strategy happen very often. Such departures were either instances of passive resistance through the traditional mode of 'privileged obstruction' or situations in which a woman has dared to act boldly on her own behalf because those formally responsible for her have defaulted on their obligations.[24]

Thus, though certainly constrained by ideological structures, women often act boldly. They often sell their husband's crops, use modern contraceptives without their husband's knowledge etc. According to Sarah LeVine, women often 'misbehave' in order to invoke Gusii norms on their behalf:

> Laying responsibility for their own acts on the failures of their husbands to fulfil basic material obligations, they intended their indiscretions to dramatize these failures, heaping disgrace on their husbands in order to force their compliance with the norms (1979:380).

Women often portray themselves as afflicted sufferers and pitiable victims and by so doing heap disgrace on their husbands. They tend to conceal information that is to their advantage. It is more socially acceptable for women to complain than to boast (1979:377). This is in sharp contrast to male

---

[24] The term 'privileged obstruction' is 'borrowed' from Philip Mayer's description of Gusii marriage rites: traditional wedding ceremonies can be held up by an essential participant who extorts gifts from the other parties in return for permitting the ceremony to continue (cf. Mayer, 1950 in LeVine, 1979:380).

'owner' behaviour and strategies. In addition, men are very vulnerable about their wives' sexual and moral behaviour.

It can be argued that this style of manoeuvring whereby women dramatise their plight as neglected or abused wives is questionable as a long term strategy. However, it should not be overlooked that if a wife dresses in rags, lives in a crumbling house with a leaky roof and has malnourished and disorderly children—she is not the one to be blamed. It is her husband's reputation that suffers. This fact was confirmed by Dr. Badia, who also argued that while male identities are suffering because of the clash or lack of fit between present and traditional norms and values, women's identity is not exposed to such 'lack of fit': 'women's identity is much more tied to the labour process which keeps one going'; or as pointed out by a female nurse in the psychiatric ward at Kisii hospital 'women have much less time than men to nurse their psychological problems'.

Practices of subordination and manipulation

For a deeper understanding of what takes place between the sexes in Kisii, the observations of Villarreal from her work in a Mexican village are very relevant. According to Villarreal a society is composed of actors, thinking agents, capable of strategizing and finding space for manoeuvre in the situations they face and manipulating resources and constraints. And she concludes that women often use 'women's weapons' not only in order to avoid drowning—in deep waters—but also to use the current in order to steer the boat in their direction (Villarreal, 1991:27; 1994). This is very much in line with my own observations. As shown above, Gusii women constantly manipulate and try to rework their constraints, and in their struggle and constant manipulation women often choose to project a non-threatening image of themselves.

This raises the question of what are 'men's weapons' to create space and be respected in a situation in which they feel pressured and threatened. Men also manipulate but they are not so subtle as women. For a woman it is essential to manipulate delicately in order for her to project the image of a 'real' woman. Women accept such roles for themselves to win battles elsewhere (1991:27).

> Despite their daily frustrations, the indications are that the Gusii women ... find some emotional comfort in their status in society that they might not receive in a more independent role (LeVine, R., 1966:188).

In order for a Gusii man to acquire the image of a 'real' man, he should not be delicate—on the contrary. And women often let men play their male role. Women do not want to show that they have the upper hand in the household: it disturbs the image of a woman. Besides,

> (A) man will have more possibilities of being respected in the village because he
> is obeyed and respected at home. The woman also will be seen as a good woman
> because she accords her man 'his place' (Villarreal, 1991:20).

In 'feminist' literature women are often described as striving for autonomy
from male domination: they struggle to achieve control over their lives and
over their bodies. Rather than arguing that women are struggling for autonomy, Villarreal emphasizes the importance of looking into the efforts of
women in the creation, appropriation and conservation of space for themselves (Villarreal, 1992:263). Looking into the limitations that Gusii women
are faced with, into the meanings they assign to their agricultural or household activities, into their representation of the kinds of roles they are willing
to see themselves playing, women seem to use a double strategy. On the one
hand, they accept the norms and standards by which they live; not breaking
these norms unless it is really necessary; working through their networks
and creating new ones. On the other hand, women are also demarcating the
limits to what they will put up with in order to survive with their children;
to the extent that men feel threatened.

New social roles

The Kisii household, its functions, the sexual division of labour, and the
social roles of genders as well as the relations between them have changed
dramatically over past decades. While men's domain and their social role
have been drastically reduced, women's domain, including their independence, has increased. Their social role has expanded and so have their
responsibilities. Both genders, however, are deeply frustrated. Their frustrations, though, are of a different character.

   As mentioned above, different social roles entail normative prescriptions
and proscriptions enforced by positive and negative sanctions. An individual's role behaviour is either in conformity with the normative rules or
deviates from them. He/she receives special rewards and punishments accordingly (LeVine, R., 1982). Most men do not live up to either traditional or
to 'modern' roles'. The question is whether this explains men's frustrations,
dilemmas and why male identities seem to suffer more than those of
women. In precolonial times, as head of the household, the man's role was
not directly linked to economic responsibility, though men had to secure
women's access to the means of production. During colonial times, the
'provider' ideology emerged, and with it new obligations and new responsibilities for men. There was an increased need for men as providers of the
needs of the household. Male financial contributions became particularly
important. The substantial change in the need for contributions to family
support challenged the ideology of separate spheres, and a majority of men
were neither able nor prepared to deal with their new responsibilities and
obligations. However, male employment did not, per se, provide for the

families' needs and women's labour along with income generating activities became increasingly important for family support. Bearing in mind, first, that the sexual division of labour with its task allocations is mediated by a particularly powerful ideological operator, the social construction of gender identity. Secondly, that there is a close relationship between gender identity and social value. So it becomes important to investigate how male and female identity and social values have been affected differently.

Male employment did not necessarily provide a substitute for traditional male functions generating identity, status and respect from others— on the contrary (Cohen and Odhiambo, 1989:98). Moreover, male unemployment in contemporary Kisii is all pervasive. Even the few men who do have an income, have difficulties in scraping together a living to meet the needs of their family and they tend not to share their income with the household. All in all, it is clear that the lack of prestige-giving activities has 'damaged' male social values. Second, men's existential as well as role-based identities were more affected than those of women. From the point of view of women, if lack of bridewealth has affected women's existential identity adversely and negatively, then women have managed to create—if not new—then expanded social roles which give social value. These roles and values seem to compensate for other losses. Men do not speak about women with the same disrespect that women demonstrate when they speak about men. On the contrary. The majority know and admit that they are dependent on women as providers of the household, as their 'savings' etc.

> Command of material resources (including human labour power), political might, personal skill, and/or connectedness through kinship or other reliable bonds to the wealthy and mighty, and the skilled are, if conjoined with (a) effective use of these factors in dealing with others ... and (b) a modicum of largesse and concern for the social good, all sources of prestige' (Ortner and Whitehead, 1981/89:14).

Moreover,

> ... prestige structures are always supported by, indeed they appear as direct expressions of, definite beliefs and symbolic associations that make sensible and compelling the ordering of human relations into patterns of deference and condescension, respect and disregard, and in many cases command and obedience. These beliefs and symbolic associations may be looked at as a legitimating ideology. A system of social value differentiation, founded on whatever material base, is fragile and incomplete without such an ideology (1981/89:14).

Gusii men's command over resources has seriously diminished. So has their political might, their social relationships etc. The deference and respect due from their wives is questioned—and so is their control over women. The same applies to the whole ideology on which male prestige, male dominance as well as male notions about themselves are founded.

When individuals cannot live up to the expectations of their society—and their own expectations—problems of identity emerge. Recognition and acceptance by others are fundamental for identity (LeVine, S., 1979). When a person's moral universe does not 'fit' social reality, a person's identity (the conceptions of an individual self in relation to the other) will be invalidated too. Such an invalidation may be the outcome of confrontation with a changed social structure, in which the person's own role is changed too. If the self image does not correspond to the actual social reality an 'acute identity diffusion' takes place.[25]

As a result of lack of fit between the traditional moral universe, norms and values and the actual/changed social reality my data indicate that men seem to find themselves in a much more vulnerable situation than women.

Existential and role-based identities and gender relations

Using the distinctions drawn by Kopytoff it becomes possible to take a step even further in understanding how social processes affect male and female socially approved roles and identities. As mentioned above, the specific character of the features of women's and men's existential identities in any society may constrain or facilitate negotiation of their socially approved roles. Thus, the features of a person's existential identity play a crucial role when it comes to the negotiation of his/her socially approved role. The following example used by Kopytoff from the Suku is illuminating:

> When it came to the fact that Suku women did agriculture, the reason given was not that 'it is because they are women' or that there was an ancestral injunction that women should do agriculture. The reason that they gave is that it is 'social practice'. However, practices were seen as changeable (Kopytoff, 1990:83–84).

Traditionally, Suku men did some planting inside the village in the form of little gardens of herbs, tobacco and imported vegetables. In the late 1940s men had begun to plant coffee trees in the very few places in Sukuland, where the soil allowed it. Kopytoff's suggestion, therefore, that men might plant manioc, the staple food, if there was a market for it, was acceptable. The discussions, however, were filled with emotional overtones. Suku men did not like to engage in agriculture, and they felt somewhat demeaned when they did, even if as in the case of coffee, the profits seduced them into it. The point that Kopytoff makes here is that not doing agriculture was a circumstantial feature of male identity. As such it was also a socially negotiable one. Suku men were seducible for pragmatic reasons. It provided income. However, according to Kopytoff, new occupations introduced in the colonial period had no established place in Suku folk anthropology of gender. All of them lacked inherence and represented circumstantial roles.

---

[25] According to Erikson, 1959/80:132 or an 'identity-crisis' Jacobson-Widding, 1983:14).

In their Siaya study (1989) Cohen and Odhiambo argue along the same lines. New male roles introduced in the colonial period did not give social value. Certain jobs were even despised, and women would mock men because of the clothing typically worn by agricultural workers (Cohen and Odhiambo, 1989:98). If one says that men took on these jobs because it gave them money and status, such an explanation, according to Kopytoff, is too easy. The far greater status and rewards of being a Christian schoolteacher would not have been sufficient to make men even remotely consider the possibility of abandoning circumcision. The point here is that some roles can be negotiated and some cannot—depending on whether they are intrinsic to a person's existential identity.

Using Kopytoff's model in a Kisii context is illuminating. First, because it shows that not all 'circumstantial' roles give social value. To do farm work on one's own farm, to most—even if they call themselves farmers—is not a 'real' man's job. This is women's work—and thus seriously damaging for male role-based identity. However, as in the Suku case, some men in Kisii have been seduced for pragmatic reasons. Thus it is a negotiable role. The circumstantial roles of a businessman or a matatu driver have no negative connotations. The fact, though, that they have no negative connotations, and as they give access to an income is a great asset. Today, I shall argue, such roles do give social value.

Analyzing men's social roles in the context of Kopytoff's framework and comparing them with their performances in real life is difficult and a rather confusing picture emerges. For example, to be head of household is an inherent and non negotiable role. This role cannot be questioned. However, if a man does not fulfil the obligations which are today associated with this role, he would still be considered head of household—by himself and his surroundings. But his social value drops if he does not fulfil his obligations. This means that, while on the one hand, it is inherent and non-negotiable to be the head of household, it is not an inherent role to contribute to the upkeep of the household. It is not an intrinsic role to provide one's children with food and education (though it gives social value). As shall be shown in the following chapter, it is more intrinsic to father children. On the other hand, to be a person who fulfils the expectations connected to his present role as head of household gives social value, respect and, I shall argue, identity and self-esteem. Similarly, to be a breadwinner (a businessman, matatu driver) is not an existential role in itself (compared with that of being a father) but as it gives access to cash it also gives access to prestige and social value. My point here is that some circumstantial roles are now becoming increasingly important.

Comparing this with women's notions there is much more coherence between what they say and do, and even if many are frustrated and depressed, they are not confronted with an 'identity diffusion' to the extent that men are. Their active attempts to make ends meet, and their role as farm managers does not seem to upset their existential and role-based identities. On the contrary, they rather seem to reinforce them.

The consequences for the relations between genders conflicts between men and women within the household are many, and they seem to be constantly increasing. The antagonistic relations between genders observed by LeVine and LeVine seem to have augmented since they did their research. My data indicate that major reasons for this are that while husbands still are the acknowledged heads of households they do not function as such. With increasing economic pressures husband's labour and financial inputs into the household economy have become paramount. When such inputs seem to be exceptions rather than the rule, with many husbands not fulfilling their new social roles and responsibilities, tensions between the sexes often reach levels where they can no longer be controlled.

Summing up, men' role-based identities are faced with many more contradictions that those of women. At the risk of jumping to a hasty conclusion I should nevertheless suggest that a majority of Gusii men seem to be 'trapped' by the patriarchal ideology to the extent that they are prevented from actively influencing and changing their difficult situation. Moreover, they have not yet 'internalised' the fact that there is a need for them to participate in the upkeep of the household. Instead, ironically, many men seem to have 'internalised' and accepted their increasingly marginalized role in the household. To be fair, many men are actively trying to find or create jobs for themselves. Unemployment is a major problem. At the same time men are also faced with overburdened, overworked but also entrepreneurial wives—and they know it. Most men seem to watch this occurring passively. As a result, men are in a contradictory situation, where they are being overtaken by women—and antagonisms between the sexes abound.

Chapter 6
Fertility, Identity and Social Value

(Your children) are your own flesh and blood, an image of your own self. In a real sense your own being is perpetuated or continued through this creative level of marriage. You become 'immortal' in and through your children, even if you die eventually. Your name is carried on and not lost, the torch of life is handed down and begins to burn anew—you are rekindled in your children. Through procreation you beat death, you bring together the three dimensions of time: past, present and future. Oh, what a sacred mystery this creative purpose and meanings of marriage is! And what joy and blessing it brings to a happy marriage, and what uncountable riches it bestows upon marriage! ... Our people may not show deep academic reflection on it, but they certainly know the value of this creative level of marriage (Mbiti, 1973/86:42–43).

Introduction

Neither reproduction nor sexuality are straightforward extrapolations of biological facts, but are the outcome of social and cultural processes. Moreover, social value and prestige 'is the domain of social structure that most directly affects cultural notions of gender and sexuality' (Ortner and Whitehead, 1981:16). Based on this, I shall try to come to grips with fertility, the social and cultural processes surrounding it, and, in particular, the relationship between fertility, identity and social value. Linked to this a number of questions will be dealt with. Have the meaning and the values attributed to fertility changed during this century? What are the current values attributed to fertility by women and men? What does fertility mean in terms of male and female identity?

Current Gusii cultural notions of gender identity and social value closely interact with fertility. However, not in the same way as with sexuality, as shall be shown in the next chapter and not in an obvious, direct and straightforward way as in precolonial times. The way in which both identity and social value interact with fertility is often very paradoxical. Moreover, while men and women often share the same values linked to fertility, they frequently have what seem to be different and contradictory priorities—as shall also be shown below.

The cultural construction of 'biological facts' about women's and men's bodies, their sexuality and fertility are important parts of how gender is constituted. But such 'biological facts' are rarely questioned because they are associated with nature and thereby placed beyond dispute (Moore, 1986).

This observation is not self-evident and requires discussion. While male and female fertility is fundamental to both genders, these 'biological facts' have become sensitive issues which are increasingly being questioned and disputed.

Fertility patterns in present day Kisii

Birth rates in Kisii are among the highest in the country. Fertility in Kenya reached a peak of over 8 children per woman of child-bearing age in the late 1970s. Then fertility started declining slowly. By 1989, the total fertility rate had declined to an estimated 6.7 children (Brass and Jolly in Egerö and Hammarskjöld, 1994:37). Fertility rates in Kisii have not decreased significantly (7.6 in 1991). Women express the wish for four to six children.[26] According to our own survey data collected on women, 21% said that they wanted four children, 11.9% wanted five, and 20.2% said that six children was the ideal number. 22.4% wanted more than six. Some said 'according to God's will'. Comparing the number of children that women wanted with the number they *thought* their husbands wanted, there is a discrepancy. Only 11.6% of the husbands were said to want four children: 6.7% said their husbands wanted five children while 10.2% said that their husbands wanted six children. More than 40% of the women, though, had never discussed the subject with their husbands.

Using the survey method on these types of question is problematic. People's life situation changes, and so may their desire for children. When a 25 year old woman with 4 children says that six are enough, by the age of 35 she may end up with at least 8 . Moreover, the survey method will never disclose the real reasons or preferences. A Gusii woman would never dare to admit that she really wanted 10 children. Apart from the fact that the interviewer would probably not think much of her if she said that she wanted ten children, she could be accused of boasting—and therefore subject to bewitching—and she might end up with her children dying. On the other hand, a woman who admitted that she wanted a more modest number would also be afraid of being bewitched for arrogance. 'Never tell a stranger how many eggs you have in your basket; never tell how many children you have or they might die', women would often say.

Comparing the ideal number of children with the number of each sex which was desired, the vast majority said that, ideally, they wanted at least two or three children of each sex. These are much more reliable figures to deal with; and they are clearly supported by my qualitative data. If women do not get the desired number of each sex, the majority will just continue to give birth. But still, this does not answer the question of why women get so many children, when women and men agree that children constitute a

---

[26] According to the *Kenya Contraceptive Prevalence Survey* undertaken in Kisii in 1983/84 targeting women only.

heavy economic burden. While some studies document that the value of children decreases when children become economic burdens (Caldwell, 1982) or when school fees increase (World Bank, 1991), other studies maintain that the value of children depends more on functional changes in the family and changes in the family structure (Frank, 1990). In Kisii children have become an economic burden and family structures are changing. Yet birth rates have not been affected so far.

Controlled fertility is part of a strategy of life which may vary according to events or disruptions affecting the life cycle of parties to a marriage (Locoh, 1988). Before considering the possibility of limiting the number of one's children, some capacity for foresight is necessary. This is possible where a family life cycle is reasonably stable. But in the absence of such stability, decisions are reconsidered whenever there is a disruption in the life cycle. When a man fails to pay brideprice, takes an additional wife, or a woman leaves in order to live with a new husband, the strategies relating to fertility of both parties may be modified. Children continue to be the cement of a union, but they are also weapons in the struggle for power among polygamous wives. Marital insecurity and competition among co-wives prompt women to have many children.

The area of 'decision-making' on the number of children is a no-man's land. People's views are not static. They change according to the circumstances they find themselves in. Moreover, it may well be that each spouse believes the other wants more children, but that neither bothers to verify that assumption. This is exactly what happened in a very poor family I visited. The wife had just given birth to her ninth son one hour ago. She was lying on the ground inside the hut. Her bed consisted of some plastic bags and old rags. She was in a state of despair. She had been so tired and weak during her last pregnancies, and she wanted so much to 'be done completely' (i.e. sterilized). But her husband wanted daughters, and 'now she had tried once again—without success'. The husband was sitting outside the hut. We were all prepared to have a serious word with him. However, as it turned out, he was also in despair. How could he manage nine sons, with only three acres of land? He was convinced, though, that his wife wanted a daughter badly. He wanted her to go for family planning, but did not dare to mention it for fear that she might think that he wanted to take a second wife.

Traditional fertility beliefs and values

Traditionally, as mentioned above, the religious beliefs and practices of the Gusii were related directly to the desire for large families, and men were commemorated by their sons in the ancestor cult. In the ancestor cult it was a religious and moral duty to offer sacrifices regularly so that the father or grandfather 'will not be forgotten' and 'his name lives'. Since nobody but the sons and grandsons could offer these sacrifices, the name of a man who died without leaving such offspring was forgotten. The desire to be commemorated was seen as axiomatic. It represented the desire to leave a certain influence after death—to be regarded as 'somebody' in the world of living men. This is still the case. As mentioned above, even those Gusii who refer to themselves as Christians have by no means given up the beliefs and practices of their traditional religion.

The cultural association of fertility was good, right and proper behaviour. Infertility was associated with evil and wickedness. Just as fertility signified the blessing of the shades, so infertility signified their righteous anger with descendants who impiously 'forgot them'. A childless wife or impotent man would consult a diviner to learn whether and how the family shades required placating. The dwindling of a family through child death and miscarriages could also be seen as the result of a curse sent by Nyasae (God) or the sun. The punishment was not necessarily aimed at the parent couple themselves, but at any senior (especially male) member of the family. It might also be sent to innocent people by vindictive enemies. By and large, family misfortune indicated guilt. Conversely, a large number of children growing up and thriving helped to indicate that one was virtuous and innocent (Mayer in Molnos, 1972–74, Vol. 3, No. 2:125).

Plurality of wives and offspring was a major ambition for men. Men wanted wives for their reproductive capacity. They wanted daughters because the bridewealth cattle paid for them enlarged the family herd and could be used to acquire wives for the homestead head and his sons, and they wanted sons because they expanded the minimal lineage and took care of their parents in old age. The more children a man fathered the more he was respected and valued in the community. There was enough land, enough food, no school fees to pay, and goat skins were used for clothing. In spite of occasional famines, droughts and locusts, the household economy was not strained, and even if there might have been conflicting interests within the households, male and female attitudes as to the number of children did not seem to differ. Four wives with three or four children each meant more for a man's status than one wife with a dozen children (1972–74:123). Although it was clearly the women who carried the fetuses in their bodies, and nursed the children after birth, it was obvious that women were only a vessel, while the father was the true parent. Nevertheless, this did not impede men from blaming their wives for not giving birth to sons—or from taking another wife. Consequently, the husband also had the custody of the children. Fertility used to be ruled by three basic principles:

- a woman should begin to bear children almost as soon as she was able and continue as long as she was able.
- every man (even if old, married and father many times over) should invest almost all available wealth (cattle, goats, surplus grains etc.) to pro-

cure childbearing wives for himself or his sons by way of bridewealth payment.
– children born 'irregularly' or 'out of wedlock' would always find a man willing to claim them as legal father.

The childbearing capacity of a woman was the main value transferred in exchange for bridewealth. If she died prematurely the number of cattle reclaimed was reduced proportionately to the number of children she had borne. It was legitimate to divorce her, send her home and reclaim the bridewealth cattle, if she did not become pregnant within a reasonable amount of time. But a loving husband might decide to adopt a child rather than divorce his wife as he was legally entitled to do. Such a child would be 'bought for grain' from some famine-stricken family in a far-off locality. Pregnancy before marriage was not a serious crime. 'The child goes with the cattle' paid by the prospective husband whether or not he had fathered the child. Older men, widowers and polygynists might be pleased to get a wife's premarital child for nothing. Likewise, if a girl was married to a man who was impotent or too old to beget children, it was tacitly assumed that he would connive at her 'getting children in the bush' by another man but born for his own sake and hers (Mayer, I., 1974:123).

Ideally, men and women wanted equal numbers of sons and daughters. Sons were wanted to 'carry on the Egesaku'. A man wanted at least two sons: 'with fewer than two, the Ekgesaku does not stand'. But an equal number of daughters were needed because the sons were to marry with the bridewealth cattle paid for the daughters. 'The house with only daughters is not poor' in food and cattle, 'but loneliness will come to it' since the daughters are to marry away, while sons will stay and carry on the family line. Thus the cattle and inheritance laws made it desirable for every wife to have at least two boys and two girls, and she would be proud if she contributed more than this number to her husband's egesaku. Childbearing was a matter of invidious distinction among co-wives in a polygynous family, and wives would be sensitive to any inequalities in the distribution of living children. Suspicions of witchcraft would arise among the wives if one of them had a miscarriage or stillbirth. Children were so desired by women that, in polygynous families, childbearing was competitive and gave rise to many hostilities among co-wives (LeVine, R. and B., 1966/77:112–13).

While women were supposed to be sexually faithful to their husband during his lifetime, they were not to stop bearing children after his death. On the contrary, a widow of childbearing age had to go on producing children 'to the name' of the dead husband. Within about a year of the husband's death, his brothers or cousins had either to accept the widow(s) as wife/wives themselves, or allow each to choose a 'warmer of the house'. The 'warmer' would then visit the widow in her hut regularly, help her in the domestic sense, and beget children, though legally they were not his

children but the dead man's (1966/77:124). As mentioned above, the practice
of getting a 'warmer' of the house still exists today. A widow with some
land can always find a poor and landless man. I met a few women who had
'chosen' hard working men to 'help' around the house, including giving
them children.

So fertility was considered a blessing by both women and men, and infertility was a disaster. Women as well as men had a common interest in
getting many children in order to extend social relations, to fight in feuds,
for herding cattle, as extra hands in the fields and as a security in old age—
not to mention identity and social value. Social esteem for both women and
men came later in life as grandparents rather than parents, but much more
as parents than as adults and as married much more than unmarried. With
many surviving sons and daughters men as well as women were highly respected. Thus the need for procreation throughout their fertile years was felt
so deeply by both men and women that irregularities in the ideal reproductive cycle aroused anxieties and caused disruptions in family relations
(1966/77:113) so it is difficult to imagine a traditional Gusii couple making a
decision, separately or together, about how many children they would have.
Normally it would be assumed that both would want to have several or
many children and they would fear the frustration of their hopes through
sterility, miscarriages, disease or death (Mayer, I., 1974).

The phenomenon of women marriages, which is still practised today,
has probably been adopted in order to cope with difficult situations, where
for example the children in a family died or if there were no sons to inherit
the land. What is meant by Women marriages is that the children of another
woman are made legal heirs if a family or a woman is not able to produce
heirs. An often heard of example today is if a wealthy widow has no sons.
Then she can 'marry' another woman and 'adopt' her children, so they become her heirs. Josephine, one of my assistants, who was in her mid-thirties
had just 'married' an elderly widow with several acres of land. Josephine
lived in town, worked at the hospital and had no land. She was a widow
herself and had two sons (aged 12 and 14) and three younger daughters.
Now her two sons had moved to the farm of the old widow who paid their
school fees.

'Traditional' family planning

In the past, Gusii women never had unlimited numbers of children. There
was a clear check to procreation. if a woman got pregnant too soon after her
last birth this was not approved of. In spite of the fact that it was important
to have many children—also because child mortality was considerable—
some sort of 'family planning' was practised—as in almost all cultures.

Abstinence was used to limit births. The husband was supposed to stay
away from his wife during breast-feeding, stay away and herd the cattle or

be with the other wives until the nursing period was over. It was up to the woman to summon her husband again. When she sent her last born with a small bowl of porridge for the husband he would know that he was expected to resume his marital duties. Thus, while women were required to abstain from sex until their last born was weaned, men just acquired another wife, or went to their other wife or wives who went on producing children. Women, though, were not totally dependent on abstinence. Natural herbs with contraceptive effects were also used by women as a means to space or limit births. Little is known on this issue, and it was not possible to find out the extent to which women in the past 'managed' their fertility 'on their own' or spaced their children. Gusii men were also known to eat certain types of food which reduced their sexual appetite. But this was only occasionally successful (Were and Nyamwaya, 1986:146).

A man had to tend to all his wives, and he was supposed to honour each wife's desire to have children at regular intervals, *regardless of his preference* (Mayer, I., 1974). This observation is interesting. It is normally argued that through marriage, men are in control of both women's fertility and sexuality. If Mayer's observation is true—which is very difficult to substantiate today—it means that women were in fact in control of their own fertility. On the other hand, women also seem to have been held responsible if they gave birth too often. Women who violated the limits on procreation were viewed as lacking proper sexual inhibition (LeVine, R. and B., 1966/77:115). I shall return to this issue in the next chapter.

Fertility in Kisii today

Even today, fertility is extremely important for both men and women. From childhood on, they are surrounded by folklore reflecting the tremendous value set on the blessing of fertility. As shown above, the circumcision rituals put strong emphasis on male and female fertility. For both male and female initiates it is crucial that the initiation fire in the hut does not go out—'or you may not get any children'. When an infertile woman was referred to, I was always told that her mother had not tended the fire properly during initiation. One 'married' infertile woman in her mid-twenties had taken all kinds of different herbs to become fertile—but with no results. Now she was planning to see 'somebody' (a sorcerer) hoping that he could 'undo' the curse.

A woman's progress in gaining respect and social value depends on a number of factors. When she marries, her domestic and agricultural skills are scrutinized in her new home, particularly by her mother-in-law. But in the long run her acceptance requires giving birth to children early and regularly. Motherhood is highly rated and prestige giving. A young woman who has not yet given birth may often be more concerned about being able to give birth than about protecting herself from getting pregnant. It is extremely important for a woman to 'prove' her fertility. Just as an unmarried woman has no status, a woman with no children has no status. A woman's ability to bear children gives her respect and social value in the masculine as well as the feminine world. A demonstrable capacity to bear and raise (many) children, especially sons, is still the primary criterion by which a woman defines herself and acquires social acceptance and respect. An infertile woman will be sent back to her parents and end up as a spinster—or rather—like a few that I met—become second wives, who could only stay on a husband's land if they accept their fate as labourers with no status. Traditionally, a woman who died without ever conceiving would have a thorn stuck in her nipple with the words 'this is your child' (Mayer, I., 1974:126). Just as there is no status for women outside 'marriage' so there is no status for a woman without children. Infertility is a disaster. If a woman cannot produce any children, the husband is in his full right to send her back. Joyce, a very entrepreneurial woman whom I first met in 1985 had by then just got married to Peter. By 1990 she had not yet conceived. The year before, her husband had brought another wife to the house. She soon got pregnant. One day Joyce tried to kill her. As she did not succeed, she set fire to herself. When she did not succeed in this either, she was sent back to her parents. By 1992, I was told that she had gone mad. Of course Joyce was terribly jealous; but there was more to it than that. Her whole identity as a woman was wiped out. She was not respected by her husband, her in-laws, the society. Her own parents treated her as a misfit.

Just as motherhood is still fundamental for the identity of a woman, fatherhood is just as fundamental for the identity of a man. Without a child of their own, a couple are still considered children of their parents and hence dependents. Men still argue that 'no man's name is lost if he leaves sons and grandsons'; and 'we only remember names of the ancestors, who became many—the names of others get lost'. A man with no children 'has no say'. Even if the men interviewed had no income and only a tiny plot of land, the majority would still want to have many children: 'only rich people do not need to have children'; 'poor people need children'. A few young husbands with only a couple of children so far had very 'modern' views. They stressed that according to the President, family size should be reduced, and they certainly intended to 'stop' after 3 or 4 children. Checking this information with their wives, they did not believe it: 'husbands always change their minds later'.

Gusii women do not expect their husbands to be faithful and have no culturally prescribed right to demand fidelity, but they certainly do expect their husbands to be able to give them children. The worst thing for a Gusii man is to be impotent. Men are greatly concerned with their potency. Women are also concerned about male potency. Women complain about men not being able to fulfil their obligations. Men who have been weakened by alcohol, and who are not able to 'perform properly'; who keep their wives awake all night. In most local markets, there will always be all kind of remedies against impotence.

While barren women are a well known and frequently mentioned phenomenon, barren men are a subject not often spoken of in spite of the fact that an increasing number of men have become barren because of the frequency of venereal disease.[27] It is a disgrace for a man to be barren and procreative failure on the part of the husband disrupts the marital relationship (LeVine, R. and B., 1966/77:113). Zachary, a well respected farmer with quite a lot of land, had turned out to be sterile. The need for his wife to have children was solved by a clandestine breach of her obligation to remain faithful to her husband. Thus, the problem was solved by one of his friends. Esther got four children by him; two sons and two daughters. They are now adults. That was a socially accepted practice. What was certainly not acceptable, (and what I learnt by accident when I visited a very old woman known for making herb mixtures with contraceptive effects), was that Ester did not engage in an extra marital relation just to get pregnant. She continued to have affairs with other men and this was known because she continued to be a customer of the old woman. Two of my assistants were with me on that occasion, and they kept on talking about these shocking facts, though perfectly aware of the fact that the husband was known to have numerous extramarital relations.

The value of children

> The Nyansongan desire for children is one of the strongest motivations in their culture ... . The high value which they set on human fertility and reproduction is exemplified by their attitudes toward sterility, impotence, infanticide, infant mortality and abortion (1966/77:115).

Twenty years later, children still remain the most valued possessions of their parents and represent the continuation of religious and moral life as well as economic hope for the future (LeVine, S. and R., 1981). However, my data clearly indicate that today men and women increasingly recognize that children have become economic burdens. With smaller and smaller plots and hardly any land to inherit, the education of children becomes paramount as security for the old age of the parents. And education is expensive. Thus while the value of children is still paramount, large numbers are becoming questionable. But, as noted above, this is not reflected in Kisii birth rates.

Linked to this, men and women are struggling with conflicting rationalities and ideals which seem to compete with each other. On the one hand, both men and women want to have many children—in principle. On the

---

[27] Personal communication with health staff at Kisii hospital and at health centres in the district.

The family planning room at Kisii District Hospital where the client is adviced about what type of preventive method she should use.

other, both sexes recognize that it is a problem to educate, feed and clothe their children. In earlier times, children were very important assets in terms of labour. Today parents—or rather mainly women—complain that they cannot count on help from their children. Children start school at 7 in the morning, and they only return at 5 o'clock. Even if there are long vacations around harvest time, a general complaint is that 'school takes all their time and energy'. When there is no more money for school fees, uniforms or books, children are sent back from school by their teachers. Then they may help around the house, collecting wood, fetching water and looking after smaller siblings. Often, though, the children are so disappointed and frustrated that their assistance at home is irregular and limited.

Thus, from a rational point of view, a large number of children does not make sense and there is a need to curb procreation. If parents cannot educate their children, they are of little help when parents get old. So the benefit of many children is no longer so obvious. The benefits have started to be questioned—but more in theory than in practice.

Fertility and the consequences for women and men

In spite of the fact that men and women may have the same values as to fertility, the consequences of having children are not the same for men and women. Women, of course, bear all the burdens and health risks of giving birth. And these are many when daily life is strenuous, food often scarce, anaemia frequent and health services inadequate. But apart from this, there are different domains of responsibility. As emerges from the previous chapters, children are often cost free to men while women tend to bear more than their share of the daily costs of rearing children.

Thus, the member of the family most often responsible for its subsistence is the wife and mother. This generally means that the mother is not only responsible for her own livelihood, but she also has to be economically active enough to produce or purchase the necessary sustenance for her family—her children and often her husband. Raising children has increasingly become an exclusively female domain. This means that after husbands have secured right over children and the labour of a woman to raise them (if some bridewealth has been paid), childbearing becomes virtually cost free for men. This is becoming a general phenomenon which has also been observed elsewhere (Frank, 1990).

Modern family planning in Kisii—Knowledge, attitude and practice by women and men

In the 1960s it was (naively) believed that, within a period of 10–15 years, family planning programmes might result in drastically lower fertility levels. In 1966, as one of the first sub-Saharan countries, Kenya introduced modern family planning. In Kisii the first government clinics appeared in the late 1960s. Right from the start, women were the targets and family planning was mainly introduced through MCH (mother and child health care). As mentioned above, there is a traditional knowledge of contraceptive herbs. However, today this knowledge is dying out. In our survey of 723 women, only two women said that they had tried traditional herbs. It may be that women did not want to admit to such 'old fashioned' attitudes, but my assistants did not know of anybody practising such methods. Consequently, it was by sheer accident that we found the old herbalist mentioned above. The old woman (somewhere in her 80s) said that more than 40 years ago she had many clients to whom she gave her own mixtures. She dried and burnt special leaves and roots from certain plants which then were to be found the District. Her main activity today consisted in preparing medicine from plants found in Kakamega District to make infertile women fertile and to provoke abortions.

The family planning programmes introduced in Kenya were based on two contradictory principles: a means to control population growth by controlling women's fertility, and a means whereby (married) couples could plan their families on the basis of free choice. The choice of contraceptive methods was very limited. Until 1990, those who accepted family planning were mainly given pills. Injections with depo provera and noristerad were also available and became increasingly used—even on young mothers although this is against the rules. IUDs (intra uterine devices) were not popular; 'they go to the head', 'they disappear in the body' or husbands complain

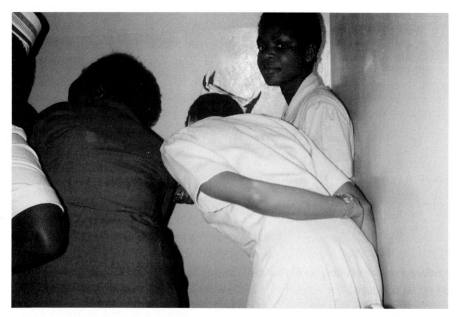

There is not much privacy when a client is being examined in the family planning section.

that they are uncomfortable (they could feel the thread), women would argue. Moreover, most health centres did not have the facilities to make
proper gynaecological examinations (examination tables and instruments
were lacking) or educated personnel to undertake such examinations.

Until the early 1980s, a women was only allowed a contraceptive
method provided her husband had given his approval (signature). Today,
this requirement has been abandoned (except for sterilization—see below),
and many women use a contraceptive method without the husband's
knowledge. Even today, family planning is still only for 'married' women
according to government policy. In practice this means women who have
already given birth. 'No permanent method should be given, before a
women has proven that she is fertile'. 'Unmarried' young women are not
allowed any contraception, and certainly not adolescents. 'It will induce
immoral behaviour' the health personnel maintained—at the same time being very concerned about their reputation in the local community. They
were afraid of being accused by parents of inducing young women to lead
an unrestrained sexual life. None of them wanted to contribute to adolescents' immoral behaviour. Young school girls died regularly from induced
abortions (drinking ink, inserting sticks in their uterus or taking an overdose
of anti-malarials). Abortions are illegal, and many newborn babies are found
in the latrines.[28]

---

[28] Pregnancy is increasingly becoming the main determinant of female secondary-school
dropout rates in Kenya. Pregnant primary- and secondary-school students are expelled from
school and may experience difficulties re-enroling after giving birth. Although female students

Women's reasons for use of modern contraceptives

In spite of its introduction almost 30 years ago, the use of modern contraception is a very delicate subject in Kisii. While awareness of family planning methods is high, acceptance is low. Only 8% of women in their reproductive age made use of a contraceptive method at the time of the survey (Silberschmidt, 1991a; *Kenya Contraceptive Prevalence Survey*, 1992). 13.4% of all women interviewed in our survey had at one point tried some kind of contraceptive method. Among these users, 70% had been using a modern method (oral contraceptives (52), injectables (10), IUD (10); 20 had been sterilized and 10% had been relying on a combination of methods (breast-feeding, natural family planning i.e. Billing's method introduced by the catholic missions).

Trying to decipher who were the women who did make use of modern contraception there seems to be a marked difference between FP-users and non-users in terms of bridewealth paid. With bridewealth paid—or part of it—women feel more secure and accepted. Therefore they are more inclined to try to use modern contraceptives—at least as a spacing method. While a general and well established assumption is that the educational level of women constitutes a determinant factor in terms of their use of FP, this was not the case in our study. There was no significant difference in FP use between women with no schooling and those with schooling.[29]

Thus, despite the expansion of family planning services in Kisii, both by government and also by private organizations, these services are only used to a surprisingly limited extent. The reasons given by the majority of women for use of contraceptives were first of all economic pressure (school fees, the cost of food and lack of land). The second set of reasons were enough children (of the right sex), that pregnancies are a burden, and the need for longer intervals between births. About half of the women using a contraceptive method did so without the husband's knowledge. Some of them had to stop, because of irregular bleedings which could not escape the attention of their husbands.[30]

The magnitude of the problems that women face is huge. There are increasing numbers of female-headed households, unstable relationships, elopements, little bridewealth transfer, male withdrawal from their eco-

---

at institutions of higher learning are not expelled when they get pregnant, they are nonetheless often subject to penalties by the government. For example they might be suspended from school for one year, after which they lose boarding privileges. Male students are not punished for impregnating women (Gage and Njogu, 1994:41).

[29] This links up with findings by Molnos from her large KAP study. (knowledge, attitude and practice). The Molnos study underlines the fact that there is no necessy correlation between fertility matters and educational level (1972–74). This is is supported by Young (1978) as well as by a number of recent studies carried out in Sub-Saharan Africa (Egerö and Mburugu, 1994; Kirumira, 1995) and also in South East Asia (Nafis Sadik, UNFPA, Danida conference on population, Copenhagen, May 1994).

[30] For more details, see Silberschmidt, 1991a.

nomic responsibilities, increasing workload, increasing pressure on land with hardly any land left for the coming generation and increasing difficulties in providing money for food, clothing and especially school fees. One might expect that such conditions would lead women to line up in front of the family planning units, eagerly asking for access to family planning devices. This, however, was not the case. It raises the question of why women are reluctant to make use of modern contraceptives.

In the 1984 Kenya Contraceptive Prevalence Survey a most important conclusion was that there are strong indicators of unmet needs (by women) for both permanent and temporary methods of fertility regulation.[31] This is not in contradiction with our findings. However as this study also indicates there may be a considerable step from women's 'so called' unmet needs in theory to make use of a contraceptive method to their conscious use in practice. Not to mention the fact that women are often confronted with incredible obstacles.

For example, in 1986 a privately financed team of six doctors from Nairobi arrived in Kisii to perform about 100 laparoscopic tubal ligations in one day (i.e. sterilizations by a special apparatus where only small incisions are made in order to "tie" the tubes). This procedure did not require the normal hospitalization but could be done on an out-patient basis. One hundred women got an appointment for a gynaecological examination at Kisii Hospital to precede the laparoscopy. Theresa, who was 34 years and had 9 children, was one of them. A message was sent to Theresa, and she turned up for the examination on the agreed day. All women in the waiting area, however, were told to come back another day, because nobody was there to give the examinations. Another consultation was arranged the following week, and this time, after the examination, Theresa was told that she could have her tubal ligation the following week. Turning up one week later at 7 a.m. for the big day, she was told that since the sterilizations were carried out on an official basis, the husband's signature was required. Theresa rushed back and caught her husband, Jim, still asleep. He refused to come with her to give his signature. Besides, he had no trousers to wear. Theresa rushed to her brother-in-law. He agreed to go with her and give the signature. He only needed a wash, then he would join her. Returning to home to wait for him, she found that Jim had left the house. Peter, the brother-in-law, never turned up to join Theresa. Jim had sneaked to his house and started accusing him of having an affair with Theresa. Theresa was bewildered because Peter refused to tell her why he had changed his mind. Only a few

---

[31] Unmet need is a very slippery term. Though most often referred to as an unproblematic category and used to make official estimates by the *World Fertility Survey and Contraceptive Prevalence Survey* the term is far from clear. In literature, the concepts of unmet need and KAP gap are used interchangeably even though conceptually they are not at all identical. Moreover, definitions are numerous (for more details see Dixon-Mueller and Germain, 1993; Silberschmidt, 1994).

days later, Peter's wife told Theresa what had happened: 'Before, people were laughing because Jim always said that I was the one refusing and just went on producing and producing. Now, people will laugh again and say that it is my husband who is refusing'. 'Anyway', Theresa concluded, 'he is the weak one. He will have to accept. I am stronger than him'. Having missed her chance on that fatal day, the local gynaecologist gave us his word to undertake the tubal ligation on Theresa the following week—without her husband's signature.

Women's reasons for not using contraceptives

Some women would say that they could not make up their minds to use any contraceptives, because of all kinds of rumours about side-effects (irregular bleedings, nausea, backache etc.). Such rumours were not without some truth. The choice of contraceptives was very limited and not very suitable for women with very strenuous work. In general, nurses would say that they used two types of pills: one type for the fat ones and another type for the thin ones. The quality of the services was poor, the staff overburdened, and priority would be given to antenatal clinics and acute health problems. Often the staff had no opportunity to attend follow-up courses, and their knowledge of contraceptive methods was inadequate. Family planning clinics were given once a week and often women were afraid of meeting neighbours or friends who might then find out that they were (prospective) family planning users. At the Kisii District Hospital, there were long waiting lists for tubal ligations. The majority of women who lined up for these operations were in their mid-thirties, and already had the number and sex of children that they wanted. These women were determined that 8 children (or more) were enough.

In our survey, and in the qualitative interviews, the most frequent reasons given by women for non-use were that 'children are not enough'. The reason why children were not enough differed. They were not enough, if there were not enough children of the desired sex. As mentioned above, two sons are a minimum, and even if a poor woman has 5 daughters, this is not enough. Sons are considered a security in old age. Catherine, the handicapped widow mentioned above, had three daughters (Stella was one of them) and one son when I first met her (in 1984). By 1986 she had decided that she wanted to be sterilized. The only payment she could offer for help in the shamba was her sexual services. This had resulted in her last born daughter. Now she had realized that she could not afford more children. So by 1986 she went through a very uncomfortable sterilization on the day when the doctors from Nairobi came to Kisii and undertook the 100 laparoscopic tubal ligations. They had no time to wait for the local anaesthesia to take full effect, and many women suffered considerably. Catherine was one of them. On my return in 1990, she complained of a stomach ache. When I brought her to the local gynaecologist, he discovered that she was pregnant. As was the case with many women who had a tubal ligation, the 'knots' had 'un-knotted'. The gynaecologist offered her an abortion. Catherine refused. She had two reasons. Her one son, Julius, was not enough. Besides, if she gave birth to another son, she could put pressure on her 'helper' to give her more assistance in the shamba. On my return in 1992, Catherine had given birth to another daughter, and her 'helper' had been killed in a road accident.

Paradoxically, the risk and uncertainties that a majority of women are exposed to seem to create a powerful incentive to continue to produce children and constitutes part of a broader calculus to improve their situation. As also mentioned above, when bridewealth has not been paid, a woman's (desperate) strategy to stabilize her situation may take the form of giving birth. One of the most consistent arguments of women for not using any contraceptive methods were that 'husbands are against'; 'husbands want all the eggs in a woman's womb to be used'.

Male attitudes

In addition to a large number of qualitative interviews, 180 men were also interviewed by questionnaire on fertility beliefs, values and attitudes to family planning at the same time as the above survey on women was carried out. When family planning and modern contraceptives were discussed, a surprisingly large number of men accepted the idea—in theory. And they were all for it if it was for their neighbour's wife. When the discussion turned to the question of their own wives using modern contraceptives, men were much more reluctant, arguing that it would induce their wives to 'roam about' and 'families would break up'; 'women are responsible for all the broken homes nowadays'. However, as will be shown in the following chapter, it is much more common (and acceptable) for men to 'roam'—and men have more time to roam.

A number of studies document that men who take their paternal responsibilities lightly, will not be interested in family planning. In fact, their attitude may be very hostile since they feel that a woman's use of a contraceptive method may result in loss of power over their wives. They still want to ensure that their spouses do not benefit from the ultimate freedom which control over their own fertility would give them. But there may be more to it than that.

I once attended a baraza (Meeting) during which some men spoke with great concern about the side-effects of contraceptives. They were even indignant on behalf of their wives. I was very impressed at their concern, until they told me that 'side-effects are bad for women; then they cannot work hard in the shamba'; and 'they bleed all the time and that is no good for a man'.

According to men, a wife's use of modern contraception 'undermines a man's authority in his own house'; 'the wife gets the upper hand, and the husband has no say'; 'women go looking for other men'. Faced with the question of why they would have such high numbers of children, in particular sons, for whom there would be no land, most men did not seem to make the link—or did not want to make the link. It was rather a matter of them getting sons who would achieve in life what they themselves had never been able to achieve. Men would say over and over that 'if all the eggs in the womb of my wife are not used how would I know if I have prevented the birth of a son who would once become president of Kenya?'. As to the question of how they would feed, clothe and educate their children if they had no prospects of land—the majority of men would leave this problem 'in the hands of God. He will look after them'; 'I do not want to know anything about the future of my children; I am a sheep of God—and so are they. So God will take care of them'.

Speaking about male contraception (i.e. condoms) with men and women a general comment by both sexes was, 'men do not like such things'; 'they make a man not function'. As family planning information and devices were delivered through the MCH (mother and child health clinics), men were directly approached. A young mother who did not have her period at the time she went to the H/C to ask for a contraceptive method was provided with 5 condoms to last the rest of the month. Then it was her (impossible) job to convince her husband to use them. In the storage room of the H/C there were at least large 50 boxes filled with condoms from SIDA. When I asked why the woman was not given more condoms, the answer from the female nurse was that 'women should learn to control themselves'.

Contraception is not a man's problem: 'It is a woman's problem'. From that point of view, control of men's fertility and sexuality is not a matter of male concern. 'Condoms hurt a man's self-esteem'. 'They are unpleasant' not only men but also women agree. 'Condoms are not for home use'. 'If somebody gets hold of a condom with my semen they could use it for bewitching', many men would argue. Besides 'male semen is good for women'; 'women complain if they do not get the male semen'; 'it is women's right'; 'it gives strength to the baby, if a woman is pregnant', both men and women agree. 'Condoms are for extra-marital sex'. 'You don't use a condom when you have sex with a wife'; 'it is insulting to a woman if her husband uses condoms. It implies lack of trust'. Sure enough, everybody agrees that if a husband uses condoms at home he has been roaming around and has perhaps contracted a venereal disease. If a woman should suggest to her husband that he should use a condom, she implies that she is the one who has been 'roaming'. So male use of a contraceptive is neither popular nor acceptable.

As mentioned above, sexually transmitted diseases flourish, and the AIDS epidemic has not left Kisii untouched. In 1992, according to the local gynaecologist, 30% of all his clients were HIV infected.[32]

Identity, social value and fertility

As demonstrated above, reproduction and fertility behaviour are the outcome of complex social and cultural processes. Moreover, cultural notions of social value and identity often do not interact with fertility in a direct and straightforward way and there is often a difference between men's and women's fertility interests.

While fertility is attributed great value by men and women, reproductive goals are often different and conflicting. The differences in fertility interests have already been explained, partly in the above, and should be seen in relation to socio-economic pressure coupled with the breakdown of traditional family structures, lack of bridewealth transfer and the increase in the number of female headed households. All combined with the fact that women are left alone to support their children.

However, I shall argue that behind these more obvious reasons for conflicting fertility interests are also a number of more obscure reasons which seem to be related to questions about social value and identity. These questions have not received much attention in the vast amount of literature on family planning. In the following, I shall discuss these features in more depth by relating them to male and female social value and male and female identity.

While men's domain, their social role, their responsibility towards the household and with it their social value have been drastically reduced, new prestige giving activities have not replaced the old ones, and male authority is increasingly being questioned. There is no immediate possibility that men will recapture social roles that would enable them to acquire a more prominent role in the household and fulfil the expectations of them as heads of households. So men in particular seem to resort to the old prestige-giving values of the past.

As mentioned above, men were commemorated by their sons in the ancestor cult. It was a religious and moral duty to offer sacrifices regularly so that the father or grandfather 'will not be forgotten' and 'his name lives'. A man wanted to be assured of this posthumous commemoration in the same natural and elementary way as he wanted to be 'somebody' in his lifetime' (LeVine, R. and B., 1966/77; Mayer, I., 1974). Men argue the same today: 'no man's name is lost if he leaves sons and grandsons'. Even when the men interviewed had no income and only a tiny plot of land, most would still want

---

[32] Personal communication.

to have many children—even if they were also fully aware of the fact that they could not afford to educate them.

This raises the question of why so many husbands are reluctant to accept their wives' use of contraception. Modern contraception has opened up for women the same vista of sexual opportunities that had been available for men—at least in principle. Even if women do not make use of them men feel threatened. A man's identity is deeply rooted in his ability to control his wife's fertility. His identity and social value are also closely linked to having many children. Even if he is poor, has no authority and respect, a man feels even poorer and with less authority if he does not have many children (according to my interviews). On top of this he also gets social value by controlling his wife's fertility and sexuality. Consequently, my data suggest that even if a man cannot educate and feed his children, the ability to father many children may act as a compensation for lack of other prestige giving roles.

As to women, my data indicate that their expanded social and economic roles within the household do not put them in the same position as men. Moreover, women's importance is recognized at all levels, from government level down to the household level. While fertility is fundamental for a woman's identity and social value, a women does not need eight children to acquire social value. But if she gives birth to eight children a number of different reasons may be intertwined. As shown above, women may use their fertility strategically, particularly when bridewealth has not been paid. If so, women use their fertility as a weapon to gain or maintain control over their life situation, though under the present condition of deepening poverty this strategy may fail to provide the economic shelter that they are desperately trying to create.

Control over fertility—Who is in control?

Most literature on Sub-Saharan Africa maintains that, through marriage, men are in control of women's fertility and this means control over wives. Moreover, control of female fertility is inextricably linked to control of female sexuality (Caplan, 1987/91:24). Based on my Kisii data these seem to be half truths as it can be argued that women may be in control of their fertility precisely by their use or non-use of contraceptive methods.

Men's preoccupation with fertility made them want to control sexuality—not dominate women (Berman and Lonsdale, 1992:393). In Kisii men are preoccupied with fertility—both their own as well as that of their wives. They want to control the fertility of their wives and they also want to dominate her (including her fertility and sexuality). A man's social value and identity are deeply rooted in his ability to control his wife's fertility, and women's use of modern contraception is a challenge to male control and authority. But do men really control women's fertility?

Gusii men control women's fertility in the sense that it is through her fertility that a woman can get access to land. Men also exercise control over their wives fertility in that, if the wife wants sterilization, their signatures are still needed (at least theoretically—this practice is increasingly being dropped). But many women told me that they brought their brothers to sign—without their husband's knowledge. However, with the introduction of modern contraceptives, male control over female reproduction is modified. Contraception is a threat to male dominance and control. And many of the women using a contraceptive method, did so without their husband's knowledge. Men are very aware of this fact, and it makes them uncomfortable. Men fear that contraception makes their wives 'loose'. And a man with a 'loose' wife is one who has lost control over his wife's fertility and thus has lost social value.

Are women then in control of their fertility? According to my data women do not use a contraceptive method to limit their births. On the contrary: women use their fertility strategically: as a means of pressure when bridewealth is not paid; to avoid their husband taking a second wife; to see to it that he cannot afford it. Women's strengthened position within the household and the fact that their control has increased seem to act as a motivation for women to control their fertility one way or the other. According to a study in Uganda, many men feel that in terms of deciding on children, 'it is women's decision in the end' (Kirumira, 1995). I never heard any men in Kisii admitting this, though men may increasingly be faced with such a situation.

Conflicting fertility interests?

I argue along with Kopytoff, (1990) that it is an inherent feature in the existential identities of both women and men to have children. In his conversations with the Suku, Kopytoff argued that there emerged a kind of operational definition for existential identities and their inherent features. This definition rested on the form taken by explanations of a role's raison d'être. The simplest reason given for the fact that women bore children was that 'they are women'. The role of child bearer was seen as flowing directly from the woman's identity—out of her state of being a woman. The appeal to this existential identity constituted a crucial explanation for her role of child bearer; the statement was sufficient and nothing more need be said (Kopytoff, 1990:81). Few inherent roles were linked to the man or the woman qua existential identities. Among these, the one that loomed largest for a woman was childbearing—fundamental for female identity (1990:81). This is also the case in Kisii. The childbearing role is an inherent role for women, it is difficult to negotiate.

For a man it is a "natural" role to provide his wife with children. So it is to be a father. Thus the husband's pressure to use all the eggs in a woman's womb. The immanence of these roles for both men and women explains why men are against modern contraception when it comes to their own wives but readily accept it for their neighbour's wife. It also explains why many women, in spite of the burden of continuous pregnancies, still continue to give birth.

On the other hand, my data indicate that the "natural" role of childbearing may be changing slowly, particularly when it comes to women. In the Kisii example, new female social roles have clearly been emerging over the past decades. This could entail a new important sense of identity linked to women's social role is emerging, and—if not competing—then interacting with women's childbearing role. That 'biological facts' are increasingly being questioned and women have become interested in at least spacing their births, may suggest that women are prompted by difficult economic circumstances. It may also suggest that their social role as provider of the needs of the household (often solely responsible) is creating a new important sense of identity.

Men's increasingly ambiguous role as head of household, the fact that children are often cost free to men and men take their 'fertility responsibilities' lightly—(the majority not being concerned with *how* they perform their role as fathers)—may also explain not only conflicting fertility interests but also the hostilities and antagonism between the sexes.

Chapter 7
Sexuality, Identity and Social Value

Letter to AMANI: Daily Nation, August, 28, 1991
"Should I go on loving this man?"

Dear Amani,
My husband is unfaithful to me. My mother told me not to worry or think of leaving because she says that all men are promiscuous. Is this true?

Answer:
Much depends on what you mean by "promiscuous". The term means the compulsive seeking of sex from random partners. This compulsion is always based on feelings of low self-esteem and on anxiety related to an uncertain sense of identity. Promiscuity exists among men and women alike. The vast majority of people are not sexually driven and are not compulsively promiscuous. Of course, both men and women are capable of being attracted to any number of people. What they do about such attraction largely depends on individual values. Talk to your husband and remember—communication is the key between husband and wife.

Introduction

The relationship between gender, systems of prestige/social value and sex-related beliefs has not been totally overlooked in the anthropological literature. But most studies do not seem to have accomplished more than just adding another determinant of gender ideas to a long list of suggested determinants—a list that includes the productive system, inheritance, the dominant social ideology, cosmology, kinship organization, and the patterns of warfare (Ortner and Whitehead, 1981/89:13). A sex-gender system has been described as a set of arrangements by which a society transforms biological sexuality into products of human activity and in which these transformed needs are satisfied (Rubin, 1975:159). This definition has been widely quoted and used. A revision of this definition argued that it is essential to separate gender and sexuality analytically to more accurately reflect their separate social existence. But there is some doubt as to whether it is possible to separate gender and sexuality in non-western societies, since, in kinship-based societies, kinship shapes sexuality which is embedded in numerous other social relations. Ortner and Whitehead agree with this position, emphasizing that in such societies the power of social considerations override libidinal ones (Ortner and Whitehead, 1981/89:24).

Sexuality is here conceived as a cultural construct constituting the cornerstone of marriage, and as such marriage and sexuality are closely interrelated and particularly important for male prestige and social value. Moreover, social value and prestige are the domain of social structure that most directly affects cultural notions of gender and sexuality (1981/89:16). Most importantly, in relation to this study:

> For men ... although the issue of sexual control does not actually generate categories of masculinity, there is nonetheless a correspondence between status and sexual activity that is the inverse of the female system ... (1981/89:9)

While the emphasis on the correspondence between male status and male sexual activity—which is the inverse of the female system—seems particularly relevant in a Kisii context, the argument that sexual control does not actually generate categories of masculinity seems questionable, particularly in contemporary Kisii. But what happens when the institution of marriage is changing?

In this chapter I shall explore what sexuality *means* in Kisii today. When the institution of marriage is falling apart, how does this affect sexuality? Does the power of social considerations still override libidinal ones? Assuming that there is a correspondence between male status and sexual activity that is the inverse of the female system, how have social change and particular changing social roles affected this asymmetry? What are the present values attributed to sexuality by women and men? What are the consequences of sexuality for women and men respectively? Since social value is fundamental to women's and men's identity, self-esteem as well as gender relations , what does sexuality mean in terms of current male and female identity? With the emergence of HIV/AIDS, an understanding of the different sexual behaviour patterns of men and women and the norms and values pertaining to them has become increasingly urgent.

Sexuality in past and present times

What do we know about sexuality and social value in the past? Did social considerations override libidinal ones? With fairly limited sources dealing with sexuality in Kisii in precolonial times,[33] I shall start by suggesting that sexuality was to a much larger degree than today an activity kept within the framework of the homestead i.e. within the framework of the polygynous household, and surrounded by strict norms and values. The belief was—then as now—that there is a profound biological difference between women and men. Linked to this, morality in Kisii was gendered, just as the social value system was gendered. What was appropriate sexual behaviour for

---

[33] Based mainly on accounts by Robert and Barbara LeVine, 1966/77 and Sarah LeVine, 1979 as well as Iona Mayer, 1974.

men was and is certainly not appropriate for women—and vice versa. In addition, it was/is a morality in which virtue was at stake. Not men's virtue—but women's: in particular, that of a wife.

The description of the traditional morality of the Gusii by Iona Mayer does not directly address sexuality. But it 'situates' sexuality within the Gusii culture where the Gusii 'traditional' homestead represented a proto-typical moral order: one which involved a highly prescriptive organization of activities. This organization was viewed as the embodiment of the highest moral ideals and normative prescriptions by which Gusii were supposed to live. Restrictions regarding sexual modesty and respect represented a code of propriety which was effective throughout the clan, and which enforced incest rules, marital rights, respect for paternal authority etc. (Mayer, I., 1974). The 'code' words here are sexual modesty and respect.

Marital fidelity was enforced by beliefs in supernatural retribution. Adultery with a married woman was feared, in contrast to adultery with an unmarried woman. Since marriages were exogamous, single males avoided sexual relations with their clan girls for fear of incest. Masturbation was rare and highly stigmatised. Homosexuality was inconceivable. Bestiality was a sexual conduct which young boys resorted to, harmlessly, for their sexual debut (LeVine, R. and B., 1966/77). All these norms and values are also known today—though not observed.

As discussed above, traditionally, there was a certain permissiveness among adolescents. Premarital sex and discrete incomplete sex were permit-ted, provided that the female hymen was not broken and pregnancy did not occur. The traditional permissiveness was in stark contrast to the sexual control of women later in life. This is still the case in Kisii today. As long as women are not 'married' a certain amount 'promiscuity' is expected, if not accepted. The increasing number of pregnant adolescent girls today shows that, over the past 30–40 years, the curbs on female sexuality are no longer observed. Traditionally, during female initiation ceremonies, adolescent boys would sneak into houses where adolescent girls were sleeping and attempt to have intercourse with them. Some girls would succeed in brush-ing the boys off—or some boys would succeed in pursuing a hurried inter-course while the girl would often pretend to be sleeping. Even if such a practice was more or less condoned, if a boy made a girl pregnant this was considered a serious offence. Today, this is still so. But even if such promis-cuity is not accepted, it happens all the time, and not only in relation to the initiation ceremonies.

Male virginity was never an issue, and adolescent boys used to encour-age each other to conquer girls. Today, premarital or rather adolescent sex is expected and feared by many parents. In a study of the Kikuyu, it has been argued that, because 'institutionalized' permissiveness has disappeared, this has had a destabilizing effect on the regulation of premarital sex and mate selection (Ahlberg, 1991).

The traditional strict moral code did not interfere with the abduction of young marriageable girls against their will by young men—their friends or brothers—who would 'kidnap' a young woman and often 'help' the 'groom' to perform intercourse. Birisira (32 years old) whom I first met in 1984 told me that she had met Joseph when she was 18. One Sunday after church, Joseph, one of his brothers and a cousin convinced her to come for a visit to his home. In the afternoon, when Birisera wanted to leave, she was locked up in a hut with Joseph and she had to spend the night there together with him. Birisera was very upset. She knew that her parents would be very angry, and she was ashamed to go back to them. Nevertheless, the next morning she insisted on returning home. Joseph would not let her go. Instead he, the brother and the cousin took her to the house of Joseph's sister far away. The next eight days Joseph did what he could to make her pregnant—and he succeeded. Birisira's parents did not have much choice, and they agreed to her living with Joseph. Joseph turned out to be a good man. After 14 years of marriage he had succeeded in paying 7 of the promised 12 cows as bridewealth. By 1992, he had not paid additional cows, but he had bought a piece of land in Kitale. Every three months he went off for at least one month to look after his land. Birisira worried that he 'roamed' during his absences.

Colonialism, and following it male migration out of Kisii, started a process whereby sexuality took on other meanings, and sexuality was taken out of the homestead. Migrant husbands became used to having girlfriends and frequent prostitutes, or prostitutes were put at their disposal (White, 1990). Women started roaming. As a result, whereas sexuality had primarily been an activity within the homestead, sexuality was now taken out of the homestead.

Men, sexuality and identity

Polygyny, as mentioned above, used to be the norm, and a man would have from 2–4 wives. Some had up to 20 wives. Findings from the survey study indicate that only 10% of the women were second wives while 2% were third and fourth wives. Men like to boast about having many wives—and if not wives then girlfriends. Strangely enough, in my questionnaire survey, only three men said that they lived in 'legal' polygynous unions. It was not possible, though, to find out how many 'steady' girlfriends or unauthorized second or third wives men had.

In earlier times, polygyny permitted men to have sexual relations with several women, and men are not used to sexual abstinence. Consequently, men are very open about their sexual activity (except to their wives). Having relationships with more than one woman is a sign of virility and a way for men to demonstrate their maleness and their ability to 'manage'. Typical comments from men are: 'I do not remember how many women I have had sex with, but they were many'. Many claimed—or boasted—of having had 40–50 partners. 'If you cannot manage more than one woman—you are not a real man'. 'It is a man's right to misbehave'. A majority of men said that they had started their sexual activity at an early age, even at ten years old.

George, a medical officer, boasted of having had between 300–400 sexual relationships. He had been married to a school teacher for 4 years, and they had 2 children. Every time George went to Kisii hospital to pick up medicine for the health centre where he worked, he always stopped at one of the bars, where there were women around, and where rooms could be rented on a 2 hourly basis. In one afternoon, George could manage 5–6 women: 'as soon as I have finished with one, I feel that I need another one'. He was also interested in marrying a second wife, and he had already found one he was very keen on. When I asked him what this woman's particular attraction was, he said: 'she is a typist and she earns her own money'.

Thus, polygyny seems to have been replaced by promiscuity, and 'misbehaviour' is associated with maleness, virility and not being hen-pecked. 'Misbehaviour' is expected and tolerated, not only by wives—even if they disapprove—but also by the wider society. Sexual activity and status also seem to be closely related. Higher ranking or rather rich men—(whether they are already married or not) are certainly expected to have many girl-friends.[34] It is obvious, though, that poor men are unattractive, simply be-cause sexual services are considered a lucrative activity and girlfriends' al-ways expect some kind of economic benefit in return.

But there are 'mixed messages' and double standards: "If a man moves, he cannot raise his hand at the baraza'(if a man is promiscuous, he has no right to talk at community meetings), some would argue. On the other hand 'a man cannot be expected to stay with just one woman'. While a woman is not allowed to have intercourse with any other man than her husband, the husband is free to engage in extramarital sex—men and women agree on this. At the same time, men would often fear that 'if wives find husbands are moving they risk being poisoned by their wives'; 'sometimes men do not dare to take food from the wife's hand'. Men's infidelity, however, was not the most important issue of discussion among women. What upset women was that the men used their money on other women instead of paying school fees, clothes and food for the family.

The belief is that a man *needs* a lot of sex and a variety of sexual partners. Faithfulness is not an issue for men, as it is for women. There is a sense, conveyed more by men than women, that regular sex with a variety of part-ners is a man's right—a logical extension of the commonly held view that men are naturally polygynous (while women should be monogamous by nature). Men would point to the 'Gusii way' of polygynous marriage which they would use to justify their need—not to say right—to have regular sex

---

[34] In line with the observations of Ortner and Whitehead, 1981/89.

with a number of partners. Men who migrate to town without their wives take it for granted that they will have sexual liaisons in town. And wives resign themselves to this.

Thus, there is a strong tendency for men to redefine polygyny into a situation of one 'legal' or rather 'official' wife—to whom they have a variety of long-term socio-economic responsibilities, at least in principle—combined with a number of relationships for whom they have only short term responsibilities or even shorter term commercialized sexual relationships. A very interesting comment (excuse) from men—legitimizing their extramarital affairs—is that 'wives are not nice to you'; 'they turn the back to you in bed'; 'wives are not affectionate'.

Men, potency and contraception

'How an amazon woman can make a man impotent' (Headlines in *Daily Nation*, May 27, 1990).

As mentioned in the previous chapter, men are greatly concerned with their potency, and impotence is a serious concern of many men. Impotent men are said to be deserted by their wives, and a man who is confronted with such a misfortune usually spends most of his property trying to cure himself. Impotence, just as infertility, is considered a curse from the ancestral spirits, a curse of a father on his disobedient son, a curse inflicted on people by elders as a result of serious criminal offences or the taking of false oaths in which the ancestral spirits have been called as witnesses. If the spirits are content with sacrifices, they can withdraw their punishment. Impotence is not considered a medical matter. Even if it were so, it is not a condition that could be treated by the local health services. If the infliction is caused by witchcraft, which is a commonly held belief, this can be cured by medicine men or by contacting diviners who can give advice on what to do.

Sexual offences

Kisii is renowned in Kenya for the high incidence of rape, despite sexual prudishness and maintaining strict sexual prohibitions in many areas of life. By local and cross-cultural standards, Kisii had a very high frequency of rape already in the 1940s (LeVine, R., 1959). Today, women are scared to walk alone after dark, but also during the day. Even my female assistants felt insecure about walking around on their home visits. If the maize fields were dense, they insisted on wearing their uniforms (as 'institutional' protection) and always paid their visits together with another assistant. During my many stays in Kisii, rape seemed to be an almost daily phenomenon.

Socialization of sex is strict and repressive concerning public manifestations of sexuality. But it is relatively permissive concerning clandestine sexual acts. But this was predicated on the existence of enforcement procedures

(inter-clan feuding) that had broken down during the British colonial administration. At the beginning of the 50s the strict sex-training practices did
nothing to prevent inter-clan sex offences and could even be seen as promot-
ing rape by raising the average level of male sexual frustration and making
females resistant to heterosexual advances. Hence, the paradox of an ethnic
group notorious for both its prudery and its sex crimes (1959: 130).

An extremely conservative estimate of the annual rate of rape, based on
court records for 1955 and 1956, was 47.2 per 100,000 population (1959:336–
57; 1959:965–990). LeVine defines rape as 'the culturally disvalued use of co-
ercion by a male to achieve the submission of a female to sexual intercourse',
and he traces the genesis of this problem to four factors:

– institutional forms of sex antagonism

– traditional and contemporary limitations on premarital sexuality

– the differing motivation of rapists and

– the role of bridewealth in delaying marriages

As mentioned above, Gusii people were traditionally organized in exogamous clans which had a history of hostilities and blood feuds between
themselves. Marriages were therefore contracted among members of alien
and unfriendly groups. Based on this, LeVine concludes that there are
sadomasochistic aspects of Gusii nuptial and marital sexuality. For example,
on the wedding night the bride is expected to resist the groom's sexual advances as a measure of her innocence. A man on his part takes pride in
hurting his wife as a demonstration of his sexuality. In addition, men also
have an exaggerated expectation of sexual performance, demanding coitus
at least twice a night. Men's sadistic sexual behaviour should be seen in
relation to their experiences at the time of circumcision, when they are
visited by naked girls who dance and take pleasure in teasing and arousing
them at a time when they are incapable of coitus. Most Gusii men think that
the girl's ceremonial behaviour is intended to cause pain.[35] The girls have
their triumph if a resulting erection causes the partly-healed wound to burst
open with acute pain to the novice. According to LeVine, such institutionalized forms of sex antagonism lead to legitimate heterosexual encounters
often involving force and pain, which under other circumstances could
easily be construed as rape.

The high level of bridewealth—in the form of cows—has also been
identified as a factor in Gusii sex offences. The men marry at a relatively ad-
vanced age since they cannot afford to buy cattle. Meanwhile they elope or
rape. This leads LeVine to conclude that it is likely that the high rate of rape
indictments is in part a function of the economic barrier to the marriage of
young men which excessive bridewealth entails.

---

[35] LeVine here cites Philip Mayer.

Whether this argument is justifiable or not, I will not discuss here. I shall limit myself to the question of why rape still figures prominently in Kisii. With increasing elopements and no bridewealth—rape does not seem to have decreased. This, combined with the near disappearance of lengthy postpartum sexual abstinence, should have greatly reduced not only rape but also male demand for non-marital sex and hence the degree of sexual networking (promiscuity). However, this has not happened. I shall discuss this in more detail. But first I shall look at women, identity and sexuality.

Women, sexuality and identity

Just as it is an inherent role for a man to have exclusive sexual rights over his wife, be potent and provide her with children, it is an inherent role of a woman to provide the husband with children and sex. 'A woman should always be ready anytime the husband wants it'. 'It is a woman's duty to be ready whenever the husband is ready'.

A woman, though, should never initiate sexual intercourse with her husband. Women were never to take an active part in the sexual act—which is customary among many other tribes—and customarily they should always make a token objection before yielding to their husband's advances. A Woman who takes the sexual initiative lacks the proper sexual inhibition and, both sexes agree, 'husbands will believe that their wives have been roaming'.

A general observation by women was that 'husbands need sex several times during the night—and even during the day with the children around', and 'husbands want sex right after a woman has given birth, and if women are stubborn men just go to Kisii town' (to find a prostitute). The prescribed time for resuming marital relations after giving birth is 6 weeks according to health staff in Kisii. In our survey, a majority of women say that they resumed marital relations after one week—or the husband would go to other women. 'In no relationship does a woman perceive herself as more victimized than in a sexual one' (LeVine, S., 1979:362).

In my qualitative interviews, surprisingly many women expressed frustration in relation to 'playing sex' with husbands, and a recurrent complaint of women was that it was painful for them to have intercourse. As one woman put it 'men nowadays do not know how to treat their wives; they do not understand that a woman's body is like a shamba: first you prepare, then you wait for rain—then you can plant'.

My health worker assistants told me that major complaints from women were that 'most men do not know how to play sex'. As Clementhia said 'I keep telling James, don't behave like a cock'. It has been noted that the sexuality of many African women is seldom realized through the sex act: 'the fact that most patriarchal societies taught young women how to please the man during coitus does not necessarily mean that women were taught to get pleasure out of sex in their own right' (McPhadden, 1992:179–180). However, according to the literature on Kisii and the information that I have been able to acquire, Gusii women are not taught to give men pleasure either. They are taught to resist men's approaches and not show much interest and initiative. Some husbands complained and said that 'having sex with a wife is sometimes like having sex with a dead body'.

In their study LeVine and LeVine quote some interesting remarks from a 36-year old husband. The husband asks his wife

> What do you feel? Don't you think it's good? The wife says, Don't ask me that'. She will never say yes. When the woman cries and protests during intercourse you are very excited .. We are always mystified as to whether women enjoy it. But the wives in polygynous homesteads complain when their husbands neglect them, so they must like it (LeVine, R. and B., 1966/77:54).

However, women's resistance is not necessarily a conventional pose or an attempt to arouse their husbands. It could be both but I suggest that there is good reason to believe that the reluctant sexual pose of Gusii wives is not always feigned. Many Gusii wives have a sincere desire to avoid coitus (LeVine, R., 1959:970).

I often heard the remark—by women as well as men—that women do not like to be neglected by their husbands. And again 'men create jealousy among women'. From most women's point of view, though, it is not a matter of emotional neglect but rather 'if a wife refuses her husband, he spends money on other women'. This seems to be a major reason why women complain if they are neglected. In polygynous unions, women are often extremely jealous of each other. They fight over resources for their sons and they compete in making themselves sexually available in order not to be neglected materially. Traditionally, and as mentioned above, women had several sanctions against their husbands, provided bridewealth was paid. Today these sanctions have disappeared to a certain extent. However, women do use their sexuality to negotiate and bargain. And one type of sanction against husbands is to refuse sexual services: 'a woman can be very stubborn'.

But not only women are victimized. Poor men with no income have also become increasingly dependent on their wives for sex. From that point of view, women exercise considerable power, and many 'do what they can to undermine a man's self-confidence'—according to male health workers. Men's sexual performance is questioned, and women complain not only about painful intercourse: 'so many men cannot function'; 'when men drink too much they keep wives awake all the night because they cannot perform'; 'women get exhausted—when they have to get up early'. Others (as I experienced when weeding with a group of women) were giggling over husbands' 'difficulties'. They slapped their thighs and laughed, using the whole morning to exchange among themselves stories about their husbands' difficulties. Again this is precisely where women exercise their power over men, and men lose face if it becomes known that they do not 'perform' well. 'A man who does not perform well brings shame to his ancestors'.

The 'performance' of women is not questioned in the same way. Women, though, seem to be in a very ambiguous situation. On the one hand, they are expected to be passive and reluctant, on the other, a general complaint from husbands is their wives' passivity, and many claim that this is a reason for their need to have girlfriends. Luo prostitutes in Kisii town are very much in demand. 'They really know how to play sex', I was told in confidence by several men. Luo women are not clitoridectomized—and from the point of view of Gusii women, Luo women are uncivilized and promiscuous. But no Gusii man would want an uncircumcised woman as his wife.

If Kisii women are not affectionate enough—as many men complain—the same certainly applies to men. And there are ample reasons for lack of emotional warmth between spouses. Given the rough and unaffectionate way children are raised in Kisii, Gusii women might be uncomfortable with any activity directed toward pleasure rather than some specific utilitarian goal—because they were never confronted with affection (LeVine, S. and R., 1981:53). Babies that are given little affection soon learn to protect themselves by adopting a 'low profile' (1981:53). That mothers remain aloof must be the result of a number of factors: for example, a reluctance to spend valuable time in play when so many domestic tasks await their attention, and a perception that playful behaviour, in and of itself, is not appropriate to the maternal role. If this is the reason why women are not affectionate, the same may be applicable to men.

So a wife cannot be a respectable woman if she is not faithful to her husband. A woman's respectability is first of all linked to her sexual behaviour. A woman's sexual behaviour determines to a large extent her social value. It is decisive for her attraction in the marriage market and determines her possibilities of becoming a respectable wife and mother. If female premarital virginity is losing its importance, fidelity within marriage is not. Among other things, it determines the social position of men as husbands.

The case of Josephine is rather special and contradictory. She was very much respected in her village. Her livelihood came from brewing *changaa*. She 'serviced' the village with her much appreciated high quality *changaa*. She was around 40 years of age and had six children, two of them in secondary school. Her husband lived in Nairobi, and came home about once a year. Everybody knew that he did not pay school fees for the children, and it was entirely through *changaa* brewing that Josephine on her own was able to send her two oldest children to secondary school. And she was given credit for that. It was said that she sometimes had to be 'nice' to her clients and that she had occasional 'visitors', but the fact that she raised the children on her own and succeeded well, overshadowed the fact that her 'respectability' could be questioned.

But who are the women that men "move" with? To move with married women is not without difficulties but takes place increasingly. Theresa had ended up making herself available to anybody who offered her a jug of *busaa* because she was hungry. 'Unmarried women make themselves available', 'married' women complain. 'Divorced' women and young unmarried women often seem to make themselves available when searching either for a husband or money, believing in the myth that women are in surplus and at the risk of being called prostitutes. It gives prestige to have a wealthy 'boyfriend', and it is extremely easy for a man to have a number of 'dedicated' girlfriends—that is if he is 'generous'—'gives them a ride in his car' and provides them with 'creams and other female necessities' as one sophisticated 'mistress' put it. Even if wives do not expect their husbands to zero graze (be faithful), they feel extremely threatened by the husband's girlfriends. Not from an emotional point of view, but simply because they know that mistresses are costly.

In the past, being a second wife was not desirable, though it was the only option for a woman who had already given birth illegitimately. Now, however, new trends are emerging. As one young unmarried woman told me (and as confirmed by Helen above) 'I prefer to become the second wife of a rich man than the first wife of a poor man. As second wife of a rich man I will have enough to eat for myself and my children but as the first wife of a poor fellow I will have to struggle to make ends meet'.

Sexual behaviour and AIDS

In Kisii in the late 1980s, AIDS was not a subject of debate. Some people had heard about AIDS, but it was not at all a matter of concern. Malaria and other diseases were a matter of much greater concern. At Kisii District Hospital methods for diagnosing AIDS were inadequate, and when I inquired at the hospital I was told that only about a hundred cases had been identified as AIDS. The medical personnel, though, suspected that many more had died from AIDS in Kisii. While gonorrhoea and other venereal diseases are very well known and frequently treated in local dispensaries, they were seldom discussed in public. However, people had started talking about an increasing number of people suffering from serious weight loss. Some had died from 'mysterious cancer', 'tuberculosis'—or what some expected was witchcraft.

In 1992, AIDS was being talked about much more openly. An increasing number of people had died, and they all had the same symptoms. Most people seemed to know somebody who had died from AIDS. There were of course no statistics but according to the local gynaecologist 30% of his clients were infected with HIV, and about 30% of the sexually active population in

Kisii was HIV positive.[36] My health assistants and many other women were terrified. Many of their friends had died; particularly women. This is because, for biological reasons, women are more vulnerable to infection than are men. Medical personnel tend to focus on the symptoms of the disease as manifested in men—mouth ulcers, tuberculosis, weight loss—while the gendered symptoms of the disease in women, such as persistent vaginal thrush and genital ulcers are often assumed to be symptoms of curable sexually transmitted diseases. This means that there is a strong tendency to overlook the fact that women develop other symptoms than men. In addition, while HIV is a virus affecting both genders, rich and poor, it is those who have least access to information, to choices, the health services, and to the right to make critical decision, who are the easiest victims of the disease. Poor women and children are the most prone to HIV (McPhadden, 1992:158). Men complain that women are not affectionate. But it is frequently women's fear and anxiety linked to AIDS that makes them less sexually responsive. Women's' attitude is in great contrast with the high risk character of male sexual behaviour. The concept of zero-grazing introduced recently refers to no grazing outside the household. The men that I spoke to agreed that it was probably a good idea—but not for them. Considering the state of women's sexual and reproductive health, which has seriously deteriorated over the past decades and resulted in a new sexual and reproductive government health strategy,[37] men may fear that the Kenyan government—in collaboration with donors—will try to interfere with their sexual behaviour.

George, the medical officer, was very well aware of AIDS and he confessed that recently, when he had been 'playing sex' with various girlfriends, he had been a little worried. As a man of some education, he had now started using not only one condom but two (and sometimes even three). His girlfriends, however, were highly dissatisfied, and he was now considering the possibility of returning to the use of only one condom.

Adultery in the past and today

'A man cannot commit adultery. Only women can slip'.

Adultery in Kisii has different meanings for men and for women. In fact, the term 'adultery' is not applicable to a man. 'A man cannot commit adultery' men say—with the modification 'unless he has a relationship with another man's wife'. Relationships with unmarried women do not count as adultery.

---

[36] Personal communication.

[37] According to the strategy adopted at the International Conference on Population and Development, Cairo, 1994.

But women can commit adultery—though they are certainly not supposed to, and many dangers are connected to female adultery.

Adultery by a woman was, when discovered, was a very serious offence. Apart from disgracing the husband, his family and the woman's own family, it was dangerous for the husband to eat food prepared by her. He could even die from it. Moreover, female adultery was said to affect pregnancy, and it was thought that adulterous women would have difficulties in conceiving or risk continuous miscarriages. If a woman committed adultery after she had already born children, they might die. They would all die eventually, unless she confessed and went through a cleansing ceremonial, the 'amasangia'. If a woman had continuous miscarriages she was asked to confess to adultery or she would never give birth (even if she had not committed adultery). If she refused to confess, the husband would go to the diviner, who would reveal everything to him. The woman was then asked to reveal the name of the man with whom she had committed adultery, otherwise the cleansing could not be performed.

The 'amasangia' was performed by the village elders, the husband's parents, the husband, the adulterous wife and the man with whom she had committed the offence. A goat was sacrificed, and the woman was asked to confess in the presence of everybody, calling the ancestral spirits as her witnesses. She had to tell exactly how many times and where she had committed adultery. Following this, she, the husband and the lover had to remove all their clothes, remain naked in the middle of the hut and stand closely together. One of the elders then passed a basket filled with beer first to the husband, then to the lover. Both had to drink from the same basket. Then a piece of meat was cut from the goat and passed to the three of them. As they had been sharing the same woman, now they had to share beer and meat in front of the parents and the elders. The woman was then to swear that she would never again have anything to do with her lover—or any other man except her husband. The lover had to do the same. To seal this promise the adulterous man had to go down on his knees and creep through the woman's legs. 'If the man enters between that woman' thighs again, he will die'. Then the elders and all present sipped beer and spat it on the naked woman and her lover to show that they had witnessed the confession. If they disobeyed, the ancestral spirits would impose a more serious punishment.

Though an increasing number of women 'move' with other men today, female adultery is profoundly feared by husbands: 'if your wife behaves like a prostitute, you may even die from the food she cooks for you', I was told by many worried men. In terms of present 'coping mechanisms' if a wife has 'slipped' and in case a husband had decided not to chase his wife or kill her—I was given the following version which according to my informant had taken place 'just the other day' (in 1992):

> If your wife has "gone astray", she has to bring a white cock and prepare it for
> eating. Then husband and wife have to make an incision (with a razor blade) on

the lower back just above the buttocks, mix the blood and suck it. The head of the wife is shaven with the same razor blade, a bird's nest is placed on the wife's head and fire is put to the nest. When it has burnt down she can be accepted by the husband.

Sexuality and social value

It is too shameful for a man if his wife moves with other men. Some will kill, others will even commit suicide. (A Kisii woman interviewed.)

The 'honour-shame' concept—frequently used in Latin American and Mediterranean contexts—is intimately bound up with female sexual behaviour (Peristiany, 1965; Brandes, 1981; Archetti, 1988). In societies where concepts of honour and shame are deeply embedded, repercussions of sexual behaviour affect others than those immediately involved, and there are fundamental asymmetries. Male sexual behaviour is not 'controlled' whereas female sexuality and female sexual behaviour are strictly controlled by men. Traditionally, the honour of a man is involved in the sexual purity of his mother, wife and daughters and sisters, not in his own (Archetti, 1988:10). There is a correspondence between status and sexual activity that is the inverse of the female system in which female sexual activity has very negative connotations (Ortner and Whitehead, 1981/89:9, 12, 16). Furthermore, sexuality is fundamental for male existential identity (Kopytoff, 1990:83).

My interest in the 'honour and shame' debate is prompted by the fact that men in Kisii are increasingly preoccupied with women's sexual behaviour and the control of it. Women's sexuality represents an active and threatening power, and male reputation depends on female sexual conduct. Men are vulnerable to the capacity of women to bring 'shame' upon them. A man's honour, his masculinity, his reputation is severely affected if he cannot 'make her stay away from other men'. When men are not successful in this, their prestige in the society is diminished and they lose honour. Honour is not only the value of a person in his own eyes, but also in the eyes of society (Pitt-Rivers in Goddard, 1987/91:167). Male honour and sexual control in Kisii, though, are not so much linked to the virginity and protection of young girls as in Catholic or Islamic cultures, but rather to the chastity of their wives. Thus, wives, and women as potential wives, pose the greatest threat to men, the family and to the social order. Female fertility is the socially essential productive and reproductive powers of womanhood and the threatening, potentially destructive nature of female power and sexuality (Moore, 1986:113). Thus, male honour is intimately bound up with the behaviour of the wife.

A wife's infidelity threatens the moral reputation of her entire family. But it affects no one so profoundly as her cuckolded husband (Brandes, 1981). If men are socially superior to women, and throughout all stages of life actually enjoy a good deal more freedom of action than do women, why do they then often portray themselves ideologically as potentially vulnerable and weak, and women as hostile and aggressive? Why do they assume a psychologically defensive position, when their appropriate behavioural role is assertive? (1981:234) But is male fear of women's sexuality a projection? Do men attribute to women motives that they themselves may hold? Men believe that women constantly crave men, even though there is little in female words or deeds to confirm their opinion. Moreover, men complain about being tied down to a single wife and to family obligations. Do men project their own feelings onto their wives thereby helping to alleviate whatever guilt those feelings might evoke? Is that why female purity and fidelity must be maintained at all costs? (1981:235) However, my data suggest that Gusii women do not crave men sexually (though some men may have that fear). What women crave are responsible husbands. And while the 'conquering' of women seems to have become increasingly important for the self-esteem of men, women's self-esteem is not linked to the 'conquering' of men. Women want husbands who pay bridewealth. That is important for their self-esteem and social value.

In order, though, to put the present Kisii honour-shame notions in a wider perspective I shall first argue that for a Gusii man to defend his own (and his family's honour), wives must preserve their purity i.e. they must not be loose. Men's relationship to honour can therefore be said to involve an active role, whereas the role of women in the theatre of honour is a passive one. The code of honour is associated with self-defence against encroachment from the outside, and men are projected into an active role, the role of defender, controller and aggressor (Goddard, 1987/91:171). Gusii men seem to identify with such a role—and they respond with 'ultra-male' behaviour. Honour and shame are crucial elements in small scale societies where face to face relations are dominant. The total social personality of the individual is relevant for social interaction, and domestic behaviour and reputation and honour in the wider society are particularly important in situations where political and economic activities are based on trust. (Peristiany , 1965). In Kisii a man's reputation is a central resource, and how a man behaves within his family and his ability to protect it, certainly provides a guide to his reliability and effectiveness in the public sphere.

In all the above studies, 'machismo' (the quality of being 'macho') is an underlying concept. 'Machismo' is defined as the cult of virility characterized by aggressiveness and intransigence in male-to-male interpersonal relationships, and by arrogance and aggression in male-to-female relationships (Stölen, 1990). Machismo describes both the ideology, the man and his acts— the virile, sexually aggressive, fearless and even violent man. It underpins and renders comprehensible men's sexual violence against and exploitation of women in order to achieve social value (Melhuus, 1991:5). But it is also related to male grief and alienation. This links up with the complaints by frustrated Gusii men: 'wives can be very stubborn nowadays'; 'they do not give a husband what he needs'; 'they turn the back to you in bed'; 'women know how to hurt a man's self confidence'.

Though a number of authors argue that the 'machismo syndrome' is only fully developed in Latin America, both the concept of honour-shame and the concept of machismo are illuminating in a Kisii context. They throw light on male behaviour and contribute explanations to clarify why the relations between the sexes in Kisii are so tense and aggressive. Though there may be cultural variations between Kisii, Latin American or Mediterranean communities, there seem to be common characteristics. To my knowledge, 'honour-shame' or 'machismo' have not been debated in studies of East Africa.

It has been argued that men's preoccupation with fertility made them want to control sexuality—not dominate women (Lonsdale in Berman and Lonsdale, 1992:393). However, I would suggest—on the basis of the honour/shame/ machismo debate—that this argument is highly questionable in a Kisii context. Gusii men are preoccupied with fertility—both their own and that of their wives. They want to control the fertility of their wives and they also want to dominate both her fertility and her sexuality. It is a question of honour. It is a question of social value. It is a question of identity.

> Sex is one of the most basic human activities, bringing us closest to other members of the animal world in its commonality as well as in its essentially instinctive nature. The biological component of sexual need is generally overlooked or underplayed, because humans would like to emphasise their unique characteristics of choice and decision-making. But both these elements exist at much lower levels of development among all animals, so that even among the least developed of the animal species, sex is not completely random. Among human beings however, the sexual act is not simply for the purpose of reproducing the species. Over past millennia, sex has assumed a complex and varied character, impacted upon by culture, custom, norms of behaviour, morals and by the commoditisation process (McPhadden, 1992:167).

As demonstrated in this chapter, sexuality is an integral part of female and in particular male identity—both on a personal and a social level. Sexual relations in Kisii, however, are not relations between two equal partners. They are based on social and cultural norms and values; and closely related to control over women.

Extreme male control over female sexuality in cattle societies is widely documented in the literature (LeVine, R. and B., 1966/77; Gluckman cited in Caldwell, 1990:12). As Kisii was a cattle society female sexuality was strictly controlled—at least in principle. Today, Kisii can hardly be called a cattle society any longer, but male control over female sexuality is still there—perhaps even stronger than before. In cultures in which affinal role definitions and emphasis on female sexuality dominate the notions of femininity, women are generally viewed and treated with less respect than cultures where women are construed largely as kin. Thus, women in roles with a major sexual component are more easily seen as different kinds of 'natural' beings than men, whereas kinswomen are more easily seen simply as different social actors. Consequently, cultures in which kinship definitions of womanhood are dominant vis-à-vis sexual and marital definitions appear to be more sex-egalitarian and less sex-antagonistic than cultures in which the opposite is the case (Ortner, 1981:23). As shown above, Gusii kinship definitions of womanhood *do not have* hegemony over sexual and marital definitions, and Kisii society is therefore not sex-egalitarian. However, this raises another question: when having a wife is the prerequisite to full adult male status, and marriage and sexuality are inextricably linked, in particular, for male prestige and social value, what happens then to sexuality and sexual control when the institution of marriage is breaking down as is the case in Kisii?

As demonstrated in this chapter, a man's identity is deeply rooted in his ability to control his wife, and his 'honour' is intimately bound up with the behaviour of his wife. With increasing land shortage, poverty, unemployment, with women's access to modern contraception—at least in principle—male role-based and existential identities are threatened. Linked to this, my data indicate that violent (sexual) 'macho' behaviour, even rape, seems to have become men's strategies in their pursuit of control, identity, self-esteem and social value. Male sexual activity does generate categories of masculinity. Because of lack of social roles and role-based identities coupled with lack of respect from women, my data seem to indicate that sexual control over women has become even more important to male existential identity and social value. According to Kopytoff, a man's identity is closely linked to his (culturally defined) sexuality: it is an immanent (inherent) feature of his existential identity which cannot be negotiated. This argument is greatly supported by my own findings. Kopytoff, however, stops here and does not deal with questions of male sexual activity as a compensation for loss or lack of other role-based and existential identities. That is a central issue, which needs further investigation.

In a study of the cultural construction of sexuality in Jamaica, it has been observed that, when men (as well as women) do not have any status-giving economic roles then sexuality becomes an important alternative to the creation of an identity. With the collapse of many traditional structures, including polygyny, and the disappearance of former male roles, male sexuality and male sexual control over women seem to have become an alternative to the generation of a new identity and male self-esteem.

While it gives social value to men to be in control of female sexuality, it also gives social value to women to submit to sexual control. Although an analysis of honour from a female perspective has been totally absent in the literature, Gusii women certainly also have a system, if not of honour, then of self-appraisal and self-esteem in terms of sexual behaviour. This system is related to their judgement not only of others—but also of themselves. Moreover, women are actively trying to shape their own lives. Linked to this it is tempting to suggest that men's anxieties not only reflect that they cannot totally control women, but also represent a recognition of women's oppression at the hands of men, an oppression which women are likely to want to overthrow. Women in Kisii may not openly have the ambition to attain command and liberty. They may not openly wish to change 'the order of nature'—but by means of manipulation they may attempt to do so.

Women may also bring disgrace by wilfully going against the rules. They have the capacity to provoke crises precisely through their sexuality. It is because of an awareness of the danger of the capacity of women to break the rules that it is thought that they must be controlled (MacCormack and Draper, 1987:146).

While it gives social value to men to be in control of female sexuality, it also gives social value to women to submit to sexual control. Although an analysis of honour from a female perspective has been totally absent in the literature, Gusii women certainly also have a system, if not of honour, then of self-appraisal and self-esteem in terms of sexual behaviour. This system is related to their judgement not only of others—but also of themselves. Moreover, women are actively trying to shape their own lives. Linked to this it is tempting to suggest that men's anxieties not only reflect that they cannot totally control women, but also represent a recognition of women's oppression at the hands of men, an oppression which women are likely to want to overthrow. Women in Kisii may not openly have the ambition to attain command and liberty. They may not openly wish to change 'the order of nature'—but by means of manipulation they may attempt to do so.

Women may also bring disgrace by wilfully going against the rules. They have the capacity to provoke crises precisely through their sexuality. It is because of an awareness of the danger of the capacity of women to break the rules that it is thought that they must be controlled (Goddard, 1987/91: 190). However, this being said, with the existing norms and values pertaining to male and female sexuality and behaviour, women—in spite of their 'capacities' and in spite of the fact that they seem to have acquired control and even power in other spheres of their lives—seem to be at the mercy of men when it comes to their sexual relations. Women may be able to control their fertility, but in their sexual relations women are exposed and victimized—much more than in any other relationship.

Chapter 8

Gender Antagonism, Social Value and Identities

Introduction

A main objective of this study has been to come to grips with the reasons for the antagonistic and aggressive relations between women and men in Kisii today. The underlying theme of the study has been that socio-economic transformations in Kisii have been even harsher for men than for women and that female identity and self-esteem have been strengthened whereas male identity and self-esteem have weakened. A main hypothesis has been that social values linked to men and male identity have become more complex and contradictory than those linked to female identity.

Let us assume that social value is fundamental to women's and men's identity, self-esteem as well as to gender relations. Further, that social value is the part of social structure that most directly affects cultural notions of gender and sexuality. Hence the concept of social value developed by Ortner and Whitehead has been an important key to understanding the construction of gender and gender relations. In addition, concepts of identity, in particular those of Igor Kopytoff, have been another set of important keys in developing a more sophisticated understanding of the dynamics of gender identity in Kisii and the implications for the relations between men and women. None of the above authors deal with issues of antagonism between the sexes. However, their concepts have provided important tools for understanding the underlying reasons for the antagonistic relations between Gusii men and women.

Findings

Colonialism and socio-economic change had profound implications for male and female social roles, social value and identities. Traditional male activities closely linked to men's identities disappeared. Men became migrant workers and often lived under humiliating circumstances in their new surroundings. In this process, they became marginalized from the rural household. New social values emerged and men's social role became closely associated with contributing financially to the needs of the household. This new role had no place in the Kisii value system. Women's new social role as daily managers and often sole supporters of the household was not in contradiction to the traditional image of the 'entrepreneurial and strong woman'.

Women's active response to their new situation seems to have strengthened their identity and social value. A new situation emerged which did not conform to traditional gender roles, norms and values. This had fundamental consequences not only for male and female gender identity but also for the relations between the sexes.

The ritual of circumcision had a fundamental but also very contradictory role in the construction of role-based and existential gender identities and social value. Crucially, the ritual emphasizes more social roles, identities and responsibilities for men than for women with women's roles much more narrowly defined. Moreover, the ritual has very strong sexual connotations with different values for women and men. The emphasis of the female ritual is on control of female sexuality. Women are circumcised because their sexuality must be controlled: contrary to that of men. Women, though, are also circumcised in order for them to control not only their own sexuality (and fertility) but also that of men, because 'men cannot control themselves'. As the female initiation ritual allows women to mock men and to protest against male (sexual) control, initiation 'messages' are contradictory. This has implications for the relations between the sexes.

All features of marriage are under redefinition—and renegotiation. Marriage is increasingly being replaced by cohabitation and no bridewealth transfer. With male social value deeply involved in cross-sex relations, and the cross-sex bond most critical to a man's social standing being marriage, the emergence of cohabitation has a negative impact on male social value. The impact on women is even more severe. Women's access to her husband's land is insecure, their social value becomes questionable, and female existential identity and self-esteem are seriously affected. Women, however, are actively manoeuvring and manipulating in their daily lives in order to stabilize their position within the household. This leads to continuous negotiations between the sexes.

The pattern developed during colonialism has continued. The traditional complementarity between men and women has disappeared. While male migration has become insignificant, men's role as head of household has become closely associated with economic responsibility. A provider/breadwinner ideology has emerged and a new type of social value system has emerged whereby men's social value is most readily measured in economic terms. With land shortage and economic pressure, there is a greater need for both genders to contribute to the upkeep of the household, and from this point of view their interdependence has increased. Faced with unemployment and with a general tendency for men to use whatever (irregular) income they may have on investments outside the household (often on alcohol and girlfriends), deference and respect from wives are decreasing. Men's roles are becoming peripheral, and their authority as head of household is increasingly challenged. In this situation male social value and role-based and existential identities are also under threat. In contrast, as daily shamba(farm) managers, traders trying to make ends meet etc., women's role-based identities and self-esteem increase. As a majority of men do not identify with their breadwinner role and seem to have 'internalized' and accepted their increasingly marginalized social role, tensions and negotiations have become daily phenomena adding to the escalating antagonism between the sexes.

Fertility and children are fundamental for male and female existential identities and social value. With a lack of prestigious social roles, it seems to have become particularly important for male existential identity and social value to have descendants (sons) to commemorate them in the ancestor cult and also to control female fertility. With the emergence of cohabitation, no bridewealth transfer and men tending not to shoulder the costs of children, fertility interests often differ. Women have developed many fertility strategies and are, with contraceptives, in control of their fertility. The fact is that If women have access to modern contraception (at least in theory) this, in combination with conflicting male and female fertility interests, presents a threat to male control and contributes to the tense relations between the sexes.

Women and their sexuality represent an active and threatening power to male existential identity, social value and 'honour'. Thus, as women, they acquire power over men. However, there are different norms and values linked to male and female sexuality, sexual behaviour, social value and identity. A man's identity, self confidence and social value are closely linked to his sexuality and his sexual control over women. This is an inherent and non-negotiable feature of his existential identity. Given the loss of social roles (including that of a polygynist), 'ultra' male sexual behaviour (including violence) and sexual networking (promiscuity) outside the household seem to compensate for the loss of role-based identities and social value. In spite of the fact that women have acquired control and even power in other spheres of their lives they are exposed and victimized in their sexual relations—much more than in any other relationship. All these factors exacerbate the already antagonistic relations between the sexes.

Gender antagonism, social value and role-based and existential identities

The antagonistic relations between the sexes are closely related to the exogamous structure of Kisii society. The Gusii have always been exogamous, and the relations between the sexes have always been antagonistic (LeVine, R. and B., 1966/77:184). Men married women from other clans (and for these women it was often a traumatic experience to be removed from their place of birth) in order to stabilize relations to potential enemies. Men would say 'we marry those we fight'.

Now, LeVine and LeVine take sex antagonism as almost axiomatic—a given—as if it was an inherent characteristic of the relationship between men and women. They also stress that interpersonal hostility and the insufficient training of children in positive responses to others are inherent characteristics (1966/77:196). There is a particularly close association between sex and aggression. Coitus is as an act in which a man overcomes the resistance of a woman and causes her pain. This act/behaviour is not limited to the wedding night but continues to be important in marital relations (1966/77:54).

Today, fights between clans have been stopped. Men no longer marry or cohabit with 'those they fight'. I suggest that antagonism is neither a given nor inherent feature in the relations between Gusii men and women. However, this being said, my study shows that antagonism still seems fundamental to the relations between the genders. Gusii men fight those they marry—and women fight back tooth and nail. Antagonism even seems to be steadily increasing. However, the premises on which men and women fight are no longer the same. The antagonism is based on a different set of reasons than before.

Based on my theoretical approach, it has become clear that it is not socio-economic change per se which has provoked the antagonistic relations, but rather some more complex and obscure reasons. These are linked to changing and contradictory male and female social roles, and new social values which have affected the identities of both sexes profoundly—but also very differently. Thus, a combination of economic pressure, changing or contradictory social roles (or lack of same) and new norms and values which are given different priority by men and women, have forced the sexes into more confrontation with each other—and more interdependence. There is a greater need for sharing responsibilities. But it is precisely this 'sharing' of responsibilities and pooling of resources which is lacking, and women are often left to support the household singlehandedly. With the emergence of the breadwinner ideology vis-à-vis men, new expectations have emerged. As breadwinners, men are expected to contribute to the needs of the household. Thus, the breadwinner role entails certain social functions. In earlier times women were able to provide the family with the 'daily bread'. Today, with dwindling landplots, there is a need to supplement with store-bought food items. Moreover, the 'daily bread' also includes clothes and school fees. Most men, however, do not pool whatever resources they may have (if any) for the common benefit of the household. As a result, they ignore their social functions, and they do not live up to expectations.

So my study shows that Kisii is a strongly male dominated society and that today men are left with a patriarchal ideology bereft of its legitimising activities and not able to fulfil new roles and expectations. Men and women are caught in a quagmire of conflicting, obscure values and paradoxes, and their lives are filled with contradictions. New social values have been introduced in this century. These values, though, have changed much more radically for men than for women. In addition, social values linked to male identity have become very complex and contradictory. Moreover, the fact that men have more social roles than women (in principle and emphasized in the initiation ritual) entails greater responsibilities for men. This also explains why women would say that 'husbands have so many burdens. Therefore they break'. In practice, though, men's role as head of household is becoming more theoretical than practical; their role-based identity is weakened, contrary to that of their wife. With men often reduced to 'figureheads' of households, their authority has come under threat and so has their identity and sense of self-esteem. While men often seem to be in a position of authority—and wives may show public deference—my study shows that a majority of men wield little authority and no real power. What seems to be left to many men is a 'powerless' authority often accompanied by a felt sense of powerlessness and a certain fatalism: 'I am a sheep of God. He will take care of me and my children'.

Female identity is also unstable. With no bridewealth a woman's position in her husband's household is insecure. Her role as wife is questionable. So is her role as a daughter because she has not provided her parents with bridewealth (for her brothers to marry). So her relations to her parents are tense. In sum her social value, her existential identity and self-esteem are very negatively affected. On the other hand, it can be argued that female power is enhanced by the fact that women feel little identification with the patrilineage and seem less reluctant to bring shame on it and 'break the home'—as men accuse women of doing. Moreover, because women *de facto* tend to be in control of the daily household economy—though often under extreme economic pressure—their identity and self-esteem have not suffered as those of men have. This seems to have reinforced their role-based identity: 'men cannot plan, they need to be monitored by women'. Women have not resigned as many men have: 'women have no time to break'. Of necessity women behave as social actors who use whatever resources are available, often using their 'appropriate' behaviour in pursuit of survival.

This does not mean, though, that women are not subject to male control and dominance. They are. While having children is fundamental for both male and female identity, and perceptions of such identity influence men's and women's reproductive and sexual behaviour—male existential identity is particularly influenced—men are especially concerned about controlling female fertility. Male and female fertility interests, however, often differ because men benefit from the privilege of having children but take their father role lightly and leave women to carry the burden of children. While female existential identity is closely linked to fertility, women also use their fertility strategically. Linked to this, my data suggest that as women's role-based identity has been reinforced, fertility as an inherent feature of their existential identity may then take on new dimensions. Particularly when combined with the fact that women are often left with the sole support of their children. Thus, while motherhood is an immanent feature—how many children she has is negotiable. This seems to suggest that fertility is negotiable.

As male sexuality and sexual control over women seem to have become particularly important for male existential identity, it can be argued that this is because of the positive connotations linked to male sexual activity, contrary to that of women. However, my data rather suggest that in situations of instability, unemployment, lack of social roles and role-based identities, and with male authority under threat, male (aggressive) sexuality and male control over women's fertility and sexuality become more closely tied to male existential identities. My data even seem to suggest that male sexuality/sexual activity and sexual control over women seem to become a possible alternative to the generation of a new identity and male self-esteem.

In sum, with traditional gender roles and values becoming increasingly ambiguous, with new and often obscure role-based and existential identities, and with existing structures and 'myths' no longer fitting with the realities of contemporary Kisii, traditional boundaries are no longer self-evident. This suggests that while women's role-based identities have been strengthened, the existential identities of men—in a situation of reduced access to role-based identities and with male authority under threat—increase in importance.

Reproduction and sexuality are symbols invested with meaning and they reflect male dominance (Ortner and Whitehead, 1981/89). Thus, when men feel that their dominance is threatened, these symbols become increasingly important for male existential identity. Kisii is a kinship and gender-based society in which the existential identities of both sexes always used to be very dominant and essential. During this century a majority of men have not been able to develop new role-based identities, and the need for men to hang on to their existential identities seems to have become increasingly essential to their self-esteem.

Theoretical concepts revisited

While Ortner and Whitehead argue that gender identity and social value are closely linked to a person's roles they do not deal with changing roles, changing social values and the consequences for identity. From this point of view, Kopytoff's distinctions between role-based and existential identities have brought me further in my analysis. According to Kopytoff, many new occupations imposed by the colonial system had no established place in the particular representation of gender; they represented circumstantial roles and as were not inherent. Thus, while Ortner and Whitehead's approach becomes 'immobile' and static, Kopytoff's distinctions allow me to explore how new roles affect identities, how identities formed by complex ongoing processes may change and, not least, how they may interact with each other. Thus, Kopytoff's model provides operational tools which permit one to identify change and the impact of change on role-based and existential identities.

Analyzing my findings, it becomes clear that new role-based and existential identities are coming to the fore in Kisii. Women's new 'managerial' roles within the household seem to have become even more powerful and important for women's role-based identities. This particular role has taken on totally new dimensions, and from this point of view it has had a profound effect on women's role-based identities. The breadwinner role (whatever form it may take), is not inherent (compared with that of being a father and fathering children) but it does give access to social value and self-esteem. Some circumstantial roles (a businessman, matatu driver) are now becoming increasingly integrated in Kisii culture. Even if they have no 'counterparts' in any traditional activities they are increasingly recognized and accepted—because they entail social value.

However, while Kopytoff points out that to be circumcised is inherent to a man's existential identity—a non-negotiable feature—he does not discuss whether this non-negotiable feature is eternal. While my data show that circumcision of both sexes in Kisii are still inherent for male and female existential identities, the practice of female circumcision is a practice which in the face of 'development' may not continue. Eventually, this non-negotiable feature will become negotiable.

This raises a number of questions: to what extent are existential identities constant and to what extent do they change? Can non-negotiable identities become negotiable? To what extent can new role-based identities substitute or replace non-negotiable existential identities? For example how do women's role-based identities 'compete' with their existential identities? If, as I have suggested, male sexuality and reinforced control over women's reproductive and sexual capacities seem to compensate for a loss of role-based identities—is the reverse then also possible?

Thus, to what extent is male control over female reproduction and sexuality non-negotiable and immutable (in particular if men realize that their sexual behaviour is threatening women's reproductive health—and ultimately their ability to produce children). If children are fundamental for male identity and social value, what happens to a man's existential and non-negotiable identity as a father when he no longer supports his children?

Kopytoff does not deal with such questions. This dimension is not developed in his model. However, it is fundamental for the dynamics of his 'ideal types'. From this point of view, his model becomes too simple. Returning to the question of the social functions which are attached to a person's roles, I suggest that the social functions create a link between Kopytoff's two 'ideal types'. Social functions are a mediating link between the existential and the role-based identities, a link which makes his model dynamic. It is precisely in terms of men's social functions that fundamental changes have taken place in Kisii. And it is these social functions that men have difficulties in fulfilling. As Colette Suda, a Kenyan social scientist, observed: Our men need to be domesticated—but how can they be domesticated without being stripped of their maleness? (personal communication, 1992). Maleness is strongly linked to men's existential as well as role-based identities. Maleness and men's identities, however, are also bound up with the way in which a man performs his social functions: it is not only a question of *being* (a father) and *doing* (a matatu driver); it is also a question of *how*. Consequently, it is not enough just to *be* a father, a husband, a head of household or *do* a job. It is important *how* a man is a father; *how* he contributes to the household with his income from driving a matatu; *how* he performs as a head of household.

Kopytoff's approach does not allow for a discussion of the relations of power between genders. However, by introducing 'social functions' the question of the relations of power between genders presents itself. 'Social functions' initiate a discussion of negotiation and bargaining. If men are to fulfil social functions it entails obligations and duties. If men do not fulfil their expected social functions a tug-of-war and antagonisms between the genders are provoked.

Finally, how can we deal with the fact that male authority seems to have become hollow; what are the implications for Gusii male and female gender identity? what happens to the asymmetric gender relations which favours men? Will women now be favoured? Addressing these types of questions not only Ortner and Whitehead's approach but also that of Kopytoff fall short and more refined tools are needed. To go deeper into an exploration of how to deal with such questions is not within the scope of this study. However it indicates new research areas.

Final words

> I think that when we talk about the position of women in Africa and see how miserable it is, quite often we forget that these miserable women are married to miserable men. (Wanagari Mathai, 1992, Kenyan women's activist cited in Gordon, 1995)

In this study I may have raised more questions than I can answer. However, I hope that they will serve to indicate new areas where future research may be needed.

The study emphasizes a need to examine in depth changing African social contexts with collapsing traditional structures, the emergence of new unstable situations, new social roles, norms and values. And there is a need to explore how these changes affect male and female gender identity, the relations between sexes and, in particular, fertility and sexual behaviour. My study stresses, in particular, the need to reconsider and reconceptualize conventional and stereotyped assumptions about the relationship between men and women not only in Kisii but also in other social, cultural and economic contexts in Africa where there is instability and transformation. In these situations, the notions of the dominant and all-powerful male and the subordinate and dominated woman: such notions must be re-thought.

The stereotypes of male domination and women's subordination are dangerous. They are static and do not allow for change. They hide the fact that there are cultural variations. They help to naturalize inferiority and may end up being internalized by the subordinates themselves.

There is an enormous gap between the dominant ideology and the great range of possible actions, tactics and negotiations. Patriarchal ideology may be embodied in the lives of socially dominant men and subordinate women. But this does not mean that all men are successful patriarchs or that all women are passive victims.

Bibliography

Ahlberg, Beth Maina. 1991. *Women, sexuality and the changing social order. The impact of government policies on reproductive behavior in Kenya.* International studies in global change; 1. Philadelphia: Gordon and Breach Science.

Archetti, Eduardo P. 1988. *Argentinian Tango. Male sexual ideology and morality.* Working Paper No. 1. Oslo: Department of Social Anthropology, University of Oslo.

Beckmann, Vanna. 1988. *Alcohol, another trap for Africa.* Örebro: Libris Publishing.

Beneria, Lourdes and Marthe Roldàn. 1987. *The crossroads of class and gender.* Chicago: The University of Chicago Press.

Berman, Bruce and John Lonsdale. 1992. *Unhappy valley: conflict in Kenya and Africa.* Book 1: State & Class. London: James Curry Ltd.

Billetoft, Jørgen. 1989. *Rural nonfarm enterprises in Western Kenya. Spatial structure and development.* CDR Project Paper 89.3. Copenhagen: Centre for Development Research.

— 1995. *Between industrialisation and income generation: The dilemma of support to micro activities. A policy study from Kenya and Bangladesh.* Ph.D. dissertation. Centre for Development Research and Aalborg University Centre.

Bogonko, S.N. 1976. "Grazing grounds and Gusii indigenous education", *Education in Eastern Africa*, Vol. 6, 2, 176, p. 191–206.

Boserup, Ester. 1980. "African women in production and household", in Presvelou, Clio and Saskia Spijkers-Zwart (eds.), *The household, women and agricultural development.* Wageningen: H. Weenman & B. V. Zonen.

Brandes, Stanley. 1981. "Like wounded stags: male sexual ideology in an Andalusian Town", in Ortner, Shirley and Harriet Whitehead (eds.), *Sexual Meanings.* New York: Cambridge University Press.

Burnes, Carolyn. 1976. *An experiment with African coffee growing in Kenya: The Gusii 1933–50.* Ph.D. dissertation. Department of History, Michigan State University.

Caldwell, John C. 1982. *Theory of fertility decline.* London/New York: Academic Press.

Caldwell, John C., Pat Caldwell, and I.O. Orubuloye. 1990. *The family and sexual networking in Sub-Saharan Africa: Historic regional differences and present day implications.* Wealth Transition Centre Working Papers No. 5. Canberra: Australian University.

Caplan, Pat (ed.) 1987/91. *The cultural construction of sexuality.* London: Routledge.

Cardinal Otunga Historical Society. 1979. *Reprints*, Vol. 1.

Carney, Judith and Michael Watts. 1991. "Disciplining Women!" *Signs*, Vol. 16, No. 4.

Central Bureau of Statistics. 1986. *Economic Survey*. Nairobi: Ministry of Planning and National Development.

— 1989. *Impact of socio-economic development on fertility in rural Kenya*. Nairobi: Ministry of Planning and National Development.

Cohen, David William and E.S. Atieno Odhiambo. 1989. *Siaya: the historical anthropology of an African landscape*. London: James Curry.

Collier, Jane Fishburne, and Sylvia Junko Yanagisako. 1987. *Gender and Kinship. Essays toward a unified analysis*. Stanford: Stanford University Press.

Dixon-Mueller, Ruth and Adrienne Germain. 1993. "Defining the 'unmet need' for family planning", in Dixon-Mueller, Ruth and Adrienne Germain (eds.), *Four essays on birth control needs and risks*. New York: International Women's Health Coalition.

Egerö, Bertil and Mikael Hammarskjöld (eds.) 1994. *Understanding reproductive change*. Lund: Lund University Press.

Egerö, Bertil and E. Mburugu, "Kenya: Reproductive change under strain", in Egerö, B. and M. Hammarskjöld (eds.), *Understanding reproductive change*. Lund: Lund University Press.

Erikson, Erik H. 1950/63. *Childhood and society*. New York: W.W. Norton & Company.

— 1959/80. *Identity and the life cycle: Psychological issues*. New York: International Press.

Etienne, Mona and Eleanor B. Leacock. 1980. *Women and colonization: Anthropological perspectives*. New York: Praeger.

Frank, Odile and Geoffrey McNicoll. 1988. "Fertility and population policy in Kenya", *Population and Development Review* 13, No. 2.

Frank, Odile. 1990. "The childbearing family in sub-Saharan Africa, Structure, fertility, and the future", *World Bank working paper*, WPS 509.

Fuglesang, Minou. 1994. *Veils and videos: Female youth culture on the Kenyan Coast*. Stockholm Studies in Social Anthropology. Department of Anthropology, Stockholm University.

Gage, Anastasia J. and Wamucii Njogu. 1994. *Gender inequalities and demographic behaviour. Ghana/Kenya*. New York: The Population Council.

Gennep, Arnold van. 1908/60. *The rites de passage*. University of Chicago Press.

Gluckman, M. 1950. "Kinship and marriage among the Lozi of Northern Rhodesia and the Zulu of Natal", in Radcliffe-Brown A.R. and D. Forde (eds.), *African systems of kinship and marriage*. London: Oxford University Press.

Goddard, Victoria. 1987/91. "Honour and shame: the control of women's sexuality and group identity in Naples", in Caplan, Pat (ed.), *The cultural construction of sexuality*. London: Routledge.

Gordon, April. 1995. "Gender, ethnicity, and class in Kenya: 'Burying Otieno' revisited", *Signs*, Vol. 20, No. 4, pp. 883–912.

Gudykunst, William B. and Stella Ting-Toomey. 1988. *Culture and interpersonal communication*. Newbury Park, NY: Sage Publications.

Guyer, Jane I. 1981. "Household and community in African studies", *African Studies Review*, Vol. 24, No. 2/3.

— 1988. "Dynamic approaches to domestic budgeting", in Dwyer, Daisy and Judith Bruce (eds.), *A home divided*. Stanford: Stanford University Press.

Gwako, Edwins Laban Moogi. 1995. "Continuity and change in the practice of clitoridectomy in Kenya: a Case Study of the Abagusii", *The Journal of Modern African Studies*, Vol. 33, No. 2, pp. 33–337.

Harris, Olivia. 1981. "Households as natural units", in Young, Kate, Cool Walkowitz and Roselyn McCullagh (eds.), *Of marriage and the market*. London: CSE Books.

Hay, Margaret Jean, and Sharon Stichter (eds.) 1984. *African women south of the Sahara*. London & New York: Longman.

Hill, Polly. 1975. "West African farming household" in J. Goody (ed.), *Changing social structure in Ghana: Essays in the comparative sociology of a new state and an old tradition*. London: International Africa Institute.

Håkansson, Thomas, 1985. "Why do Gusii women get married? A study of cultural constraints in a rural community in Kenya", *Folk*, Vol. 27.

Håkansson, Thomas, 1988. *Bridewealth, women and land: Social change among the Gusii of Kenya*. Doctoral dissertation. Uppsala: Acta Universitatis Upsaliensis.

Håkansson, Thomas. 1994. "The detachability of women: gender and kinship in processes of socioeconomic change among the Gusii of Kenya", *American Ethnologist* 21 (3): 516–538.

Jacobson-Widding, Anita. 1983. *Identity: Personal and socio-cultural*. Stockholm: Almquist & Wiksell International.

Kandiyoti, Deniz. 1988. "Bargaining with patriarchy", *Gender & Society*, Vol. 3, No. 3.

Kenya Contraceptive Prevalence Survey 1984. Central Bureau of Statistics. 1986. Nairobi: Ministry of Planning and National Development.

Kenyatta, Jomo. 1938/61. *Facing Mount Kenya. The tribal life of the Gikuyu*. London: Secker & Warburg.

Keesing, Roger M. and Felix M. Keesing. 1971. *New perspectives in cultural anthropology*. New York: Holt, Rinehart and Winston.

Kirumira, Edward Kasujja. 1995. *Familial relationships and population dynamics in Uganda: a case study of fertility behaviour in the Central Region.* Ph.D. thesis, University of Copenhagen.

Kisii District Development Plan1984–88. Ministry of Planning and National Development, Kenya.

Kisii District Development Plan for 1989–93. 1992. Ministry of Planning and National Development, Kenya.

Kisii District Socio-Cultural Profile. 1986. Institute of African Studies, University of Nairobi.

Kitching, Gavin. 1980. *Class and economic change in Kenya.* New York: Yale University Press.

Kongstad, Per and Mette Mønsted. 1980. *Family, labour and trade in Western Kenya.* Uppsala: Scandinavian Institute of African Studies.

Kopytoff, Igor. 1990. "Women's roles and existential identities", in Sanday, Peggy Reeves and Ruth Gallagher Goodenough (eds.), *Beyond the second sex: New directions in the anthropology of gender.* Philadelphia: University of Pennsylvania Press.

Kuper, A. 1982. *Wives for cattle.* London: Routledge and Kegan Paul.

LeVine, Robert A. 1959. "Gusii sex offenses: A study in social control", in Lieberman, B. (ed), *Human sexual behaviours.* John Wiley and Sons Inc. 336–357. Also in *American Anthropologist*, 1959 61(6):965–990.

LeVine, Robert A. 1966. "Sex roles and economic change in Africa", *Ethnology*, Vol. 5.

LeVine, Robert A. 1982. *Culture, behaviour and personality. An introduction to the comparative study of psychosocial adaption.* New York: Aldine Publishing Company.

LeVine, Robert A. and Barbara B. LeVine. 1966/77. *Nyansongo: A Gusii community in Kenya.* Huntington NY: Robert E. Krieger Publishing Company.

LeVine, Sarah, and Robert A. LeVine. 1981. "Child abuse and neglect in Subsaharan Africa", in Korbin, Jill E. (ed.), *Child abuse and neglect: Cross cultural perspectives.* Berkeley: University of California Press.

LeVine, Sarah. 1979. *Mothers and wives: Gusii women of East Africa.* Chicago: University of Chicago Press.

Llewelyn-Davies, Melissa. 1981. "Women, warriors, and patriarchs", in Ortner, Shirley and Harriet Whitehead (eds.), *Sexual meanings.* New York: Cambridge University Press.

Locoh, Thérèse. 1988. *Obstacles to the acceptance of family planning in West Africa.* Paris: CEPED.

MacCormack, Carol P. and Alizon Draper. 1987. "Social and cognitive aspects of female sexuality in Jamaica", in Caplan, Pat (ed.), *The cultural construction of sexuality.* London and New York: Tavistock Publications.

Maendeleo Ya Wanawake. 1992. *FGM in Kenya*. Washington, DC: Population Crisis Committee.

Mayer, Iona. 1965. "From kinship to common descent: Four- generation genealogies among the Gusii", *Africa*, Vol. 35.

— 1972. "How to introduce family planning among the Gusii?" in Molnos, Angela, *Cultural source material for population planning in East Africa*, Vol. 2:149–156. Institute of African Studies. University of Nairobi. East African Publishing House.

— 1973. "The Gusii of Western Kenya", in Molnos, Angela, *Cultural source material for population planning in East Africa*, Vol. 3:122–138. Institute of African Studies. University of Nairobi. East African Publishing House.

— 1974. "The patriarchal image: Routine dissociation in Gusii families", *African Studies*, Vol. 34, No. 4.

Mayer, Philip. 1949. *The lineage principle in Gusii Society*. Memo. 24 of International African Institute. London & Oxford: Oxford University Press.

— 1950. "Gusii bridewealth law and custom", *Rhodes-Livingstone Paper* No. 18. London: Oxford University Press.

— 1953. "Gusii initiation ceremonies", *Journal of Royal Anthropological Institute*.

— 1961. "Migrancy and the study of towns", *American Anthropologist*, Vol. 64.

— 1961. "Migrancy and the study of towns", *American Anthropologist*, Vol. 64.

Mbiti, John S. 1973/86. *Love and marriage in Africa*. London: Longman.

McPhadden, Patricia. 1992. "Sex, Sexuality and the problems of AIDS in Africa", in Meena, Ruth (ed.), *Gender in Southern Africa: Conceptual and theoretical issues*. Harare: Sapes Books.

Melhuus, Marit, 1991. "Machismo and maranismo." Paper presented at 7th Nosalf conference, Sundvollen, Norway.

Mitchell, J. Clyde. 1959. "Labour migration in Africa south of Sahara: The cause of labour migration", *Bulletin of the Inter-African Labour Institute*, Vol. 6.

— 1987. *Cities, society and social perception: A central African perspective*. Oxford: Clarendon Press.

Molnos, Angela. 1972–74. *Review of socio-cultural research 1952–72*. Nairobi.

Moore, Henrietta L. 1986. *Space, text and gender: An anthropological study of the Marakwet of Kenya*. Cambridge: Cambridge University Press.

Moore, Henrietta L. 1988. *Feminism and anthropology*. Cambridge: Polity Press.

Nafis Sadik, Opening speech, UNFPA, Danida Conference on Population, Copenhagen, May 1994.

Ndetei, *Sunday Times*, May 13, 1990

Njonjo, A. 1983. *Consultancy Report*, Africa Research Institute, Nairobi.

Nyansani, Joseph M. 1984. *The British Massacre of the Gusii Freedom Defenders*. Nairobi Bookmen.

Oboler, Regina, S. 1985. *Women, power and economic change: The Nandi of Kenya*. California: Stanford University.

Ochieng, William Robert. 1974. *A pre-colonial history of the Gusii of western Kenya C.A.D. 1500–1914*. Nairobi: East Africa Literature Bureau.

Ominde, S.H. 1984. *Population and development in Kenya*. London/Nairobi: Heinemann Educational Books.

Ortner, Shirley and Harriet Whitehead. 1981/89. *Sexual meanings: The cultural construction of gender and sexuality*. Cambridge: Cambridge University Press.

Ortner, Shirley. 1981. "Gender and sexuality in hierarchical societies: the case of Polynesia and some comparative implications", in Ortner, Shirley and Harriet Whitehead (eds.), *Sexual meanings*. New York: Cambridge University Press.

Orvis, Stephen. 1985a. *Men and women in a household economy: Evidence from Kisii*. Working Paper No. 432. Nairobi: Institute for Development Studies, University of Nairobi.

— 1985b. *A patriarchy transformed: Reproducing labour and the viability of small-holder agriculture in Kisii*. Working Paper No. 434. Nairobi: Institute for Development Studies, University of Nairobi.

— 1988. "The development debate and household reproduction in Kenya". Paper presented at the African Studies Association Conference on Change and Continuity, 28–31 October, Chicago.

Otieno, B., J.A. Owola and P. Oduor. 1979. "A study of alcoholism in rural setting in Kenya", *East African Medical Journal*, Vol. 56, No. 12, pp. 665–670.

Paige, Karen Erickson and Jeffrey M. Paige. 1981. *The Politics of reproductive ritual*. Berkeley: University of California Press.

Parkin, D. 1978. *The Cultural definition of political response*. London: Academic Press.

— 1980. "Kind, Bridewealth and Hard Cash", in Comaroff, J.L. (ed.), *The meaning of marriage payment*. New York: Academic Press.

Peristiany, J. G. (ed). 1965. *Honour and shame: Honour and social status: the values of Mediterranean society*. Chicago/London: University of Chicago Press.

Population and Development in Kenya. 1980. World Bank Report No. 2775-Ke.

Raikes, Alanagh. 1990. *Pregnancy , Birthing and family planning in Kenya: Changing patterns of behaviour. A health service utilization study in Kisii*

District. CDR Working Paper 88.7. Copenhagen: Centre for Development Research.

Raikes, Philip. 1988. *Savings and credit in Kisii, Western Kenya*. CDR Working Paper 88.7. Copenhagen: Centre for Development Research.

— 1990. "State and civil society in Western Kenya. Preliminary notes on freedom and control in Kisii". Paper presented at FAU-seminar on State and Civil Society.

— 1992. "Notes on the construction of gender and ethnicity in Kisii, Western Kenya". Draft not published.

Rubin, Gayle. 1975. "The traffic in women: Notes toward a political economy of sex", in Reiter, Rayna (ed.), *Toward an anthropology of women*. New York: Monthly Review Press.

Sacks, Karen. 1982. *Sisters and wives: The past and future of sexual equality*. Chicago: University of Illinois Press.

Safilios-Rothschild, Constantine. 1983. "Female power, autonomy and demographic change", in Anker, Richard, Magre Buvimic and Nadic H. Yanssefo (eds.), *Women's roles and population trends in the third world*. London & Canberra: Croom Helm.

Sanday, Peggy Reeves. 1981. *Female power and male dominance: On the origins of sexual inequality*. New York: Cambridge University Press.

Silberschmidt, Margrethe. 1991a. *Women's position in the household and their use of family planning and antenatal services. A case study from Kisii District, Kenya*. CDR Project Paper 91.4. Copenhagen: Centre for Development Research.

— 1991b. *Rethinking men and gender relations. An investigation of men, their changing roles within the household, and the implications for gender relations in Kisii District, Kenya*. CDR Research Report. No. 16. Copenhagen: Centre for Development Research.

— 1993. *Survey on research concerning user's perspectives on contraceptive services with emphasis on Sub-Saharan Africa*. Report prepared for SAREC (Swedish Agency for Research Cooperation with Developing Countries), Stockholm and DASA, Copenhagen.

— 1994 . *Female genital mutilation: a harmful act of trust*. Background study for Danida's strategy on FGM. Copenhagen.

Southall, Aidan W. 1960. "On Chastity in Africa", *Uganda Journal*, 24:207–216.

Strathern, Marilyn (ed.) 1987. *Dealing with inequality*. Cambridge: Cambridge University Press.

— 1990. *The gender of the gift*. Berkeley and Los Angeles: University of California Press.

Stölen, Kristiane. 1990. "Gender sexuality and violence in Ecuador". Paper presented at Nordic Symposium on Gender and Social Change in the Third World. Granavolden, Norway.

Sørensen, Bo Wagner. 1990. "Folk models of wife-beating in Nuuk, Greenland", *Folk*, Vol. 32. Copenhagen.

— 1992. *Magt eller afmagt? Gender, sentiments and violence in Greenland*. Ph.D. dissertation. Institute of Anthropology, Copenhagen.

Talle, Aud. 1988. *Women at a loss*. Studies in Social Anthroplogy. University of Stockholm.

— 1991. "Kvinnlig könsstympning: Ett sätt att skapa kvinnor och män", in Kulik, Don (ed.), *Från kön til genus*. Borås: Carlsson Bokförlag.

Tostensen, Arne. 1986. *Between shamba and factory*. Working Paper No. 423. Nairobi: Institute for Development Studies.

Villarreal, Magdalena. 1991. *The forging of a project. Women's struggle for space in a Mexican Ejido*. Wageningen: Department of Rural Sociology.

— 1992. "The poverty of practice: Power, gender and intervention from an actor-oriented perspective", in Long, Norman and Ann Long (eds.), *Battlefields of knowledge: The interlocking theory and practice in social resarch and development*. London: Routledge.

— 1994. *Wielding and yielding: Power, subordination and gender identity in the context of a Mexican development project*. University of Wageningen.

Were, Gideon S. and David Nyamwaya (eds.) 1986. *Kisii District socio-cultural profile*. Government of Kenya. Nairobi: Lengo Press.

White, Luise. 1990. "Separating the men from the boys: Constructions of gender, sexuality, and terrorism in central Kenya 1939–1959", *International Journal of African Historical Studies*, Vol. 23, No. 1:1–27.

Wolf de, Jan. 1977. *Differentiation and integration in Western Kenya*. The Hague: Morton and Co.

Young, Kate. 1978. *The social determinants of fertility*. IDS working paper. University of Sussex.